The Wow Climax

The Wow Climax

Tracing the Emotional Impact of Popular Culture

Henry Jenkins

NEW YORK UNIVERSITY PRESS

New York and London

NEW YORK UNIVERSITY PRESS
New York and London
www.nyupress.org

"Games, the New Lively Art" originally appeared in Jeffrey Goldstein, ed., Handbook for Video Game Studies (Cambridge, MA: MIT Press, 2005).

"Death-Defying Heroes" originally appeared in Sherry Turkle, ed., Evocative Objects: Things We Think With (Cambridge, MA: MIT Press, 2007).

"Never Trust a Snake: WWF Wrestling as Masculine Melodrama" originally appeared in Aaron Baker and Todd Boyd, eds., Out of Bounds: Sports, Media, and the Politics of Identity (Bloomington: Indiana University Press, 1997).

"'Going Bonkers': Children, Play, and Pee-Wee" originally appeared in Camera Obscura 17 (May 1988).

"'Complete Freedom of Movement': Video Games as Gendered Play Spaces" originally appeared in Justine Cassell and Henry Jenkins, eds., From Barbie to Mortal Kombat: Gender and Computer Games (Cambridge, MA: MIT Press, 1998).

"'Her Suffering Aristocratic Majesty': The Sentimental Value of Lassie" originally appeared in Marsha Kinder, ed., Kid's Media Culture (Durham, NC: Duke University Press, 1999).

Library of Congress Cataloging-in-Publication Data
Jenkins, Henry, 1958–
The wow climax : tracing the emotional impact of popular culture / Henry Jenkins.
p. cm.
Includes bibliographical references and index.
ISBN-13: 978-0-8147-4282-2 (cloth : alk. paper)
ISBN-10: 0-8147-4282-3 (cloth : alk. paper)
ISBN-13: 978-0-8147-4283-9 (pbk. : alk. paper)
ISBN-10: 0-8147-4283-1 (pbk. : alk. paper)
1. Popular culture—United States. 2. Popular culture—United States—Psychological aspects. 3. Emotions—Social aspects—United States. 4. Affect (Psychology)—United States. 5. Aesthetics—Social aspects—United States. 6. Mass media—Social aspects—United States. 7. Mass media—United States—Psychological aspects. 8. United States—Social conditions—1933–1945. 9. United States—Social conditions—1945– I. Title.
E169.12.J46   2006
302.230973—dc22   2006022413

New York University Press books are printed on acid-free paper, and their binding materials are chosen for strength and durability.

Manufactured in the United States of America

c 10 9 8 7 6 5 4 3 2 1
p 10 9 8 7 6 5 4 3 2 1

Contents

Introduction
Wow!

Consider the singular beauty of the word "wow." Think about the pleasure in forming that perfectly symmetrical phrase on your tongue. Imagine the particular enthusiasm it expresses—the sense of wonderment, astonishment, absolute engagement. A "wow" is something that has to be earned, and in the modern age we distribute standing ovations far too often when we are just being polite, but we have become too jaded to give a wow. The term takes on a certain irony, as if it can only be uttered in quotation marks. Perhaps we are not as jaded as the *Variety* critic who was asked to review a performance by a pair of Siamese twins who did impersonations, sang, did ballroom and tap dancing, and juggled, all in the course of a ten-minute vaudeville act. All the critic could muster was, "Not bad for an act of this kind," a phrase that falls far short of a wow.

There's a wow-worthy sequence near the beginning of Zhang Yimou's 2004 film *House of Flying Daggers*. A blind courtesan has been brought before a local magistrate who suspects that she may be a member of the secret Flying Daggers organization, and not a brothel entertainer. He demands a performance, challenging her to what he calls the "echo game." She is brought to the center of a room lined with drums on poles. The crowd gathers on the balcony to watch. The magistrate flings a bean and hits one of the drums. The blind woman thwacks out her long sleeves and slaps them against the same drum. A group of musicians signal their enthusiasm for her perceptual mastery. Then, he throws a second bean and this one ricochets across several drums before dropping to the floor. Again, she flings out her long sleeves and hits the first and then the second drum, followed by grand leaps and twirls. Finally, the magistrate flings the entire bowl of beans, which rain down upon the drums. She listens carefully, waits a beat, and then goes into an elaborate dance, hitting drum after drum, trying to map their trajectory. And then she flings out her sleeves one more time, wraps them around a sword that lies on the table, and uses it to threaten the magistrate, a gesture that leads into a spectacular martial arts sequence.

Throughout the scene, we are left seeing but not quite believing. Much of the pleasure comes from the sequence's larger-than-life qualities—with its wire-work stunts, slow-motion cinematography, and special effects. It is easy to understand why we would be impressed to see such a performance improvised live before our very eyes. It is harder to understand why it holds such wonderment for us in an age where we know every element could be faked, yet the sequence is so spectacularly executed on the screen that it becomes a showstopper. It has its own trajectory: each gesture builds on the one before; each action is just a little more spectacular than what precedes it. The scene is constructed so there is an internal audience—the people lining the balcony—whose oohs and ahs stand in for our own astonished responses toward what we are seeing. Arguably, Yimou makes an aesthetic mistake—putting this sequence so early in the film, he has to struggle to top it in subsequent scenes and never quite overcomes this war of expectations.

The scene can be extracted from the film as a set piece and watched with almost equal pleasure. At the same time, Yimou uses the sequence to set the stage for everything that follows. He returns to the "echo game" later in the film, when the magistrate himself is blindfolded and forced to try to duplicate her virtuosity. In the end, we discover that the protagonist is a woman pretending to be blind, that the magistrate and the woman are former suitors, that the performance is a kind of lovemaking, and that they are being forced to pretend that they are strangers even though they yearn to be in each other's arms. The narrative adds more and more layers to our appreciation of her virtuosity. Yimou amplifies the martial arts film tradition of playing with identity until none of the characters is what they seem and they find themselves actually feeling the emotions they have been feigning. All of this builds toward a tragic ending where these divided loyalties result in the deaths of all of the primary characters. All of this is to say that the scene works both within and outside of the narrative structure of the film.

The essays in *The Wow Climax* are about things that make me go "wow." I am someone who cries intensely at movies, even bad movies, especially bad movies on airplanes. I am someone who laughs loudly, even at bad jokes, especially bad jokes, and I am someone who gasps and applauds loudly when I see an acrobat do a back flip or watch someone eat fire. When I was little, my mother let me go inside the sideshow tent at a local carnival; an hour later she came inside, the manager in tow, looking for me, convinced I had been kidnapped, and instead found me sitting there, eyes open wide, watching a man drive a nail up his nose. In short, I am someone who is passionate about popular culture.

Most popular culture is shaped by a logic of emotional intensification. It is less interested in making us think than it is in making us feel. Yet that distinction is too simple: popular culture, at its best, makes us think by making us feel. We saw this in the scene from *House of Flying Daggers* described above, in which what once seemed to be a set piece turns out to be the key to understanding the film. Popular culture can generate a fair amount of effortless emotion by following well-trod formulas, but to make us go "wow," it has to twist or transform those formulas into something marvelous and unexpected. Several recent books, most notably Steven Johnson's *Everything Bad Is Good For You*,[1] have made the case for the complexity of contemporary popular culture and for the demands it makes on consumers. My first response to this book was to embrace the argument as consistent with my own long-standing interests in helping people better appreciate the complexity and diversity of popular culture. My second response, however, was to challenge the argument that this was anything new. Popular culture has enjoyed complexity and diversity throughout its history; it is simply that most intellectuals lack the knowledge and competency to consume it with any real appreciation. The only time we are truly brain-dead in our response to popular culture is when it becomes so formulaic that it no longer provokes an emotional reaction; and at that point, it has failed on its own terms and any other we want to apply. Whatever anyone has told you, it is certainly not the case that to see one work is to see them all. It is almost certainly the case, though, that to fully appreciate a piece of popular art, you need to have seen enough other examples to observe the ways it builds upon and breaks with existing formulas. The ability to fall back on the tried and the true frees the best popular artists to take risk with their audiences and experiment with their materials in search of the more elusive wow.

Through the years, my essays have developed a formula of their own: I almost always start by describing some element that embodies the subject's most sensationalistic dimensions, and then I unpack that moment as the launching pad for my cultural analysis. We often respond to these wow moments as if they defied any interpretation, as if they spoke to us purely on a visceral level. Yet, they may be some of the richest openings for cultural analysis. I start from the assumption that the emotions generated by popular culture are never personal; rather, to be popular, the text has to evoke broadly shared feelings. The most emotional moments are often the ones that hit on conflicts, anxieties, fantasies, and fears that are central to the culture.

This book's title comes from an old vaudeville term. The moment of peak spectacle and maximum emotional impact in an act became known as the "wow climax," the "wow finish," or simply the "big wow." Writing in the *Saturday Evening Post* in 1925, in the declining years of the vaudeville circuits, theater critic Walter De Leon explained, "An added kick at the finish of an act . . . is an elusive little thing that every vaude-villian tries to capture for the completely comprehensible reason that its possession usually guarantees long routes and pleasant profits. It is the finish of an act which does, or does not, start an audience palm-whacking. The measure and quality of this applause reveal the degree of pleasure received from the act. The acts that afford the most pleasure to the largest number of different audiences are the acts that play most steadily and continuously."[2]

Vaudeville was not about telling stories; it was about putting on a show, and more than that, it was about each performer's individual attempt to stop the show and steal the applause. Vaudeville had little use for the trappings of theatrical realism; it was about the spectacular, the fantastic, and the novel. Vaudeville had little use for continuity, consistency, or unity; it was about fragmentation, transformation, and heterogeneity. The underlying logic of the variety show rested on the assumption that heterogeneous entertainment was essential to attracting and satisfying a mass audience. The vaudeville program was constructed from modular units of diverse material, each no more than twenty minutes long, juxtaposed with an eye toward the maximum amount of variety and novelty.

Performers were responsible for originating their acts, negotiating with production specialists for materials and props, rehearsing and refining their performance skills, and transporting and maintaining scenery. This performer-centered mode of production resulted in an aesthetic strongly focused on performance virtuosity. Performers were expected to execute their specialties with a consistently high level of speed and precision. Frequently, acts were designed to focus attention upon the performer's skills, having little or no other interest. Those skills were measured in terms of the audience's outward emotional response: vaudeville had little use for nuance; everything was designed to ensure a big splash. In the old system, the local theater manager would stick his head into the auditorium near the end of each act and listen to hear how it went over; the manager's notes helped determine whether the performer would get further bookings. So the performer's economic livelihood depended on the ability to shape and control an audience's emotional trajectory through the performance in the hopes of hitting a crescendo at the moment that really mattered.

Not surprisingly, the vaudevillians developed their own folk theories of affect. Here's De Leon again: "The natural, at least customary, reserve of an American audience is comparable to the cement work damming a river. If the performer can open a sluice gate or spillway the tide of applause will rush out—we hope—in a strong compact stream. If through lack of fitting climax or showmanship no outlet for the pent enthusiasm is provided, it is very apt to trickle thinly over the top of the dam or swash around weakly in backwater bayous."[3] De Leon's language is lush, even erotic, as he talks about the relationship that emerges between the performer and their public.[4] He is, after all, talking about a climax, which causes the audience to lose control over their emotions, maybe even over their bodily functions. The vaudevillian wants us to laugh till we cry or turn red in the face or wet our pants or rock about convulsively or slap the person next to us on the back. The entire art of vaudeville performance was structured around achieving that basic emotional impact.

De Leon viewed vaudeville as a form of popular art, one with its own fully developed if sometimes implicit aesthetic principles. My first book, *What Made Pistachio Nuts? Early Sound Comedy and the Vaudeville Aesthetic*, sought to identify the defining characteristics of the vaudeville performance tradition as a way into understanding the process by which Hollywood absorbed a generation of variety performers, created vehicles that exploited their performance skills, and pulled those performers toward the classical norms that dominated American film practice.[5] I was interested in the tension between an aesthetic based on spectacle and one based on storytelling; between an aesthetic that built toward a climax that blew off the roof and one that built toward the resolution of narrative enigmas; between one that read performance in terms of virtuosity and one that read performance in terms of characterization. My goal was to develop a new critical vocabulary that would allow us to appreciate these early sound comedies for what they achieved rather than judging them by standards developed in response to other cultural forms.

Of course, De Leon was not unique in recognizing the emotional dynamics shaping the popular culture. In his essay "Montage of Attractions," Sergei Eisenstein outlines what the legitimate theater and cinema might learn from the mechanisms by which the circus thrills its spectators. Choosing a term closely associated with the fairground, Eisenstein defines an attraction as "any aggressive moment in the theater, i.e. any element of it that subjects the audience to emotional or psychological influences verified by experience and mathematically calculated to produce specific emotional shocks in the spectator in their proper order within the whole."[6] Eisenstein, like De Leon, goes on to catalogue different devices that can produce "shock" and "awe." For Eisenstein, perhaps the most vivid examples of "attractions" could be found in Grand Guignol, "where eyes are gouged out or arms and legs amputated on stage."[7] Eisenstein doesn't simply want to make us laugh; he wants to make us squirm. He saw the "living play of the passions" as the starting point for the kind of ideological transformation he wanted to achieve. Eisenstein distinguishes between "tricks," which are designed to showcase the accomplishment of performers and are often self-contained, and "attractions," which are designed as provocations and measured entirely in terms of audience response. His contemporary, Lev Kuleshov, showed a particular fascination with what he called "monsters"—performers who could exert extraordinary control over their bodies.[8]

The Soviet film theorists' fascination with the mechanics of emotion needs to be understood against the backdrop of a larger Russian formalist preoccupation with the affective dimensions of popular theater. Drama critic Sergei Balukhatyi, for example, wrote a detailed "poetics of melodrama," which, as theater historian Daniel Gerould notes, started from the premise that "all elements in melodrama—its themes, technical principles, construction and style—are subordinate to one overriding aesthetic goal: the calling forth of 'pure,' 'vivid' emotions. Plot, character, and dialogue, working in unison, serve to elicit from the spectator the greatest possible intensity of feeling."[9] Melodrama, Balukhatyi argues, depends on "foolproof emotional bases," streamlined characters, a series of jolting twists of fate, simple and recognizable conflicts, and abrupt shifts of fortune, all designed to provoke an "immediate impression." Actions in melodrama, he suggested, were justified not by ideology or narrative logic but by the sheer force of the emotion that the scene was designed to express.

David Bordwell has extended Eisenstein's interest in the attraction to talk about contemporary Hong Kong action cinema, which is similarly built around expressive performance and affective intensification: "In order to attract a mass audience, popular art deals with emotions like anger, disgust, fear, happiness, sadness, and indignation. . . . Cinema is particularly good at arousing emotions kinesthetically, through actions and music. Bruce Lee asked his students to give their fighting techniques, 'emotional content', such as purposefully directed anger. When this quality is captured in vigorous, strictly patterned movement, in nicely judged framings and crackling cutting with overwhelming music and sound effects, you can find yourself tensing and twitching to the rhythms of the fight."[10] Bordwell's celebration of the "kaleidoscopic variety," the "expressive amplification," and the sensuousness of the Hong Kong cinema would have sounded familiar to De Leon, Eisenstein, Balukhatyi, and their contemporaries.

The most famous application of Eisenstein's ideas about "attraction" came in Tom Gunning's influential 1986 essay "Cinema of Attractions," which emerged as a manifesto of sorts for a new approach to early cinema. Rather than seeing films made before 1906 as a series of stepping stones toward a more classically constructed narrative (a perspective that long shaped the historiography of the period), Gunning insisted that early cinema should be read according to a different aesthetic logic: "The cinema of attractions directly solicits spectator attention, inciting visual curiosity, and supplying pleasure through an exciting spectacle—a unique event, whether fictional or documentary, that is of interest in itself. . . . Its energy moves outward towards an acknowledged spectator rather than inward towards the character-based situations essential to classical narrative."[11] This focus on spectacle and showmanship is consistent with the logic of the "wow climax" of the vaudeville stage and the mechanics of emotion that the Russian theorists saw as shaping stage melodrama. Gunning links the "cinema of attractions" not only to the vaudeville stage but to a larger tendency toward sensationalism and stimulation in the popular culture of the early twentieth century. Gunning's account has proven widely influential for others who want to think about the place of spectacle in popular culture, and subsequent work has spread outward to encompass writing on screen comedy, the musical, animation, and pornography, among other topics.

De Leon also would have recognized many of the techniques identified by David Freeman in a recent book, *Creating Emotion in Games*, including the appeal to scientific expertise implicit in the author's reference to proven principles of "emotioneering." The book goes on to identify thirty-two categories of emotional techniques that game designers can use to intensify the game experience. As Freeman explains, "When emotion is added to a game, then the game will appeal to wider demographics. The game gets better press, gets better buzz, and is more likely to generate allegiance to the brand. The development team will have increased passion for the project. All this translates to increased profits and a much richer game experience."[12] After all, such games began—like cinema itself—as arcade attractions; their core aesthetic principles stemmed from the need to pump up players so that they kept dropping quarters into the machine. As games moved into the home, they became known as "twitch" entertainment, a phrase that refers to the need to constantly hit buttons to keep the action flowing, but also suggests the nervous energy they generate from the player.

One would be hesitant to see the ever-so-respectable C. S. Lewis among the advocates of sensationalism in popular culture, yet his essay "On Stories" seems especially interested in mapping the qualities of emotional experience that shape our encounters with literary texts. Lewis rejects, on the one hand, the tendency to reduce the details found in good stories into metaphors or allegories, and, on the other, the tendency to reduce the reading of popular fiction to some generalizable quest for "excitement." Rather, he wants us to deal with these details as part of richly constructed worlds of the imagination, each of which generate their own distinctive forms of emotional release: "different kinds of danger strike different chords from the imagination. . . . There is a fear which is twin sister to awe, such as a man in wartime feels when he first comes within the sound of guns; there is a fear which is the twin sister of disgust, such as a man feels on finding a snake or scorpion in his bed-room. There are taunt, quivering fears (for one split second hardly distinguishable from a kind of pleasurable thrill) that a man may feel on a dangerous horse or a dangerous sea; and again, dead, squashed, flattened, numbing fears as when we think we have cancer or cholera. There are also fears which are not of danger at all: like the fear of some large and hideous, though innocuous, insect or the fear of a ghost. All this, even in real life. But, in imagination, where the fear does not rise to abject terror and is not discharged in action, the qualitative difference is much stronger."[13] Good storytelling, Lewis suggests, requires a close understanding of the link between details and their emotional force, requires the teller of tales to shape the affective experience of the reader through every word.

The techniques deployed differ from medium to medium, but the vaudeville performer, the early cinematic showman, the wrestler, the action or horror film director, and the game designer are all trying to use every device their medium offers in order to maximize the emotional response of their audience. Insofar as these popular artists and performers think about their craft, they are also thinking about how to achieve an emotional impact.

The Wow Climax pulls together a range of essays written over the past decade and half that span different media (film, television, literature, games, comics), different genres (slapstick comedy, melodrama, horror, children's fiction, exploitation cinema), and different emotional reactions (shock, laughter, sentimentality). Yet, when I read back through my essays, I discovered how consistently my writing had examined the connections between affect and aesthetics. These essays, for example, talk about the sentimentality at the heart of the *Lassie* franchise; examine the ways that horror filmmakers like Wes Craven and David Cronenberg and avant-garde artist Matthew Barney create fundamentally different kinds of emotional experiences while building upon many of the same themes and images; or explore what it might mean to view professional wrestling as a form of masculine melodrama. My methods encourage me to get as specific as possible in discussing the audience appeal and cultural significance of particular forms of popular culture. But each essay also contributes to a larger theoretical project—an attempt to understand the emotional dynamics of popular art.

How do we study the "wowness" of popular art? Insofar as all elements of popular media are shaped by this push toward intense emotional experience, we need to examine popular texts from multiple perspectives. The study of melodrama, for example, has focused on emotional elements that operate on the level of the narrative and characterization; the study of games or sports or martial arts looks at kinetic elements that may or may not be fully integrated into a story; work on comedy is very interested in gags but also in the kinds of gestures that reveal the distinctive personalities of comic performers. In writing about Hong Kong action films, Bordwell urges us to examine "their moment-by-moment texture" because each moment of the film is designed to increase the immediacy of our experience.[14]

And yet, because this aesthetic is so focused on the audience's response, we can never understand it purely in formalist terms. Others have sought to understand affect through the lens of psychoanalysis or cognitive science; my preferred approach is to draw on tools of cultural analysis—to understand the contexts within which these works were produced and consumed, to map the meanings and sensations that become central to popular art at a particular historical juncture, and to explore the ways that cultural hierarchies respect or dismiss the affective dimensions of popular art or censorship codes reflect "thresholds of shame" that operate differently within different cultures.

These aspects of popular culture are difficult to understand from a stance of contemplative distance. To understand how popular culture works on our emotions, we have to pull it close, get intimate with it, let it work its magic on us, and then write about our own engagement. My personal pantheon of the best writers on popular culture (including George Lipsitz, Scott Bukatman, Richard Dyer, Alex Doty, Lynn Spigel, Robin Woods, John Hartley) almost all seem to be involved in a similar project of capturing their own subjective responses to popular texts and using them as a point of entry into understanding larger cultural processes and aesthetic issues. Unfortunately, various forms of distanciation have been built into the theoretical traditions and aesthetic categories through which we study popular culture. So much stands between scholars and the works in question, and even more stands between academics and the publics that consume popular culture. These barriers are often more imagined than real, but they deform our writing, making it harder to ask certain questions or share particular insights. These essays represent an ongoing search for a new critical language that expresses how popular art makes us feel.

In some cases, the essays are openly autobiographical, as in my reflections about how superhero comics helped me to mourn my mother's death, my memories of the dog I had as a boy, or my consideration of the differences between the kinds of play spaces my son and I had growing up. In some cases, the essays are ethnographic, as in my examination of the ways kindergarteners used *Pee-Wee's Playhouse* as a vehicle for exploring their competing feelings of pleasure and shame toward their own disruptive conduct. In some cases, the essays draw on close reading, as in my consideration of the cultural work that gets performed through sentimental constructions of childhood and pets in the Lassie books, films, and television series; or on formal analysis, as in my attempt to determine the aesthetic principles that shape contemporary game design; or on discursive analysis, as in my exploration of the scandal that surrounded Lupe Velez's screen career. Each essay comes at its topic from a slightly different angle, but when combined in this collection they map a range of core questions we might want to ask about the interplay of affect and aesthetics in popular art.

Note that I am using the somewhat archaic term *popular art* here rather than the more current and common *popular culture*. Popular art emphasizes the aesthetic and affective logics that shape the production of commercial entertainment; popular culture, as it has emerged, speaks to the integration of those commercial texts into the everyday lives of their consumers. Both concepts are worth holding onto as we attempt to understand the centrality of entertainment to life in the twentieth and twenty-first centuries. The move to talk about popular culture has been enormously valuable, helping us to think about the relations between production and consumption. Even among popular artists, there has been a tendency to reject claims of artistic status for works that were produced purely for entertainment purposes. I have several times lately found myself locked into debates with prominent game designers, for example, who were convinced that their work could not be seen as art because it was produced according to commercial impulses. This dismissal of popular art impacts the ways that art critics celebrate Matthew Barney's borrowings from the horror cinema without taking seriously the artistic ambitions of the filmmakers, such as David Cronenberg and Clive Barker, from whom he draws inspiration. You see it when judges decide that video games do not deserve constitutional protections because they do not constitute meaningful forms of expression. The power to speak about aesthetic value carries enormous political and cultural weight. The challenge is to find ways to talk about popular entertainment on its own terms, to respect the critical sensibilities of media producers and consumers without imposing top-down standards about what constitutes artistic merit.

Implicit in the subtitles I use throughout this book is an appreciation of earlier authors—Walter De Leon, Sergei Eisenstein, Gilbert Seldes, and Robert Warshow, among them—who wrote with great passion about what they saw as emergent forms of popular art. In deploying some of their core concepts to frame this book, I want to reclaim the category of popular art, with an understanding that aesthetic appreciation is complementary, not antagonistic, to the goals of understanding these works from social, cultural, ideological, or economic perspectives. The essays contained here certainly take up core concerns of gender, generation, class, race, and sexuality that have been central to the study of popular culture, but they often approach those debates from a different angle. These essays show that examining the sentimental construction of dogs, the feminist inflection of exploitation cinema, or the melodramatic dimensions of traditional masculine culture can be powerful ways of locating and understanding the "hot buttons" of a society.

The first section, "The Lively Arts," starts with a consideration of the relationship between high art and popular culture. The first essay resurrects Gilbert Seldes's concept of the lively arts to explore in what sense we might think of computer and video games as art. The second essay reverses polarities, showing how contemporary avant-garde artist Matthew Barney is indebted to his borrowings from various popular artists.

The second section, "The Immediate Experience," shifts focus to the ways popular culture plays with powerful emotions and controversial content. These essays deal with sex, violence, and trauma. At heart, they are asking who is allowed to express what emotions in what contexts.

The essays in the final section, "Welcome to the Playground," read children's culture as caught between children's desires and adult's expectations. Each essay asks us to think about the meanings associated with children's play, the ways adults shape children's fantasy lives in order to mold children's developing minds, and the gap between the reality of children's everyday experience and the world offered them through popular culture.

Let the show begin.

PART I

The Lively Arts

In 1924, the cultural critic Gilbert Seldes wrote an essential book on the popular aesthetic, *The Seven Lively Arts*, making what was then a bold argument—that America's greatest cultural contributions in the twentieth century would come not from imitating the great art traditions of Europe, but rather from exploring emerging idioms such as jazz, Broadway musicals, cinema, and comic strips.[1] Seldes sought an aesthetic language for discussing these "lively arts," one that emphasized energy, virtuosity, and kinetics rather than nuance, narrative, or thematic ambitions, and he was not afraid to apply this vocabulary to talk about what excited him about Picasso and the emergence of modern art. His book is seldom read today because it is so preoccupied with describing the emotional dynamics of specific performances rather than making grand statements, but it contains core insights that continue to shape the study of popular culture.

In "Games, the New Lively Art" I attempt to tease out some of Seldes's core claims about popular culture and apply them to the study of computer and video games. This essay emerged from a series of workshops that I and other faculty in the MIT Comparative Media Studies Program conducted with key "creative leaders" at Electronic Arts, one of the preeminent games publishers. As we sat around a seminar table with leading game designers, it was clear that they already had a well-developed framework for thinking about their craft, but they felt that discourse on games as "art" strengthened their hands in dealing with the management and marketing divisions of their own company, who were often hostile to experimentation and innovation. When I presented the earliest formulation of these ideas in *Technology Review* and in the arts section of the *New York Times*, I was struck by the public resistance to the idea that games might be considered art. I pondered yet again how radical Seldes's assertions about the value of slapstick comedy or comic strips must have seemed the better part of a century ago. Today we take such arguments for granted, but we still have difficulty extending them to newer forms of popular art. I used to joke that by the end of the twenty-first century, some guy in an arm chair would be urging Public Television viewers to think back nostalgically over a century of artistic accomplishment in game design. It turns out that I didn't need to wait so long: a recent PBS documentary, *The Video Game Revolution*, opened with a guy in an arm chair and included me as one of the talking heads helping viewers develop an aesthetic appreciation of games. Games have gone a long way toward cultural respectability and artistic accomplishment over the past few decades, but what will come in the future will boggle people's brains.

The French cultural theorist Pierre Bourdieu rather famously sets forth the differences between popular and bourgeois aesthetics in his book *Distinction*. On the one hand, he argues, the popular aesthetic reflects "a deep-rooted demand for participation . . . the desire to enter into the game, identifying with the character's joys and sufferings, worrying about their fate, espousing their hopes and ideals, living their life."[2] By contrast, Bourdieu argues that the bourgeois aesthetic values "disinvestment, detachment, indifference."[3] Bourdieu associates the bourgeois aesthetic with "the icy solemnity of the great museums, the grandiose luxury of the opera-houses and major theatres, the décor and decorum of concert halls."[4] The popular spectacles of circus and melodrama, on the other hand, are "less formalized ... and less euphemized, they offer more immediate satisfactions. . . . They satisfy the taste for and sense of revelry, the plain speaking and hearty laughter which liberate by setting the social world head over heals, overturning conventions and proprieties."[5]

Working in a different intellectual tradition, Lawrence Levine arrives at a very similar set of conclusions when he seeks to understand how Shakespeare became a central and "sacred" part of American culture. In the nineteenth century, Shakespeare's plays were quoted in vaudeville routines on the decks of showboats and performed in blackface as part of minstrel shows. The emphasis was on the broad humor and the raw emotional power of Shakespeare's stories, not necessarily on the lyricism of his language. Americans of all classes shared a fascination with the vibrant, larger-than-life personalities of the great Shakespearean performers, whose images were marketed on cheap postcards that people collected much as we collect baseball cards today. And the theatrical practices of the time encouraged the kinds of participation Bourdieu saw as so central to the popular aesthetic: "To envision nineteenth-century theater audiences correctly, one might do well to visit a contemporary sporting event in which the spectators not only are similarly heterogeneous but also . . . more than an audience; they are participants who can enter into the action on the field, who feel a sense of immediacy and at times even of control, who articulate their opinions and feelings vocally and unmistakably."[6] In the late nineteenth century, however, Shakespeare gradually became separated from popular culture by the belief that true understanding and appreciation of the "immortal bard" required specialized training and cultivated tastes. Educators argued that one needed to be taught to comprehend works that only a few decades earlier had been assumed to be immediately available to the bulk of the population. Levine writes about the "sacralization" of Shakespeare as the imposition of a kind of emotional distance and intellectual rigor on the part of the spectator and an emotional constraint on the part of the performer. Shakespeare, in other words, became an acquired taste, and over time fewer people made the effort to master these plays, until Shakespeare came to be regarded by many as something stuffy and boring.

John Kasson has similarly explored how emotional constraint and outburst came to demarcate different sets of class norms in nineteenth-century America. As the century progressed, the culture of popular participation gave way to more and more regulations on audience behavior, a process he describes as "the disciplining of spectatorship."[7] Read through Kasson's account, we might see the "wow climax" in vaudeville as holding onto the play with passions that was under siege elsewhere in the culture. Yet, how then do we explain the persistence of the "wow climax" across a range of different forms of contemporary popular culture? As I will suggest in the next section, these powerful emotions were not so much repressed as managed.

Even though popular culture is widely consumed across all levels of our society, there is still a tendency to associate it with the lower orders. As I discover almost every time I go to a cocktail party, there are people out there who are excessively proud of the fact that they do not own a television set, go to movies, play games, or read comics. Somehow, the assertion that "I don't even own a book" doesn't carry the same weight! Yet, they are equally bone-headed statements in the modern era.

Arguably, Bourdieu is at his best as a critic of the bourgeois aesthetic, stripping aside its claims to neutrality in order to demonstrate how it is bound up with class privilege. Despite his core insights into the emotional intensity of popular culture, Bourdieu falls back on the old idea that less learning and skill are needed to consume it. More accurately, popular culture depends on skills we acquire outside formal education. We can probably describe in great detail the first time we set foot in an art museum, but few of us will remember our first experience watching television. The skills needed to make sense of popular texts emerge through informal education practices as we spend time consuming media with friends and family. Yet, those who lack such skills—and this would include any number of so-called intellectuals who tend to look down their noses at popular culture—misread television every bit as badly as a country bumpkin might who finds himself trying to make sense of modern dance.

Building on this insight, cultural studies theorists have increasingly investigated the process of popular discrimination and evaluation, perhaps most vividly in the essays gathered by Alan McKee in the anthology *Beautiful Objects in Popular Culture*. As McKee writes in the introduction, "When audiences don't rely on intellectuals to guide them in their cultural consumption, they engage in detailed debates about what's good, what's bad, and how you would make these judgments. The consumers of popular culture already have aesthetic systems in place, which play a part in the intellectual work involved in making decisions about which trashy magazines to buy, which vulgar television programs to view, which dirty websites to visit."[8] McKee asked his contributors to write about what they saw as the "best" example of a particular form of popular culture and then to ground that assessment with a consideration of how evaluations get made within that popular tradition. I chose to write about Brian Michael Bendis as one of the best contemporary mainstream superhero comic-book writers, unpacking each of those modifiers to show how they represent specific criteria and contexts for evaluating comic books. I cited two competing publications that evaluate comics—*Wizard*, which praises artists and writers who work within the mainstream superhero genre, and *Comics Journal*, which celebrates aesthetic experimentation within the alternative comic books sphere. For me, personally, the most interesting work gets neglected by both publications—work that is innovative and yet accessible, that builds on genre traditions but spins them out in surprising new directions.

As the example above suggests, popular critics, no less than intellectuals, can assert too sharp a distinction between popular and high art, not recognizing the many contact zones between the two. Consider, for example, *Village Voice* film critic J. Hoberman's essay "Vulgar Modernism." Hoberman proposes a canon of American popular artists, mostly from the 1950s, whom he describes as "the vulgar equivalent of modernism itself," in some cases drawing direct parallels, as when he speaks of Tex Avery as "the Manet of Vulgar Modernism" or talks about the "distanciation devices" found in Chuck Jones's *Duck Amuck*.[9] Hoberman's essay directed overdue critical attention on folks like Frank Tashlin, Harvey Kurtzman, Will Elder, and Ernie Kovacs. Yet, he may overstate his case when he refers to such work as "vulgar modernism." Many comic-strip artists, from the turn of the century forward, came from art school backgrounds and often took classes from or alongside leading American modernist artists; they often directly quoted from and responded to specific artists and their work. In what sense can their work be called "vulgar"? They certainly are not vulgar in the sense that their work is uninformed by the practices of modern art. Perhaps they might be called "vernacular" in the sense that they choose to operate outside of that art world, adopting different aesthetic principles more appropriate to alternative contexts of production and consumption. Would we not be better off saying that these artists carried out modernist goals and impulses through other means, rather than imagining them as naïve or primitive artists who don't quite understand what they are doing?

My essay on Matthew Barney examines the increasingly blurry lines between popular culture and modern art. Barney has freely acknowledged being a fan of many forms of contemporary popular culture, particularly horror films. When I was approached by the Guggenheim Museum to write an essay on this significant contemporary artist, I was initially reluctant, arguing that I was a specialist on American popular culture and had never written about experimental art. Yet, as I began to read the critical writing about Barney's *Cremaster* cycle, it was clear that his work was often discussed in relation to popular culture by art critics who had little or no real appreciation of the genre traditions that inspired him. I was angered by the ease with which these writers dismissed David Cronenberg, Clive Barker, or Wes Craven, seeing their work not as accomplished popular art interesting on its own terms, but rather reading horror cinema as a junkyard from which Barney could raid spare parts. As someone who has written extensively about fan creativity, I had no trouble valuing Barney's appropriations as expanding the range of meanings associated with the horror genre, but I would be damned if I would see his deployment of these borrowed materials as elevating their status. The resulting essay respects both Barker and Barney, showing the commonality of their interests, while acknowledging the very different kinds of emotional responses they court—the intensification of affect in popular horror films and the dissociation in Barney's installation pieces. I was asked to rewrite it again and again; in the end, the Guggenheim bowed to Barney's own wish to avoid comparisons with other artists, high or low. I was frankly shocked that any artist could exert such great control over how his work was discussed. This essay appears in print for the first time in this collection.

1

Games, the New Lively Art

Another important element is a belief that creators are artists. At the same time, however, it's necessary for us creators to be engineers, because of the skill required for the creations.[1]

—Shigeru Miyamoto, Nintendo

Why can't these game wizards be satisfied with their ingenuity, their $7 billion (and rising) in sales, their capture of a huge chunk of youth around the world? Why must they claim that what they are doing is "art"? . . . Games can be fun and rewarding in many ways, but they can't transmit the emotional complexity that is the root of art.[2]

—Jack Kroll, *Newsweek*

Let's imagine games as an art form. I know, I know—for many of us in contact with the so-called real arts, the notion sounds pretentious. It also makes developers who are former computer science majors edgy because it challenges assumptions that games are founded upon technology. Still, it's a useful concept. It's especially useful when we start to think about the mediocre state of our profession and about ways to elevate our aims, aspirations, and attitudes.[3]

—Hal Barwood, LucasArts

Over the past three decades, computer and video games have progressed from the primitive two-paddles-and-a-ball *Pong* to the sophistication of *Final Fantasy*, a participatory story with cinema-quality graphics that unfolds over nearly 100 hours of game play, or *Black & White*, an ambitious moral tale where the player's god-like choices between good and evil leave tangible marks on the landscape.[4] The computer game has been a killer app for the home PC, increasing consumer demand for vivid graphics, rapid processing, greater memory, and better sound. One could make the case that games have been to the PC what NASA was to the mainframe—the thing that pushes forward innovation and experimentation. The release of the Sony PlayStation 2, the Microsoft Xbox, and the Nintendo GameCube signals a dramatic increase in the resources available to game designers.

In anticipation of these new technological breakthroughs, people within and beyond the games industry began to focus on the creative potentials of this emerging medium. Mapping the aesthetics of game design, they argued, would not only enable them to consolidate decades of experimentation and innovation but would also propel them toward greater artistic accomplishment. Game designers were being urged to think of themselves not simply as technicians producing corporate commodities but rather as artists mapping the dimensions and potentials of an emerging medium; this reorientation, it was hoped, would force them to ask harder questions in their design meetings and to aspire toward more depth and substance in the product they shipped. At the same time, the games industry confronted increased public and government scrutiny. If you parsed the rhetoric of the moral reformers, it was clear that their analogies to pollution or carcinogens revealed their base-level assumption that games were utterly without redeeming value, lacking any claim to meaningful content or artistic form. Seeing games as art, however, shifted the terms of the debate. Most of these discussions started from the premise that games were an emerging art form that had not yet realized its full potential. Game designer Warren Spector, for example, told a *Joystick 101* interviewer, "We're just emerging from infancy. We're still making (and remaking!) *The Great Train Robbery* or *Birth of a Nation* or, to be really generous, maybe we're at the beginning of what might be called our talkies period. But as Al Jolson said in *The Jazz Singer*, "You ain't heard nothing yet!"[5] In this context, critical discussions sought to promote experimentation and diversification of game form, content, and audience, not to develop prescriptive norms.

These debates were staged at trade shows and academic conferences, in the pages of national magazines (such as *Newsweek* and *Technology Review*) and newspapers (such as the *New York Times*), and in online zines aimed at the gaming community (such as *Joystick 101* and *Gamasutra*). Game designers, policy makers, art critics, fans, and academics all took positions on the questions of whether computer games could be considered an art form and what kinds of aesthetic categories made sense for discussing them.

Games have increasingly influenced contemporary cinema, helping to define the frantic pace and model the multi-directional plotting of *Run Lola Run*, providing the role-playing metaphor for *Being John Malkovich*, encouraging a fascination with the slippery line between reality and digital illusions in *The Matrix*, inspiring the fascination with decipherment and puzzle-solving at the heart of *Memento*, and even providing a new way of thinking about Shakespearean tragedy in *Titus*. Game interfaces and genres have increasingly surfaced as metaphors or design elements in avant-garde installations. Matthew Barney, currently the darling of the museum world, transformed the Guggenheim into a giant video game for one of his *Cremaster* films, having his protagonists battle their way up the ramps, boss by boss.[6] If critics such as *Newsweek*'s Jack Kroll were reluctant to ascribe artistic merit to games, artists in other media seemed ready to absorb aspects of game aesthetics into their work. At high schools and colleges across the country, students discussed games with the same passions with which earlier generations debated the merits of the New American Cinema or the French New Wave. Media studies programs reported that a growing number of their students wanted to be game designers rather than filmmakers.

At the same time, academics were finally embracing games as a topic worthy of serious examination—not simply as a social problem, a technological challenge, a cultural phenomenon, or an economic force within the entertainment industry, but also as an art form that demanded serious aesthetic evaluation.[7] Conferences on the art and culture of games were hosted at MIT, the University of Southern California, the University of Chicago, and the University of West England. As academics have confronted games, they have often found it easier to discuss them in social, economic, and cultural terms than through aesthetic categories. The thrust of media studies writing in recent years has been focused on the category of popular culture and framed through ideological categories, rather than in terms of popular art, a concept that carried far greater resonance in the first half of the twentieth century.

My goal here is not to argue against the value of applying concepts and categories from cultural studies to the analysis of games, but rather to make the case that something was lost when we abandoned a focus on popular aesthetics. The category of aesthetics has considerable power in our culture, helping to define not only cultural hierarchies but also social, economic, and political ones as well. The ability to dismiss certain forms of art as inherently without value paves the way for regulatory policies;

the ability to characterize certain media forms as "cultural pollution" also impacts how the general public perceives those people who consume such material; and the ability to foreclose certain works from artistic consideration narrows the ambitions and devalues the accomplishments of people who work in those media. I will admit that discussing the art of video games conjures up comic images: tuxedo-clad and jewel-bedecked patrons admiring the latest *Street Fighter*, middle-aged academics pontificating on the impact of Cubism on *Tetris*, bleeps and zaps disrupting our silent contemplation at the Guggenheim. Such images tell us more about our contemporary notion of art—as arid and stuffy, as the property of an educated and economic elite, as cut off from everyday experience— than they tell us about games.

The Lively Criticism of Gilbert Seldes

In the following pages I revisit one important effort to spark a debate about the aesthetic merits of popular culture—Gilbert Seldes's 1924 book *The Seven Lively Arts*—and suggest how reclaiming Seldes might contribute to our current debates about the artistic status of computer and video games. Adopting what was then a controversial position, Seldes argued that America's primary contributions to artistic expression had come through emerging forms of popular culture such as jazz, the Broadway musical, vaudeville, Hollywood cinema, the comic strip, and the vernacular humor column.[8] While some of these arts have gained cultural respectability over the past seventy-five years (and others have died out entirely), each was disreputable when Seldes staked out his position. Seldes wanted his book to serve two purposes: first, he wanted to give readers fresh ways of thinking about and engaging with the contents of popular art; second, he wanted to use the vitality and innovation of these emerging forms to challenge the "monotonous stupidity," "ridiculous postures," and "stained glass attitudes" of what we might now call middlebrow culture.[9]

Readers then were skeptical of Seldes's claims about cinema for many of the same reasons that contemporary critics dismiss games—they were suspicious of cinema's commercial motivations and technological origins, concerned about Hollywood's appeals to violence and eroticism, and insistent that cinema had not yet produced works of lasting value. Seldes, on the other hand, argued that cinema's popularity demanded that we reassess its aesthetic qualities. Cinema and other popular arts were to be celebrated, he insisted, because they were so deeply imbedded in everyday life, because they were democratic arts embraced by average citizens. Through streamlined styling and syncopated rhythms, they captured the vitality of contemporary urban experience. They took the very machinery of the industrial age, which many felt to be dehumanizing, and found within it the resources for expressing individual visions, for reasserting basic human needs, desires, and fantasies. And these new forms were still open to experimentation and discovery. They were, in Seldes's words, "lively arts." . . .

Games represent a new lively art, one as appropriate for the digital age as those earlier media were for the machine age. They open up new aesthetic experiences and transform the computer screen into a broadly accessible realm of experimentation and innovation. And games have been embraced by a public that has otherwise been unimpressed by much of what passes for digital art. Much as the salon arts of the 1920s seemed sterile alongside the vitality and inventiveness of popular culture, contemporary efforts to create interactive narrative through modernist hypertext or avant-garde installation art seem lifeless and pretentious alongside the creativity and exploration, the sense of fun and wonder, that game designers bring to their craft. As Hal Barwood explained to readers of *Game Developer* magazine in February 2002, "Art is what people accomplish when they don't quite know what to do, when the lines on the road map are faint, when the formula is vague, when the product of their labors is new and unique."[10] Art exists, in other words, on the cutting edge—and that was where games had remained for most of their history. The game designers are creating works that sparked the imagination and made our hearts race. And they are doing so without the safety net that inherited modernist rhetoric provides for installation and hypertext artists. They can offer no simple, straightforward justification for what they are doing or why they are doing it except by way of talking about "the fun factor," that is, the quality of the emotional experience they offer players.

Although Seldes's writing is impressionistic and evocative, rather than developing a systematic argument or framework, one can read *The Seven Lively Arts* as mapping an aesthetic of popular culture that is defined broadly enough to be useful for discussing a wide range of specific media and cultural practices, including many that did not exist when he wrote the book. Seldes drew a distinction between the "great arts," which seek to express universal and timeless values, and the "lively arts," which seek to give shape and form to immediate experiences and impressions. "Great" and "lively" arts differ "not in the degree of their intensity but in the degree of their intellect."[11] Seldes, in fact, often shows signs of admiring the broad strokes of the popular arts—where the needs for clarity and immediate recognition from a broadly defined audience allowed "no fuzzy edges, no blurred contours"—over the nuance and complexity of Great Art.[12] He consistently values affect over intellect, immediate impact over long-term consequences, the spontaneous impulse over the calculated effect.

Seldes defined art through its ability to provoke strong and immediate reactions. As popular artists master the basic building blocks of their media, they developed techniques that enable them to shape and intensify affective experience. Creativity, Seldes argued, was all bound up with our sense of play and our demands to refresh our sensual apparatus and add new energy to our mental life, which was apt to become dulled through the routine cognition and perception of everyday life. As he put it: "We require, for nourishment, something fresh and transient."[13]

From the start, games were able to create strong emotional impressions—this accounts for their enormous staying power with consumers. Early games such as *Pac-Man* or *Asteroids* could provoke strong feelings of tension or paranoia. The works of Shigeru Miyamoto (*Super Mario Brothers*, *Legend of Zelda*) represented imaginative landscapes, as idiosyncratic and witty in their way as the *Krazy Kat* comic strips or Mack Sennett comedies Seldes admired. Seldes wrote at a moment when cinema was starting to consolidate what it had learned over its first three decades of experimentation and produce works that mixed and matched affective elements to create new kinds of experiences. One could argue that recent games such as *Deus X*, *Grand Theft Auto 3*, and *Shenmue* represent a similar consolidation of earlier game genres, whereas games like *The Sims*, *Majestic*, *Rez*, and *Black & White* are expanding the repertoire of game mechanics and, by doing so, expanding the medium's potential audience.

The great arts and the lively arts share a common enemy, the "bogus arts," the middlebrow arts, which seek to substitute "refinement of taste" for "refinement of technique" and, in the process, cut themselves off from the culture around them.[14] The popular arts, he warned, often promise more than they can deliver; their commercial imperative requires that they leave us somewhat unsatisfied and thus eager to consume more. But in their straightforward appeal to emotion, they do not "corrupt." Middlebrow culture, however, often seduces us with fantasies of social and cultural betterment at the expense of novelty and innovation. Seldes wanted to deploy the shock value of contemporary popular culture to shake up the settled thinking of the art world, to force it to reconsider the relationship between art and everyday life.

At a time when the United States was emerging as a world leader, Seldes wanted to identify what he felt was a distinctively American voice. He protested, "Our life is energetic, varied, constantly changing; our art is imitative, anemic."[15] Contemporary intellectuals, he felt, had accepted too narrow a conception of what counted as art, seeing America as a new country that had not yet won the approval of its Old World counterparts. Their search for refinement constituted a "genteel corruption," a "thinning out of the blood," which cut them off from what was vital in the surrounding culture. European artists, he suggested, had often revitalized their work by returning to folk art traditions, but operating in a new country with few folk roots, American artists would need to find their vitality through a constant engagement with what was fresh and novel in popular culture. As Seldes explained, "For America, the classic and the folk arts are both imported goods. . . . But the circumstance that our popular arts are home-grown, without the prestige of Europe and of the past, had thrown upon them a shadow of vulgarity, as if they were the products of ignorance and intellectual bad manners."[16]

Seldes wrote at a time when American dominance over popular culture and European dominance over high culture were taken for granted. The aesthetics of contemporary game design, however, operates in a global context. One would have to concede, for example, that our current game genres took shape as a conversation between Japanese and American industries (with plenty of input from consumers and creators elsewhere). Increasingly, American popular culture is responding to Asian influences, with the rise in violence in mass market entertainment a property of heightened competition between Japan, India, Hong Kong, and Hollywood for access to international markets. Action elements surface, not only in games but also in film, television, and comics, because such elements are more readily translated across linguistic and national boundaries.

The need to appeal to a mass consumer, Seldes insisted, meant that popular artists could not give themselves over to morbid self-absorption. Creating works in media that were still taking shape, popular artists were not burdened with a heritage but constantly had to explore new directions and form new relationships with their publics. The lively arts look toward the future rather than toward the past. Similarly, game designers work in a commercially competitive environment and within an emerging medium. Thus, they must continually push and stretch formal boundaries in order to create novelty, while they also have to insure that their experimentation remains widely accessible to their desired audience. The context is dramatically different with middlebrow art, which often wants to build on well-established traditions rather than rely on formal experimentation, or high art, which can engage in avant-garde experimentation accessible only to an educated elite.

Seldes wrote during an era of media in transition. The cinema was maturing as an expressive medium—making a move from mere spectacle toward character and consequence, from a "cinema of attractions" to a classical storytelling system.[17] A decade earlier, many intellectuals might have freely dismissed cinema as a parlor entertainment whose primary content consisted of little more than chase scenes and pratfalls. A decade later, few would have doubted that cinema had earned its status as one of the most important contemporary arts. Seldes's respect for cinema's popular roots set him at odds with many contemporary critics, who saw the refinement of narrative techniques as essential for the maturation of the medium. Cinema, Seldes argued, "was a toy and should have remained a toy—something for our delight."[18] For Seldes, cinema was not an art despite slapstick; it was an art because slapstick demonstrated that the fullest potentials of motion pictures lay in their ability to capture motion and express emotion. "Everything in slapstick was cinematographic," Seldes proclaimed, remaining deeply suspicious of filmmakers like Thomas Ince or D.W. Griffith, who he feared had sought to impose literary and theatrical standards alien to cinema's core aesthetic impulses.[19] He explained, "The rightness of the spectacle film is implicit in its name: the screen is a place on which things can be seen and so long as a film depends on the eye it is right for the screen."[20]

The maturing of the cinematic medium may well have been what enabled Seldes to recognize its artistic accomplishments. However, in aspiring to cultural respectability, cinema ran a high risk of losing touch with its own primitive roots. Seldes sounded a warning that would seem familiar to many contemporary observers of video and computer games, suggesting that the cinema was confusing technological enhancement with aesthetic advancement, confusing the desire to reproduce reality for the desire to create an emotionally engaging experience. What had given filmgoers the "highest degree of pleasure," he argued, was "escaping actuality and entering into a created world, built on its own inherent logic, keeping time to its own rhythm—where we feel ourselves at once strangers and at home."[21]

Newsweek's Jack Kroll sparked heated debates in the gamer community when he argued that audiences will probably never be able to care as deeply about pixels on the computer screen as they care about characters in films: "Moviemakers don't have to simulate human beings; they are right there, to be recorded and orchestrated. . . . The top-heavy titillation of *Tomb Raider*'s Lara Croft falls flat next to the face of Sharon Stone. . . . Any player who's moved to tumescence by digibimbo Lara is in big trouble."[22] Yet countless viewers cry when Bambi's mother dies, and World War II veterans can tell you they felt real lust for *Esquire*'s Vargas girls. We have learned to care as much about creatures of pigment as we care about images of real people. Why should pixels be different? If we haven't yet cared this deeply about game characters (a debatable proposition, as the response to Kroll's article indicates), it is because the game design community has not yet found the right techniques for evoking such emotions, not because there is an intrinsic problem in achieving emotional complexity in the medium itself. Kroll, like the respectable critics of early cinema whom Seldes battled, assumes that realism is necessary in order to achieve a high degree of emotional engagement. The art of games may not come from reproducing the world of the senses. As Steve Poole has written:

> Whereas film—at least naturalistic, "live-action" film—is tied down to real spaces, the special virtue of videogames is precisely their limitless plasticity. And only when that virtue is exploited more fully will videogames become a truly unprecedented art—when their level of world-building competence is matched with a comparable level of pure invention. We want to be shocked by novelty. We want to lose ourselves in a space that is utterly different. We want environments that have never been seen, never been imagined before.[23]

Independent game designers such as Eric Zimmerman have argued that games need to return to a garage aesthetic, stripping aside fancy graphics and elaborate cinematics, to reclaim the core elements that make games distinctive from other expressive media. Protesting that games are more than simply "mutant cinema," Zimmerman warns that "mistaken attempts to apply the skills and methods of Hollywood to the world of electronic gaming resulted in CD-ROMs bloated with full-motion video sequences and lacking meaningful gameplay."[24] Similarly, Seldes warned that long intertitles substituted literary for cinematic values, seeking to "explain everything except the lack of action," and resulting in scenes devoid of visual interest.[25] The results were movies that no longer moved. Zimmerman and others warn that extended cinematics, often the favored means of adding narrative and character to games, cuts the player off from the action and thus sacrifice those elements of interactivity that make games unique. . . . Seldes's concept of the lively arts focuses primarily on the kinetic aspects of popular culture, aspects that can operate inside or outside a narrative frame. Poole arrives at a similar conclusion:

> A beautifully designed videogame invokes wonder as the fine arts do, only in a uniquely kinetic way. Because the videogame *must* move, it cannot offer the lapidary balance of composition that we value in painting; on the other hand, because it *can* move, it is a way to experience architecture, and more than that to create it, in a way which photographs or drawings can never compete. If architecture is frozen music, then a videogame is liquid architecture.[26]

Memorable Moments

What Seldes offers us might be described as a theory of "memorable moments," a concept that surfaces often in discussions with game designers but only rarely in academic writing about the emerging medium. Writing about the German Expressionist film *The Cabinet of Dr. Caligari*, Seldes praises not its plot but its lingering aftertaste: "I cannot think of half a dozen movies which have left so many clear images in my mind."[27] Later in the book, he writes about the pleasures of finding peak experiences within otherwise banal works: "A moment comes when everything is exactly right, and you have an occurrence—it may be something exquisite or something unnameably gross; there is in it an ecstasy which sets it apart from everything else."[28] Such peak experiences seem fully within reach of contemporary game designers in a way that complex causally integrated yet open-ended narratives or psychologically rounded yet fully interactive characters are not. If games are going to become an art, right now, rather than in some distant future, when all of our technical challenges have been resolved, it may come from game designers who are struggling with the mechanics of motion and emotion, rather than those of story and character.

As game designers evaluate games on the basis of their emotional appeal, their criteria often emphasize moments of emotional intensity or visual spectacle—the big skies that can suddenly open before you when you ride your snowboard in *SSX*, the huge shots in a hockey game when the puck goes much further than it could in real life, the pleasure of sending your car soaring off a cliff or smashing through pedestrians in *Grand Theft Auto 3*. Increasingly, games enable us to grab snapshots of such moments, to replay them and watch them unfold from multiple angles, and to share them with our friends, pushing them to see if they can match our exploits and duplicate our accomplishments. Games companies encourage their staffs to think of designs in terms of the images on boxes or in previews, the way that the demo is going to look on the trade-show floor. Yet, this may be to reduce the concept of memorable moments to "eye candy" or spectacle, something that can be readily extracted from the play experience, something that can be communicated effectively in a still image. . . .

Often, in games, those memorable moments don't simply depend on spectacle. After all, spectacle refers to something that stops you dead in your tracks, forces you to stand and look. Game play becomes memorable when it creates the opposite effect—when it makes you want to move, when it convinces you that you really are in charge of what's happening in the game, when the computer seems to be totally responsive. Frequently, the memorable moment comes when the computer does something that follows logically from your actions, yet doesn't feel like it was pre-scripted and preprogrammed. As *Deus X* designer Warren Spector explains: "Great gameplay comes, I think, from our ability to drop players into compelling situations, provide clear goals for them, give them a variety of tools with which they can impact their environment and then get out of their way. . . . That has to be so much more compelling for players—thrilling even—than simply guessing the canned solution to a puzzle or pressing a mouse button faster than a computer opponent can react."[29]

Seldes was one of a number of early twentieth-century writers who sought to better understand the "mechanics of emotion" that shaped popular entertainment. . . . The Soviet film theorist Sergei Eisenstein developed a theory of "attractions," a term he saw as broad enough to encompass any device—whether formal, narrative, or thematic—that could solicit powerful emotions from a spectator, arguing that film and theater should seek their inspiration from the circus and the music hall.[30] . . . Inspired in part by Pavlovian reflexology, the early twentieth-century entertainers Seldes discussed tried to document and master basic "surefire" stimuli that could provoke a predictable emotional response from the spectator and then to streamline their works, cutting out anything that would obscure or retard that affective impact. . . . As theater critic Vadim Uraneff explained in 1923, "The [vaudeville] actor works with the idea of an immediate response from the audience: and with regard to its demands. By cutting out everything—every line, gesture, movement—to which the audience does not react and by improvising new things, he establishes unusual unity between the audience and himself."[31]

Game designers engage in a similar process as they seek to identify "what's not in the game," that is, to determine what elements would get in the way of the game mechanic or confuse the player. Game designers speak of "hooks" that will grab consumers' attention and keep them playing, a concept that would have been familiar to vaudeville showman and circus barkers. Longtime game designers cite back to the challenges of developing games that played well in the arcades, which offered a compelling experience that could be staged in under two minutes and ramped up to an emotional high that would leave the player reaching for another quarter. Early console games also demanded economy, given the limited memory capacity of the early systems.[32] However, as consoles have developed greater capacity and thus enabled lengthier and more complex game experiences, some fear that game designers are adding too many features that get in the way of the core mechanics. The lengthy cut scenes of narrative exposition and character backstory, which academics praise for their aesthetic advancements, are often received with hostility by serious gamers because they slow down the play and result in a relatively passive experience. A great deal of effort goes into the design of the first few minutes of a game to insure that they offer a solid emotional payoff for the player rather than ending in frustration: an early moment of mastery or movement helps spark an appetite for bigger and better things to come.[33]

Play as Performance

Seldes and other early twentieth-century critics saw the emotional intensity of popular culture as emerging from the central performer, whose mastery over his or her craft enabled the performer to "command" the spectator's attention. Seldes writes about the "daemonic" authority of Al

Jolson: "he never saves up—for the next scene, or the next week, or the next show. . . . He flings into a comic song or three-minute impersonation so much energy, violence, so much of the totality of one human being, that you feel it would suffice for a hundred others."[34] His contemporary, Robert Lytell, described the characteristics of the best revue performers:

> Human horsepower, size, electricity, energy, zingo. . . . These people have a fire in their belly which makes you sit up and listen whether you want to or not, which silences criticism until their act is over, and you can start thinking again. . . . They seize you and do pretty nearly anything they want with you and while it is going on, you sit with your mouth open and laugh and laugh again.[35]

Such comments reflected the performer-centered aesthetic of vaudeville and the Broadway revue. One might well understand the pleasures of game play according to performance criteria—but as we do so, we need to understand it as a pas de deux between the designer and the player. As game designer David Perry explains, "A good game designer always knows what the players are thinking and is looking over their shoulders every step of the way."[36] The game designer's craft makes it possible for players to feel as if they are in control of the situation at all times, even though their game play and emotional experience are significantly sculpted by the designer. It is a tricky balancing act, making players aware of the challenges they confront while ensuring that they have the resources necessary to overcome those challenges. If the game play becomes transparently easy or impossibly hard, the players lose interest. They need to feel that they can run faster, shoot more accurately, jump further, and think smarter than in their everyday life, and it is this expansion of one's capacity that accounts for the emotional intensity of most games. I still recall the first time I grabbed the controls of *Sonic the Hedgehog*, got a good burst of speed, and started running as fast as I could around the loop-to-loops, collecting gold coins, and sending all obstacles scattering. I am not an especially good game player, yet I felt at that moment totally invincible, and everything in the game's design—the space, the character, the soundtrack—contributed to giving me that sense of effortless control, that release from normal constraints.

As many observers have noted, we don't speak of controlling a cursor on the screen when we describe the experience of playing a game; we act as if we had unmediated access to the fictional space. We refer to our game characters in the first person and act as if their experiences were our own. James Newman has argued that we might understand the immediacy of game play not in terms of how convincing the representations of the character and the fictional world are but rather in terms of the character's "capacity" to respond to our impulses and desires. A relatively iconic, simplified character may produce an immediate emotional response; a relatively stylized world can nevertheless be immersive. Once we engage with the game, the character may become simply a vehicle we use to navigate the game world. As Newman explains:

> Lara Croft is defined less by appearance than by the fact that "she" allows the player to jump distance x, while the ravine in front of us is larger than that, so we better start thinking of a new way round. . . . Characters are defined around gameplay-affecting characteristics. It doesn't matter that it's a burly guy—or even a guy—or perhaps even a human. That the hang glider can turn faster is a big deal; this affects the way the game plays. This affects my chances of getting a good score.[37]

A number of game designers have reminded me that Shigeru Miyamoto, whom many regard as the medium's first real master, designs his games around verbs, that is, around the actions the game enables players to perform. He wants each game to introduce a new kind of mission, making it possible for the consumer to do something that no other game has allowed before. A close examination of Miyamoto's games also suggests that he designs a playing space that both facilitates and thwarts our ability to carry out that action and thus creates a dramatic context in which the action takes aesthetic shape and narrative significance.

Many contemporary games seek to expand that sense of player mastery beyond the game space, encouraging players to dance to the rhythm, to shake maracas, twist turntables, beat drums, as the domestic space or the arcade space become performance spaces. The spectacular and performative dimensions of these games are summarized by this player's account of his experience of being a *Dance Dance Revolution* devotee:

> The first song starts and finishes, and I did well. I hear a man ask me "How in the hell do you do that?" I just laugh and pick the next

song, a harder one. I can hear people milling around behind me and I can see their reflection on screen. I hear whispers of "wow", and "damn!" The song ends. I hear a woman shout "Wooooo!" I turn and smile. Her and her friend blush and turn away. . . . Of course, Friday and Saturday nights are the big days to show off. Big crowds, loud crowds, and occasionally rowdy, mean crowds. These are the days for the big dogs, and competition is tough. Very hard songs are done, and feet fly like hummingbird wings. . . . But you take the good with the bad, and it's still fun when you get a good, loud reaction, and there's more than "hoots" to it. There's that feeling when you finally beat that tough song, or when you help a buddy learn to play. It still boils down to just having fun, whether the crowd cheers or not.[38]

Here, the player gets to enjoy the same kind of experience that fueled Jolson's performance—the pleasure of intense and immediate feedback from an engaged audience. At the same time, the game instructs the performance, giving the kinds of structured feedback that enable players to quickly master the necessary skills to impress friends and strangers alike.

The designers of *Frequency* and *Rez*, two recent music-making games, have sought to expand the sensory experience available to players. Both games start with the sensation of traveling at high speeds down winding tunnels of light and color. As we move through these stylized but representational spaces, our interactions help to shape the sound and rhythm of their techno-based soundtracks. As we get into the spirit of the game, we stop thinking simply in terms of our physical movements and become more in tune with the pulse of the music. Such games start to blur the line between play and performance, creating a context where even novice musicians can start to jam and advanced players can create complex and original musical compositions. *Frequency* designer Alex Rigopulos describes the trajectory of a player through his game:

When a gamer starts to play *Frequency*, he plays it using the gaming skills he already has: the ability to react to symbolic visual information with a precisely timed manual response. . . . What we noticed again and again in playtesting was that there is a certain point at which novice players stop playing entirely with their eyes and start playing with their ears (or, rather, their "internal ears"): they start to feel the musical beat; then, as a stream of gems approaches, they look at the oncoming stream, "imagine" in their ears what that phrase will feel like or sound like rhythmically, and begin to "play the notes" (rather than "shoot the gems"). As soon as players cross this threshold, they begin excelling much more rapidly in the game.[39]

Rez's designers have suggested that they based their designs on the theories of abstract artist Wassily Kandinsky: "*Rez* is an experience, a fusion of light, vibration and sound completely immersed in synaesthesia."[40] Here, the game controller vibrates and even develops the rhythm of a heartbeat in response to the player's actions, creating yet another dimension to what is a complex multimedia experience.

These games build on the excess kinetic energy that has always surrounded play. Watch children play games: they sway with the movement of the figures on the screen and bounce with the action, totally engaged with the moment. One could argue that such responses reflect the degree of control they feel over what happens on the screen. We speak not just of controlling the characters but of "owning" the space of the game. It is even more interesting to observe the responses of people watching them play, since they also mimic the actions that are occurring on the screen, even though their actions have no consequences on the game play. Cinema has never achieved this same visceral impact, unless we are talking about the kind of fairground attractions that are designed to give us the sensation of driving down a racetrack or riding a rollercoaster. People do sometimes feel like they are about to fall out of their seats when watching an IMAX image, for example. Games routinely create the same degree of immersion without having to surround us completely. Sometimes they achieve it by the use of first-person perspective, but one can have the same sensation watching an early Mario Brothers game that relies totally on third person point of view and a relatively iconographic landscape. One could argue that it is our knowledge of the interactive potential of games that produces these kinetic effects, yet I have observed similar kinds of behavior from people watching prerecorded clips from games, suggesting that the response has as much to do with the visual presentation of the action as any real-time engagement with the controller.

Expressive Amplification

David Bordwell makes a similar argument about the Hong Kong action film:

> We need no special training to grasp vigorous, well structured move-
> ment. More exactly, it's not so much that we grasp it as that it grabs us;
> we respond kinesthetically, as when we tap our toes to music, or ham-
> mer the air at a basketball game. These films literally grip us; we can
> watch ourselves tense and relax, twitch or flinch. By arousing us through
> highly legible motion and staccato rhythms, and by intensifying their
> arousal through composition and editing and sound, the films seem to
> ask our bodies to recall elemental and universal events like striking,
> swinging, twisting, leaping, rolling.[41]

By now, the aesthetics of the action movie and the video game are hope-
lessly intertwined: game aesthetics have clearly and directly shaped the
emergence of the genres Bordwell discusses; at the same time, game designers have consciously internalized lessons from filmmakers like Akira
Kurosawa, James Cameron, and John Woo. As game criticism emerges as
a field, it will need to address not only the stories that games tell or the
kinds of play that they facilitate, but also the formal principles that shape
our emotional responses to them. Bordwell's account of the Hong Kong
martial arts movie suggests two intertwined factors: first, the ways that
commonly staged actions appeal to bodily memories; and second, the
ways that various aesthetic devices can intensify and exaggerate the impact of such actions, making them both more legible and more intense
than their real-world counterparts.

Bordwell describes this second process as "expressive amplification."[42]
Action-film directors combine circus acrobatics and special effects with
rapid-fire editing and stylized sound effects to amp up the intensity of a
fight sequence. Similarly, game designers use movement, "camera" angle,
sound effects, and other devices to exaggerate the impact of punches or
to expand the flight of a skateboarder. The protagonists in *Jet Grind
Radio* run riot through the streets of a futuristic Tokyo, sliding up and
down ramps or along rails at high speeds, their in-line skates sending out
a shower of sparks, the sounds of the cops' boots pounding right on their
heels, and the crackle of the police radio breathing down their necks.

Here, we see "expressive amplification" at work. We take pleasure not simply in the outcome of the players' actions but the style with which they/we execute them.

Games and Silent Cinema

And this brings us back to what Seldes had to say about the cinema. The police in *Jet Grind Radio* display the exaggerated dignity and one-track thinking we associate with the Keystone Cops, as they hurl themselves onto the protagonist and end up in a heap, face down on the asphalt. Silent cinema, Seldes argued, was an art of expressive movement. He valued the speed and dynamism of Griffith's last-minute races to the rescue, the physical grace of Charlie Chaplin's pratfalls, and the ingenuity of Buster Keaton's engineering feats. He argued that each silent performer developed a characteristic way of moving, a posture, and a rhythm that defined him for the spectator the moment he appeared on the screen. Chaplin "created his own trajectory across the screen which was absolutely his own line of movement."[43] This distinctive way of moving occurred through stylization, reducing screen action to simple units of action, which could recur across a broad range of narrative situations. Moviegoers came to love the slight bounce in Chaplin's walk, the daintiness of his hands, his slightly bow-legged stance.

Games also depend upon an art of expressive movement, with characters defined through their distinctive ways of propelling themselves through space. Game designers have had to reduce character to a limited range of preprogrammed expressions, movements, and gestures, but as they have done so, they have produced characters, like Mario and Luigi or Sonic, who are enormously evocative, who provoke strong emotional reactions.

The art of silent cinema was also an art of atmospheric design. To watch a silent masterpiece like Fritz Lang's *Metropolis* is to be drawn into a world where meaning is carried by the placement of shadows, the movement of machinery, and the organization of space. If anything, game designers have pushed beyond cinema in terms of developing expressive and fantastic environments that convey a powerful sense of mood, provoke our curiosity and amusement, and motivate us to explore. The German Expressionists had to construct the world's largest soundstage to insure that every element in their shots was fully under their control. Game designers start with a blank screen: every element is there because they chose to put it there, so there is no excuse for elements that do not capture our imagination, shape our emotions, or convey meanings. Game designers are seeking inspiration from stage design, amusement park "imagineering," and postmodern architecture as they develop a better understanding of spatial design. Across a range of essays, I have made the case that games might best be discussed through a spatial aesthetic, one which sees the art of game design as a kind of narrative and affective architecture, as linked in important ways to the art of designing amusement park attractions.[44] I have argued that games compensate their players for their loss of mobility, at a time when children enjoy diminished access to real-world play spaces.[45] With Kurt Squire, I have expanded that analysis to look more closely at the ways in which a range of games create spaces that encourage our exploration and are well-designed as staging grounds for conflicts.[46]

Many of the most memorable moments in the silent films Seldes discussed centered on the struggles of characters against spatial features. Consider, for example, the extended sequence in *Safety Last* where Harold Lloyd must climb the side of a building, floor by floor, confronting a series of obstacles, and ends up hanging from the hands of a clock. To be sure, some of the sequence's fascination has to do with the photographic basis of cinema—the fact that Lloyd is actually hanging several stories off the ground (a stunt rendered all the more remarkable by the fact that Lloyd was missing several fingers from one of his hands). Yet, the scene also depends on a challenge-mastery-complication structure remarkably similar to that found in contemporary games: the higher Lloyd climbs the more intense the risk and the more likely he is to fall. Will future generations look back on *Tomb Raider*'s Lara Croft doing battle with a pack of snarling wolves as the early twenty-first-century equivalent of Lillian Gish making her way across the ice floes in *Way Down East*?

In making these analogies, I am not necessarily advocating that games should become more cinematic, any more than Seldes felt cinema should become more theatrical or literary. Game designers should study a wide range of arts, searching not only for what they have done best but also for what they have failed to achieve, for those "roads not taken" that might be more fully realized within a game aesthetic. Game designers will need to experiment with the broadest possible range of approaches and styles, breaking with the still somewhat limited conventions of the existing game genres in some cases and deepening our appreciation of their potentials in others. In the end, games may not take the same path as cinema. Game designers will almost certainly develop their own aesthetic principles as they confront the challenge of balancing our competing desires for story-telling and interactivity. As Spector explains:

> The art in gaming lies in the tension between the elements we put in our game worlds and what players choose to do with those elements. The developers who get that—the ones who aren't just making expensive, so-phisticated pick-a-path books or movies where you get to determine what the next shot is—are the ones who will expand the boundaries of this new art form.[47]

It remains to be seen whether games can give players the freedom they want and still provide an emotionally satisfying and thematically mean-ingful shape to the experience. Some of the best games—*Snood* and *Tetris* come to mind—have nothing to do with storytelling. For all we know, the future art of games may look more like architecture or dance than cin-ema.

The Future of Gaming

If we are to see games accepted as a contemporary art form, game de-signers are going to have to stop using "market pressures" as an excuse for their lack of experimentation. True, game designers need to ship prod-uct, and that can place serious limitations on how much innovation can occur within a single game. Yet, it is worth remembering that all art oc-curs within an economic context. The Hollywood filmmakers of the 1920s and 1930s often produced five to seven feature films per year, yet somewhere in that rush to the marketplace, they nevertheless came to more fully realize the potentials of their medium and developed artworks that have withstood the test of time. What keeps the lively arts lively is that they are the site of consistent experimentation and innovation. No sooner are genre conventions mapped than popular artists start to twist and turn them to yield new effects. The constant push for emotional im-mediacy demands a constant refinement of the art itself, keeping creators on their toes and forcing them to acknowledge audience response into their creative decision-making.

Seldes worried whether the conditions that had led to an enormous flowering of popular arts in the early twentieth century could be sustained in the face of increasingly industrialized modes of production. He blamed the studio system for much of what was wrong with contemporary cinema, yet he ended the book with a prediction that the costs of film production were likely to decrease steadily as the core technology of film production became standardized, thus returning filmmaking to its artisan roots. He predicted: "The first cheap film will startle you; but the film will grow less and less expensive. Presently it will be within the reach of artists. . . . The artists will give back to the screen the thing you have debauched—imagination."[48] Several decades later, in his book *The Great Public*, Seldes would be even more emphatic that the rise of corporate media had strangled the aesthetic experimentation and personal expression that had enabled these "lively arts" to exist in the first place.[49] With the coming of sound, the costs of film production had increased, further consolidating the major studios' control over the filmmaking process, and thus delaying by several decades the rise of independent cinema he had predicted.

What does this suggest about the future of innovation in game design? For starters, the basic apparatus of the camera and the projector were standardized by the turn of the century, enabling early filmmakers to focus on the expressive potential of the medium rather than continuing to have to relearn the basic technology. Game designers, on the other hand, have confronted dramatic shifts in their basic tools and resources on an average of every eighteen months since the emergence of their medium. This constant need to respond to a shifting technological infrastructure has redirected attention toward mastering tools that could have been devoted to exploring the properties and potentials of the medium. Second, despite a pretty rigorous patents war, the early history of filmmaking was marked by relatively low barriers of entry into the marketplace. Although many film histories still focus on a small number of key innovators, we now know that the basic language of cinema emerged through widespread experimentation among filmmakers scattered across the country and around the world. The early history of computer games, by contrast, was dominated by a relatively small number of game platforms, with all games having to pass through this corporate oversight before they could reach the market. The proliferation of authoring tools and open-source game engines have helped to lower barriers of entry into the game marketplace, paving the way for smaller and more independent game companies. In such a context, those emerging companies have often been forced to innovate in order to differentiate their product from what was already on the market.

At the same time as these new delivery technologies have loosened the hold of the platform manufacturers over game content, the cost of game development for those platforms has dramatically increased. We have seen rising technical standards that make it difficult for garage game designers to compete. Some have worried that the result will be an increased focus on blockbuster games with surefire market potential and the constant upgrading of popular franchises. What would contemporary cinema look like if it supported a succession of summer popcorn movies but could not support lower-budget and independent films?

2

Monstrous Beauty and Mutant Aesthetics

Rethinking Matthew Barney's Relationship to the Horror Genre

I'm less interested in skin than in fascia—connective tissue.[1]
—Matthew Barney

We've not devised an aesthetic for the inside of the body any more than we have developed an aesthetic of disease. Most people are disgusted . . . but if you develop an aesthetic for it, it ceases to be ugly. I'm trying to force the audience to change its aesthetic sense.[2]
—David Cronenberg

We have such sights to show you!

—Pinhead, *Hellraiser*

Deep in the subterranean vaults of the Chrysler Building, a creature stirs. A hand breaks through the earth and a red-haired, blue-skinned zombie pushes her way out of the ground. She is hauntingly beautiful and yet otherworldly, an object of both desire and dread. Yet, no sooner does she reach the surface than she wilts and withers in the sunlight, collapsing onto the ground again. She is surrounded by undertakers who lift her up and carry her, placing her to rest inside a 1930 Chrysler Imperial New Yorker. Thus opens Matthew Barney's *Cremaster 3*, which has been described as the culminating piece, the cornerstone, of the entire Cremaster cycle.

In e-mail correspondence with the author, Barney explained that the "dryness" of the classic zombie figure had always "repulsed" him, whereas "the creatures that attract me are wet, sensual, and more unseen" than the undead on view in most contemporary horror films. In the sequence described above, Barney focuses on the sensuality of the zombie figure, the wet earth that clings to her nakedness, the ways that decay re-sculpts her body, the stiffened grace of her movements, and the saturated colors of her thinning hair and decaying flesh. In this, he would seem to be drawing inspiration from other horror filmmakers—Mario Bava and Dario Argento come most immediately to mind—who wanted us to cele-brate the transformations that the human body undergoes after death as a thing of intense, otherworldly beauty; they wanted to blur eros and thanatos so that we could confront the natural human fascination with death not as morbidity but as desire.

Images of death and decay recur throughout *Cremaster 3*. In one of the most disturbing sequences in the entire cycle, the Apprentice is led into a dental operation chamber and forcibly stripped of his clothing to reveal his mutant anatomy underneath. The compressed metal remains of a clas-sic automobile are shoved into his toothless mouth amid pools of blood and speechless moans. His intestines are excreted from his rectum onto the operating table and are studied with strange fascination by his tor-mentors/healers. The Apprentice's body undergoes a strange metamor-phosis in which his apron is transformed into a kilt, with the tartan pat-tern formed from pulsating veins and arteries. At another point, we watch two horses whose bodies seem to consist of little more than rotting flesh sliding slowly off of their parched bones.

To be sure, *Cremaster 3*, like the other films in the cycle, is a complex work that takes its inspiration from various sources, with horror being simply one strand among many. No one viewer is apt to recognize or be able to contextualize the full range of references contained within any of the *Cremaster* films, creating the kind of openness of interpretation that Barney has described as a central goal of his art. As Barney explains, "It excites me that my work can be understood in different ways by different audiences. What operates as an abstract notion for one audience can function as a more charged cultural icon for another. I want both read-ings to be simultaneously possible, but I am more concerned with pre-serving the former (because that quality is much more elusive and frag-ile)."[3] He seems to be drawn to the materials of popular entertainment genres precisely because they are so deeply embedded in our culture, be-cause they already provoke strong associations and affective reactions, and because he wants us to look at them from a fresh perspective by re-moving them from their normal contexts.

On one level, *Cremaster 3* brings together the iconography, mythology, visual patterning, and color schemes of the earlier *Cremaster* films into one final vision—a dreamlike condensation of the series as a whole. If critics have struggled in the past to understand what the various *Cremaster* films had in common, this final work in the cycle brings them together to form one unified mythology that unfolds across the entire sequence of films and indeed, across the full body of Barney's work.

At the same time, the film represents a composite of the complex aesthetic influences that shaped American culture in the 1930s. Some images seem to recall the monumentalism with which Lewis Hine depicted the construction workers building Manhattan's skyscrapers; others the autumnal colors with which Edward Hopper depicted late-night New York; still others the brash spectacle of Busby Berkeley musicals or the strange gadgetry of Rube Goldberg or the sudsy slapstick of a Three Stooges comedy. One sequence draws inspiration from the Expressionist settings of Universal Studios monster movies, while others evoke images from gangster films or romantic comedies. And there is the recurring fascination with classic cars and Art Deco architectural details. And, for good measure, this artist throws in the Rockettes and the fashion runway. *Cremaster 3*, in other words, is entertainment for children of all ages!

Barney's aesthetic is one of appropriation and synthesis. Even that wanderlust would resonate within contemporary popular culture, where many artists construct fresh new syntheses of the heavily encoded icons and genre conventions of the past, seeking to create idiosyncratic mythologies that draw their affective power from tactical raids on earlier artworks. Such appropriations refuse to acknowledge any easy separation between elite and popular culture, seeking inspiration whenever and wherever it may be found. Barney is just as comfortable seeking inspiration from headbanger music (in *Cremaster 2*) as from opera (in *Cremaster 5*). In this essay, I want to revisit Barney's relationship to popular culture, and especially to the horror film, seeing him as involved in a conversation with other popular artists who have their own aesthetic sensibilities and thematic fixations, who are themselves involved in formal experimentation and in stretching the ways we think about how we live in our bodies.

I will admit straight out that I am a scholar of popular culture and not the avant-garde. Frankly, I knew very little of Barney's growing reputation when I agreed to write this essay, and I have had to struggle throughout the editorial process with many aspects of art criticism that seem alien to the way that I approach my own scholarship. Yet, I have come to admire Barney precisely because he respects the popular artists and genre traditions that inspire his work. What I don't respect terribly much is the way that many art critics have felt compelled to distance him (and themselves) from the popular in order to justify their own aesthetic interests in his creations. *Art in America*'s Jerry Saltz, for example, makes a passing reference to Barney's borrowings from "certain recent horror films," but assumes his readers won't know or care which ones.[4] Often, avant-garde discourse falls back on a logic of exceptionalism—for an artist to innovate, he or she has to exist outside of genre altogether. Michael Kimmelman told *New York Times* readers: "His work has nothing really to do with films in the sense that most people think of them, except, maybe, for Bunuel's and Dali's films."[5] Barney is depicted as a contemporary alchemist transforming popular dross into avant-garde gold. Dan Cameron writes: "Even our postmodern landscape of disconnected signs and referents is loaded with more of the substance of meaning than nearly any other artist has been able to locate, much less decipher."[6] There is almost no appreciation here that popular culture might itself be the site of aesthetic experimentation, or that Barney's work might be read as part of a larger dialogue between avant-garde and popular artists.

To be fair, cultural studies has paid little attention to the aesthetics of popular culture either. Much contemporary writing on popular culture addresses ideological rather than aesthetic questions, whereas art historians have felt justified in preserving relatively solid hierarchical boundaries even as they discuss "postmodernist" artists whose work freely appropriates from popular culture. Postmodernism is read symptomatically when discussing popular culture and aesthetically when discussing high arts. Much postmodernist theory assumes, in fact, that contemporary culture has suffered from an implosion of meaning, that we are dealing with relatively empty signifiers, a play with surfaces, and a flattening of affect. I have little doubt that much of popular culture looks flat and empty to anyone who lacks a solid grounding in its aesthetic traditions. Rather than seeing postmodernism as a play with empty signifiers, it might make sense to see a postmodern collage or pastiche as a memory palace, with each appropriated element bearing complex layers of meaning and association for those familiar with the genre traditions from which it originated.

The release of the final film in the *Cremaster* cycle calls for a reassessment of Barney's borrowings from popular entertainment. To fully understand what is perhaps his most complex genre synthesis to date, we would need to dig deeply into a range of different aspects in the history of popular art, including the American musical (and its roots in vaudeville and Broadway revues), the action film and its influence on the computer game, the design of classic automobiles, the heavy metal tradition, and so forth. I agree with Richard Flood that "trying to prioritize entries in Barney's syllabus is seductive but not particularly productive, as hierarchies keep mutating like the alien virus in a sci-fi movie." [7] Yet, ultimately, one has to start somewhere and see where it leads us. Inspired by the image of the zombie clawing her way to the surface at the opening of the film and by recurring evocations of horror genre elements throughout the cycle, I want to discuss Barney's relationship to recent developments in the horror genre that have similarly sought to explore bodily limits and the transformation of human identity. I will be describing horror as itself a site of artistic experimentation working within popular culture to reshape our aesthetic sensibility, reroute our erotic desires, and revitalize our perceptual norms.

Horror and the Avant-Garde

> I love horror. I love the immediacy of it. I love the traditions, the conventions, the fundamental structure of it, which involves the eruption of the fantastic, the bizarre, the unlooked-for into workaday life. It involves the throwing over of conventional standards.
> —Clive Barker (p. 124)[8]

The core definition of the horror film, according to film critic Robin Wood, can be reduced to a deceptively simple proposition: "normality is threatened by the monstrous."[9] If much mainstream horror simply reproduces a Judeo-Christian world view in which anything that steps off the narrow path of righteousness is ultimately punished, if not destroyed, Wood speaks of a subversive tradition in American horror that encourages our attachment to the monstrous and our rejection of the repressiveness of the normative. Many horror auteurs are less interested in scaring us with a glimpse of forbidden knowledge than they are with critiquing institutions, like the family or the state, that seek to regulate sexuality and eradicate difference.

The modern horror genre was born in the context of Romanticism (with authors seeking within the monster and his creator powerful metaphors for their own uneasy relationship with bourgeois culture), and the horror film originated in the context of German Expressionism (with the studios demanding that madness or the supernatural be put forth as a justification for the powerful feelings generated by that new aesthetic sensibility). The popular aesthetic's demand for affective intensity and novelty requires that popular artists constantly renew their formal vocabulary. Representing the monstrous gives popular artists a chance to move beyond conventional modes of representation, to imagine alternative forms of sensuality and perception, and to invert or transform dominant ideological assumptions. Historically, horror filmmakers have drawn on the "shock of the new" associated with cutting-edge art movements to throw us off guard and open us up to new sensations. From the start, horror films have required a complex balancing between the destabilization represented by those avant-garde techniques and the re-stabilization represented by the reassertion of traditional moral categories and aesthetic norms in the film's final moments. There is always the danger that these new devices will become so fascinating in their own right that they will swamp any moral framing or narrative positioning. For many horror fans, the genre becomes most compelling and interesting where narrative breaks down and erotic spectacle and visual excess take over. If the horror film has a moment of original sin, it came when the producers of *The Cabinet of Dr. Caligari* inserted, at the last moment, a frame story that recontextualized the film's Expressionist mise-en-scène as the distorted vision of a madman.[10] Through this compromise, they created a permanent space for modern art sensibilities within popular culture, but only at the price of them no longer being taken seriously as art.

Many leading horror artists (including David Lynch and David Cronenberg) began their careers as experimental filmmakers, often introducing themes and images that would inform their later works. Clive Barker was involved in avant-garde theater productions. Wes Craven started as a philosophy and literature professor. Many contemporary artists, including Andy Warhol, Cindy Sherman, Rita Mae Brown, Yoko Ono, and George Franju, have flirted with horror. Surrealist H.R. Giger helped design the otherworldly look of the *Alien* films, while Japanese fashion designer Eiko Ishioka has gained mainstream attention by capturing the subjective experience of a psycho killer in *The Cell*. As Cronenberg explains, "The horror genre is very kind if you are and want to be outrageous. It forgives a lot of faults and it encourages madness of a certain kind. I'm not too worried about staying within it because it encourages exactly those things that I most value about art" (p. 60).[11]

The most hardcore segments of the horror audience are, in effect, avant-garde in their tastes, with fanzine critics functioning as the low-culture counterpart of arts journals in identifying and interpreting what is distinctive about emerging figures within the genre.[12] Documenting how fanzines helped to promote the "art horror" of Lynch, Craven, and Cronenberg, David Sanjek writes, "This devotion to uniqueness of vision has led the fanzines to value most works which bear the mark of an uninhibited visionary sensibility, one which pushes the boundaries of social, sexual, and aesthetic assumptions."[13] Horror fan Mark Kermode has described the role such publications played in his own initiation into horror aesthetics, suggesting that his first encounter with horror films provoked unanticipated feelings, but that he lacked a critical vocabulary to articulate the meanings he felt lurking within the cryptic and often disturbing images: "Essentially a surrealistic genre, contemporary horror demands to be read metaphorically rather than literally. Throughout the 1980s, advanced latex special effects processes allowed directors like David Cronenberg, Brian Yuzna, and Clive Barker to stretch the envelope of on-screen surrealism with a previously impossible ease. Yet the work of all of these directors is meaningless if taken at face value. . . . The horror fan understands this, and is thus not only able but positively compelled to 'read' rather than merely 'watch' such movies. The novice, however, sees only the dismembered bodies, hears only the screams and groans, reacts only with revulsion or contempt."[14] Like the avant-garde, horror is an acquired taste, a fringe subculture whose subversiveness lies in the challenge it poses to the hegemony of more mainstream sensibilities. Also like the avant-garde, horror generates its own aesthetic discourse, positioning itself in opposition to the ideological and aesthetic norms of dominant cinema.

While Barney has told interviewers very little about his own fannish interests, he betrays an awareness of this alternative film culture simply by the films he references. One doesn't have to look very hard to see the horror influences in his work. The bleeding blade that is the logo of *Cremaster 2* recalls similar images that open the *Hellraiser* or *Nightmare on Elm Street* movies. Recall the unnerving juxtaposition of swarming bees and naked flesh in *Cremaster 2*; the strange orbs that crawl out of the driver's pockets, the closing shots of a purplish organ soaking in a vat of white goo, or the strange instruments attached to what looks like genitals in *Cremaster 4*. Consider Barney's expressed fascination with guts, connective tissue, and bodily fluids. Consider the deformed and freakish figures that creep in the corners and crawl along the floor at various points in his films. Such images draw deeply upon the generic repertoire of contemporary horror.

We might compare such moments with the "shunting sequence" in Brian Yuzna's *Society*, a film Barney has cited in previous interviews. At first glance, *Society* represents pretty blunt agitprop. Made at the end of the Reagan era, the movie depicts a world in which the wealthy literally devour the flesh of the poor and gather behind closed doors to shed their clothes, their inhibitions, and oh, yeah, their skin. We see all of this debauchery through the eyes of a rather bland boy-next-door type who is shocked and outraged to learn that his preppy classmates are part of this grisly conspiracy or that the girl he has a crush on will be "coming out" at their next blood orgy. But the film's simple moral oppositions break down in its climactic sequence, in which Yuzna draws us from dread to horror to fascination to desire as we watch these hot and sticky (well, more like melting and mutant) bodies come together, penetrate and be penetrated by each other, in every imaginable combination. Yuzna, no less than Barney, demonstrates a fascination with mixing and matching flesh and synthetic materials, luxuriating in the slipperiness and sheen of various bodily fluids, and eroticizing the dissolution of individual identity into collective consciousness. Yuzna, no less than Barney, wants to defamiliarize the ways we look at the human body and to make some fresh discoveries about the elasticity of erotic desire.

Posthumanism

> The body that scares and appalls changes over time, as do the individual characteristics that add up to monstrosity, as do the preferred interpretations of that monstrosity.[15]

> — Judith Halberstam

If, as Judith Halberstam has suggested, monsters are "meaning machines," then the introduction of new topics into cultural discourse can often result in the creation of new visual metaphors within horror.[16] Throughout the 1980s and 1990s, a number of social and technological developments have destabilized our conceptions of bodily integrity, subjectivity, and sexuality: medical advances, including heart transplants, sex change operations, new imaging technologies, and improvements in prosthetic devices; growing awareness of the threat/potential of genetic engineering; a growing discourse about the social construction of sexuality; the renewal of piercing, tattooing, and other forms of voluntary bodily modifications. Cronenberg has summed up these new attitudes toward the body: "We are physically different from our forefathers, partly because of what we take into our bodies and partly because of things like glasses and surgery. But there is a further step that could happen, which would be that you could grow another arm, that you could actually physically change the way you look—mutate. Human beings could swap sexual organs, or do without sexual organs as sexual organs per se, for procreation. We're free to develop different kinds of organs that would give pleasure and that have nothing to do with sex. The distinction between male and female would diminish, and perhaps we would become less polarized and more integrated creatures" (p. 82). Artists, both high and low, have been tempted to explore the further implications of these changes, to imagine radically different ways of living within our bodies.

Critics have labeled the popular representations of these "posthuman" identities as "body horror," pointing to a new degree of explicitness in the depiction of the body and its processes, a new anxiety about bodily invasion or transformation, a new fascination with images of mutation and plague, and a new openness about the intersection of horror and sexuality, pleasure and pain.[17] These themes have both fueled and exploited significant improvements in special effects and make-up technologies that enable filmmakers to morph and mutate the human body beyond recognition. These shifts altered our conception of what makes us human, and, in doing so, enabled new conceptualizations and visualizations of the monstrous. Now filmmakers can and do depict anything that the human mind can imagine. They don't simply want to pull out our guts and shove them in our faces; they want us to relish their distinctive texture, their pungent odor, their sensual sheen. After all, the horror film now competes with documentaries that can run fiber optics up every bodily passage and show us what the real thing looks like. As Linda Ruth Williams explains, "Contemporary horror has specialized in making the inside visible, opening it up and bringing it out and pushing the spectacle of interiority to the limit to find out what that limit is."[18] The extreme end of this tendency became known as "splatterpunk," in reference to its coupling of intensely graphic representations of violence and gore with a hip street-smart sensibility. Such works pushed the current destabilization of our thinking about bodily transformations to its apocalyptic endpoint, creating images of bodies and identities stretched, mutated, ripped open, and stitched together again.

At the same time, any stable separation between the monstrous and the normal is breaking down. What provoked unimaginable horror a decade ago might well be mundane and mainstream today. Consider, for example, how once unassemblable images—pierced genitals, say—now surface as a conventional, almost obligatory, image in mass market men's magazines. As Clive Barker explains, "liberated from the constraints of classicism, the unjaundiced eye may greet the sight of the monster much as it greets things of beauty: with awe, fascination and a little envy" (p. 223). The horror writer, he suggests, doesn't simply want to represent the new shape of human flesh but to evoke its sensations for the reader, to "get inside its impossible skin" and encourage us to see the realm of our normal experiences from a fresh perspective. It is this transformation of sensation and perception that links this popular art movement to the historical function of the avant-garde. The best artists working in the genre don't just want to provoke horror or revulsion; they want to slowly reshape our sensibilities so that we come to look at some of the most outré images as aesthetically pleasing and erotically desirable. Cronenberg joked about a future in which we might have "a beauty contest for the inside of the human body where people would unzip themselves and show you the best spleen and the best heart."[19] These popular artists wanted to confront spectators with the dark, repressed, and kinky sides of their own erotic fantasies. As Barker explains, "The monster, at its best, transforms and transforms, like a dream-mate, responding to every nuance of desire" (p. 218). Barker argues that children have "a healthy appetite for the monstrous" (p. 239), which gets repressed and turned to guilt as society exerts its constraints on the developing individual; the horror author reclaims that childlike vision of the world, allowing us to engage with pleasure in bodily difference once again.

Barker's *Hellraiser* films, for example, depict the Cenobytes, according to the film's theatrical preview, as "ageless experts in the art of refined pleasure and even more refined pain"; his human characters are restless pleasure-seekers who will pay any price for the ultimate sensation. The film's imagery constantly blurs the line between the erotic and the horrific, juxtaposing a passionate sex scene with the image of a hand scraping across a rusty nail, depicting a woman kissing and licking the bloody fingers of her newly resurrected lover, or the demons lovingly reconstructing the splayed face of the protagonist like a fleshy jigsaw puzzle. In Clive Barker's world, monsters see the world with the innocence of children, seeking out pleasure and sensation, refusing to respect the limits human morality places on the body: "The monsters concede no limitations. Amongst their tribe, eyes, ears, mouths, teeth, tongues, limbs, bellies and genitals are designed to devour experience on a scale we dream of as children, thinking it will be the reward of adulthood, only to find in maturity we were freer as infants" (p. 337).

Charles Burns's *Black Hole* comic book series takes us on a similar trajectory: one by one, a group of teenagers succumb to a sexually-transmitted "plague." The plague results in a wide range of bodily mutations, which the teens initially hide behind their clothing like so many hickeys. When the changes become too great, the infected take refuge in an outcast community, a modern-day leper colony, on the outskirts of town. Each teen initially confronts the "plague" in silent horror and self-loathing, not to mention absolute ignorance, since no one dares talk openly about the bodily changes they are confronting. Burns's self-consciously lurid style, which mimics the conventions of E.C. comics from the 1950s, suggests the contradictions of a culture that stirs up erotic desires and then refuses to discuss their consequences. Yet, as the work continues, Burns suggests more complex and ambivalent feelings about what the teens are becoming. Consider, for example, two parallel scenes. In the first, a young woman eagerly tongues the mouth-like opening on her boyfriend's neck: "Nothing about you is gross. It was warm and salty. It was like the ocean. A clean, sharp taste. And further inside, a tiny tongue. I could feel it trembling, fluttering up against mine."[20] In the second, a boy discovers that the woman he is making love with has sprouted a tail—which, without reflection, he integrates into their lovemaking: "I grabbed it and it felt good. It was strong and alive in my hand. Something to hold onto. . . . I was moving, twisting. I was holding on as hard as I could but it was slipping away."[21] Both scenes represent the remapping of erogenous zones, a blurring of male and female sexual anatomy, not simply for the fictional characters but also for the readers.

Often, these popular artists sought ways of escaping human subjectivity altogether. For example, Ernst Fuchs praises H.R. Giger's work for

Alien: "Here, for the first time, were images that I found to be completely alien in construct. There was no human trace, tool mark, or evolutionary chain to grab onto. . . . Nothing can be more difficult than to create something as a human being that has no human resonances whatever."[22] Cronenberg repeatedly discusses his work as though it were framed from the perspective of a virus: "I think most diseases would be very shocked to be considered diseases at all. It's a very negative connotation. For them, it's very positive when they take over your body and destroy you. It's a triumph" (p. 82).

These popular artists, no less than their avant-garde counterparts, are pursuing what has been one of the overriding goals of modern art: trying to brush aside encrusted layers of meaning, shatter the "glass armor" of our everyday perception, and open us to fresh experiences. It is this goal of helping us learn to stop worrying and love being posthumans that links Barney's work with the "body horror" tradition. Like Cronenberg, Barney is fascinated with the ways that new synthetic materials facilitate radically different constructions of the human body, enabling him to materialize mutant figures from his imagination. Like Barker and Burns, he is interested in exploring new forms of sensuality. And like all of these popular artists, he is interested in reconfiguring core cultural myths from an alien or mutant perspective. And to cite some of the claims made by art critics, these popular artists, no less than Barney, are "mythographer[s] of a world less recognizably human," are attempting "to tell stories of gender and generation differently," are developing "a choreography of the body's limits," and are exploring more "polymorphous" and "onanistic" structures of desire.[23] Read in that light, we may no longer wonder what an artist like Barney sees in films like *Hellraiser*, *Evil Dead II*, or *Society*, but rather why Barney chooses the avant-garde—rather than the popular cinema—to explore his pet obsessions.

Barney has himself expressed enormous admiration for Cronenberg and Barker, in particular, seeing them as artists who share his own interests in creating "internal landscapes" ripe with the possibility of metamorphosis and transformation. Yet, Barney also expresses some frustration that the horror genre does not allow them to sustain that level of abstraction for long, but instead pulls them constantly back to moral evaluation and conventional modes of thought. Barney seeks through the avant-garde the thing that eludes these popular artists: freedom from the constraints of narrative and denotation, a pure play with abstraction and connotation.

Horror without Horror

Linda Williams has proposed the category of "body genres" to refer to forms of popular fiction, such as horror, pornography, and melodrama, whose aesthetics focus around images of bodily excess. She writes, "The body spectacle is featured most sensationally in pornography's portrayal of orgasm, in horror's portrayal of violence and terror, and in melodrama's portrayal of weeping."[24] In other words, each of these body genres depends ultimately on the sounds and images of bodies out of control, "beside themselves" with pleasure, fear, or sadness.

Barney's work, on the other hand, is all about bodies under control—perhaps stretched to the limits, perhaps doing things we never imagined possible, but also perfectly regulated. He returns again and again to images of repetitive and ritualized behavior. I was struck, for example, by the bull-riding sequence in *Cremaster 2*. Bull riding in a conventional film might well conjure up a profound sensation of being unbound and out of control, as the rider is barely able to hold on and is almost inevitably going to be flung into the dust by the pounding bull. Barney, however, films the bull as if its every rise and fall had been choreographed. The rocking bull becomes the very image of bodily constraint, sinking slowly to its knees, under drugs or some other form of bewitchment. Something similar occurs earlier in the film, when we see Gary Gilmore's conception. The sexuality is explicit enough that some critics have labeled it pornographic, but it has none of the sense of bodily abandon one associates with the genre. This is sex for procreation, not pleasure. Even when Gilmore's mother throws her head back in release, it seems as much a gesture of spiritual uplift as one of orgasm. Or consider the ways that Barney films the murder sequence. There is certainly blood spilt, yet the camera seems as interested in the stacks of tires in the foreground of the shot as in the murder itself. The first gunshot is filmed through and muffled by a window. When he shows us the blood, it seems to be slowly leaking from the dead man's skull onto the tile floor.

As Williams suggests, the popular aesthetic of the horror film depends on provoking intense sensations. Its success is measured in part by its ability to shape the viewer's affective experiences. Barney's works are more open-ended; they present us with images of bodily transformations, strange couplings and unfamiliar rituals, but they do not tell us what we should think or feel about them. Barney draws visual elements from the horror film, yet he drains them of their horror. People don't scream when they encounter the monstrous in these films; there is no sense of perversity or damnation. There is something remarkably mundane about the opening images of *Cremaster 4*, in which we watch the Loughton Candidate comb and part his orangish-red hair to reveal the vestigial horns underneath.

Cronenberg, Barker, and Burns contrast the "new flesh" with what came before. Much as pornography depends on the construction and crossing of taboos, horror depends on the construction and transgression of norms. Yet, Barney's work shows only limited interest in our existing norms. He depicts the process of filling up Gary Gilmore's gas tank as if it were no more or less normal than the process by which the medium conducts her séance.

Cronenberg, Barker, and Burns all struggle against the trappings of their genre. Creating horror allows them to inject their avant-garde sensibilities into the meme-stream, to get their ideas before a larger public, but it also dooms them to a certain predetermined response from a significant portion of their audience. We may pause for a sublime moment to savor unanticipated sensations, to imagine new forms of pleasure that transcend the limits of our current bodies and consciousness, yet we are pulled back too swiftly into the onward progression of their narratives, which ultimately, in most cases, reinscribe the moral values that they sought to dislocate. Although Cronenberg, Barker, and their contemporaries have worked hard to pull the monstrous out of the shadows, these images remain, ultimately, the stuff of quick cuts and shocking revelations. The horror film always depends on an element of surprise, of being caught unawares, of seeing things we weren't quite ready to confront. By contrast, Barney prolongs the moment of our confrontation with the unfamiliar. It is hard to call his cinematography static when there is so much movement—both within the frame and of the camera itself—and yet one comes away from watching his films with a sense of stillness. We scrutinize his images; actions are performed over and over; all of the shock wears away and what we are left with is the beauty, the erotic fascination, the sense of transformation and enchantment. Even the category of the monstrous seems altogether wrong for what we see in the *Cremaster* films. Barney refuses to "other" the freakish creatures who populate his films, often taking on the most traditionally grotesque roles himself, becoming the giant, the hunchback, the psycho killer, the sheep-man, rather than holding them at a distance.

Barney doesn't so much enact his narratives as re-enact them, much as the way that a Nativity scene reminds us about a story we all already know and don't really need to be told again. He reduces the stories to holy icons, blessed sacraments, ritualized gestures, and sacred spaces. Nothing feels as if it is happening for the first time. Nothing seems spontaneous or innocent of higher orders of symbolism. Not surprisingly, many critics have found Barney's films more rewarding on subsequent viewings. We need to get inside these images, work through the complex web of associations and transformations. We need, in other words, to be initiates into the Church of Matthew Barney before we understand the full power and mystery of his iconography. Barney's enthusiasts become as obsessive as any other movie cultist—so many fan boys eagerly winding and rewinding their videos, no matter what their intellectual pretensions. As Jerry Saltz reports, "I've seen it [*Cremaster 4*] more than 75 times. Each time, I catch something new; every viewing is different and makes the experience of the work more complex and more complete."[25]

In that sense, Barney reminds me not so much of Cronenberg and Barker, or even of contemporary comic book authors such as Neil Gaiman (*The Sandman*) or Alan Moore (*Promethea*), who share Barney's desire to construct a personal mythology and who develop elaborate keys to help readers work through their various allusions and references.[26] Rather, he reminds me of the 1950s science fiction author Cordwainer Smith. Like Barney, Smith sought to link together the full body of his work—some fifty-plus short stories and several novels—into one overarching mythological vision. Like Barney, Smith was fascinated with images of bodily transformation, whether it be the complex fusion of man and machine in "Scanners Live in Vane," the horrific images of body parts being grown on and harvested from living humans in "A Planet Called Shayol," or the experiments that transform animals into half-human servants in "The Dead Lady of Clown Town." Read retrospectively, Smith's stories look forward to 1980s body horror and cyberpunk, but they are just plain weird in the context of 1950s America. Smith's narrative style was equally idiosyncratic, inspired by his studies of classical Chinese folktales but reflecting a distinctly modernist sensibility. Smith would interrupt an original short story with asides about how these same events had been represented in paintings or in stage dramas or television productions, how they had been told and retold to previous generations, and how the actual events deviated from those familiar representations. In other words, he was a revisionist within a mythology that existed nowhere outside his own imagination.[27] Cronenberg, Barker, Burns, and their contemporaries show us what it might feel like to be a posthuman, inviting us to experience new sensations, to taste new desires. Cordwainer Smith and Matthew Barney create a mythology for the posthuman world. Cronenberg and Barker address us as humans on the verge of transformation; Smith and Barney address us as posthumans who have already made the transition. They do not offer us any comfortable point of entry into their work. They are speaking, as it were, to an audience that does not yet exist and demanding of their current audience that they struggle to keep up. We do not so much consume their images as decipher them. This doesn't necessarily make Barney a better artist than Barker, only a different kind.

PART II

The Immediate Experience

Writing shortly before his death in 1955, Robert Warshow argued that "the unresolved problem of 'popular culture' . . . has come to be a kind of nagging embarrassment to criticism, intruding itself on all our efforts to understand the special qualities of our culture and to define our own relation to it."[1] Three decades had passed since the publication of Gilbert Seldes's *The Seven Lively Arts*. There was a growing recognition that Seldes had correctly identified the cultural importance of popular art, but there had not yet emerged a critical language to talk about what was most engaging and interesting in those traditions. In the introduction to his book *The Immediate Experience*, Warshow identified a need for criticism of popular culture "which can acknowledge its pervasive and disturbing power without ceasing to be aware of the superior claims of the higher arts and yet without a bad conscience."[2] On the one hand, he viewed himself as reacting against writers such as Rudolf Arnheim whom he saw as elevating film to the level of art through elitist claims of aesthetic purity; on the other, he viewed himself as reacting against writers such as Siegfried Kracauer who he claimed used films simply as indexes of mass psychology. Both approaches slighted "the actual, immediate experience of seeing and responding to the movies as most of us see them and respond to them."[3] Warshow accused both critics of denying their own personal stakes in the works they criticized, "holding the experience of the movies at arm's length."[4] For Warshow, any meaningful criticism of popular art "should start with the simple acknowledgement of his [the critic's] own relation to the object he criticizes."[5]

Warshow began his collection of essays with a description of his own relationship to the cinema: "I have felt my work to be most successful when it has seemed to display the movies as an important element in my own cultural life, an element with its own qualities and interesting in its own terms, and neither esoteric nor alien. The movies are a part of my culture, and it seems to me that their special power has something to do with their being a kind of 'pure' culture, a little like fishing or drinking or playing baseball—a cultural fact, that is, which has not yet fallen altogether under the discipline of art. I have not brought Henry James to the movies or the movies to Henry James, but I hope I have shown that the man who goes to the movies is the same as the man who reads James."[6]

What Warshow called "immediacy" we might see today as a number of distinct aspects of popular art, each of which has been the focus of its own body of theory and criticism.[7] So, for example, immediacy might be understood in terms of emotional intensification, a topic that has been examined most heavily by writers like Rhona Berenstein, Kevin Heffernan, and Eric Schaefer in their work on horror, exploitation, and trash cinema.[8] Immediacy might also refer to identification, the strong attachments fans feel to fictional characters or celebrities, a topic that has been explored by writers like Lawrence Grossberg, Jackie Stacey, or Richard Dyer.[9] We might also see immediacy in terms of intimacy, the embedding of popular culture in the fabric of our daily lives, in the ways we think about ourselves and the world around us, a topic which is the focus of my essay, "Death Defying Heroes."

My MIT colleague Sherry Turkle asked me to contribute to a book she was editing around the concept of "evocative objects," everyday things we use to reflect upon our own lives and experiences. I was still mourning the recent death of my mother, and I found myself thinking about the comics I had read in the hospice and the way that so many American superheroes get defined through their response to the death of a parent or loved one. Turkle urged me to write not about texts but about artifacts, exploring the material practices that grow up around comics rather than simply their content. The resulting essay is deeply personal, yet it also seems to articulate the shared rituals of a generation of comic book fans.

Interestingly, one of Warshow's most overtly autobiographical essays also dealt with comics—in this case, his attempt to understand his son Paul's fascination with E.C. horror comics and his outrage over the ways these same comics were being attacked by moral reformer Frederic Wertham. Warshow had no great love for these comics himself, but he wrote from the recognition that "children need some 'sinful' world of their own to which they can retreat from the demands of the adult world."[10] He pitted his own lived experiences of popular culture against Wertham's assertion of media effects. I stumbled back upon Warshow's essay at a moment in my life when it mattered the most—I had just returned from testifying before the U.S. Senate Commerce Committee in defense of games and other popular culture forms that were under fire from Wertham's descendents. It helped me to understand the cyclical nature of these "moral panics" and the recurring challenge of defending free expression.[11]

Warshow's essays often explored popular culture's reaction against the forced conformity and blind optimism that dominated official culture in Eisenhower's America. He found this countercultural impulse "in an unspecified form of expression like jazz, in the basically harmless nihilism of the Marx Brothers, in the continually reasserted strain of hopelessness that often seems to be the real meaning of the soap opera," and perhaps most emphatically in the ways that violence got represented in the gangster film.[12] Warshow argued for the meaningfulness of media violence. He saw different genres as offering different ethical framings of violence, many of which might seem superficially harmful but which in fact helped us make sense of the senseless tragedy and trauma many of us experienced in our everyday lives. Shutting down the popular representation of violence would do more harm than good: "In the criticism of popular culture, where the educated observer is usually under the illusion that he has nothing at stake, the presence of images of violence is often assumed to be in itself a sufficient ground for condemnation. These attitudes, however, have not reduced the element of violence in our culture but, if anything, have helped to free it from moral control by letting it take on the aura of 'emancipation.' The celebration of violence is left more and more to the irresponsible."[13]

We can understand the periodic moral panics about popular culture as emerging from the collision between the popular and bourgeois aesthetics. After all, as Pierre Bourdieu writes, "Tastes (i.e. manifested preferences) are the practical affirmation of an inevitable difference. It is no accident that, when they have to be justified, they are asserted purely negatively, by the refusal of other tastes. In matters of taste, more than anywhere else, all determination is negation, and tastes are perhaps first and foremost distastes, disgust provoked by the horror or visceral intolerance ('sick-making') of the tastes of others."[14] If the bourgeois aesthetic values emotional restraint, then the immediacy of popular culture is often read as a dangerous loss of control over both the physical and the social body. Instead, Norbert Elias has argued, the constraint imposed on impulses within a civilized society leaves behind a surplus of emotions that need to be expelled, and thus societies create opportunities—such as sporting events or popular cinema—for people to engage in emotional outbursts as a form of social control.[15] "Never Trust a Snake" explores the implications of Elias's analysis of the "quest for excitement" within the civilizing process. Elias emphasizes class differences in modes of emotional expression; my essay broadens this to explore gender differences in the emotional experiences of popular culture.

I had originally intended "Never Trust a Snake" as the first of a series of essays that would explore the melodramatic dimensions implicit in the forms of popular culture most closely associated with traditional masculinity. Melodrama had, at that point, been read primarily as an aspect of women's cinema, yet it seemed to me that baseball movies, hunting stories, country-and-western songs, and television wrestling all built upon aspects of the nineteenth-century melodramatic tradition, helping to facilitate and justify the expression of emotions otherwise prohibited by gender norms. I was interested, for example, in the ways that country singers function as professional mourners in a society where men experience a great deal of pain but are not allowed to cry in public.

Someday, I hope to get back to this theme, but when I was recently asked to write about wrestling again, for Nick Sammond's *Steel Chair to the Head*, I used the controversy surrounding contemporary wrestling to reflect on cultural politics, describing the ways that terms like "cultural pollution" get applied to forms of entertainment that are associated with young people, the working class, and racial and sexual minorities.[16] Drawing on Jeffrey Jerome Cohen's argument that "monsters" serve important cultural and political functions, defining the borders between cultures, and managing fear and anxiety, my essay (not contained here) suggested that wrestling is an especially difficult cultural form to assimilate because it muddies the established categories by which we organize and evaluate cultural experiences: "The WWE is a horrifying hybrid—not sports, sports entertainment; not real, not fake, but someplace in between; appealing to the 'white trash' working class and the college educated alike; courting kids and appealing to adolescents on the basis of its rejection of family values; existing outside the cultural mainstream and yet a commercial success; appealing to national pride even as it shoots a bird at most American institutions; masculine as hell and melodramatic as all get out."

Violence is, of course, only one of the most shocking and sensational aspects of popular culture. In "Film Bodies," Linda Williams deploys genre theory to explore the cinema's persistent interest in "the spectacle of the body caught in the grip of intense sensation or emotion."[17] Moral reformers often focus their most scathing comments on genres that center on the body, expressing dismay over "pornography's portrayal of the orgasm, horror's portrayal of violence and terror, melodrama's portrayal of weeping."[18] These critics are especially unnerved by the implicit invitation to audience members to have a more or less direct experience of the powerful emotions depicted on screen—" the inarticulate cries of pleasure in porn, screams of fear in horror, sobs of anguish in melodrama."[19] The films invite us to have intense, some would say excessive, bodily and affective experiences, giving way to impulses that would be censored elsewhere in our culture but are seemingly permitted by these public amusements. This is very much what I am arguing about the place of wrestling within traditional masculinity—it creates a space where men can shout or cry over tensions they experience in their own everyday lives.

Williams and I are interested in many of the same "body genres": "Monstrous Beauty and Mutant Aesthetics" explicitly references her discussion of horror movies; my wrestling essay draws heavily on the critical literature around melodrama; and I have published several essays on pornography.[20] The last two essays in this section, both published here for the first time, explore two "body genres" that Williams did not explicitly reference but which have been central to recent feminist writing about popular cinema: the exploitation flick and slapstick comedy.

By the 1960s and 1970s, producer Roger Corman had gained a reputation for taking inexperienced filmmakers, including a number of women, and giving them a chance to make their first low-budget features; the filmmakers were expected to satisfy the producer's demands for a certain amount of sex, nudity, violence, and for controversial content that could be exploited in an advertising campaign. In return, the filmmakers were given a chance to experiment with new techniques or insert their own political perspectives into their works. "Exploiting Feminism" focuses on Stephanie Rothman, whose films under Corman's supervision had been read by Claire Johnston, Pam Cook, and other British feminist critics as embodying a particular kind of "counter-cinema"—a way of working within and "against the grain" of dominant film practice. Focusing primarily on *Terminal Island*, I show how Rothman fits within the genre of exploitation cinema, demonstrating how the protofeminist themes in her work run across a whole cycle of women's prison movies produced at about the same time. Such films tapped both the early signs of feminist rage against patriarchal culture and a masculine backlash against powerful women: the same film may show images of subjugation and resistance. Returning to the concept of counter-cinema, I identify a range of strategies by which Rothman complied with Corman's hunger for nudity while dampening the voyeuristic pleasures of looking at naked women's bodies and expanding feminine pleasure in looking at naked male bodies. Rothman's tactics make sense against the backdrop of American culture in the late 1960s and early 1970s, when obscenity and nudity were widely deployed as political speech, when sexual experimentation and reproductive rights were put forth as a contrast to the government's assertion of the right to control the bodies of its citizens, and when underground comics exploited a language of exaggerated and grotesque bodies to counter a history of racial and gender stereotypes.

Yet, a politics based on transgression has its limits. In my essay on the 1930s performer Lupe Velez, I explore the ways that scandal and gossip function in the shadows of the Hollywood studio system, helping to generate "heat" around particular performers that can be exploited through their on-screen performances. Central to the essay is the contrast between the glamour photographs, which Roland Barthes celebrated in "The Face of Garbo," and the "Tijuana Bibles," early examples of underground comics that depicted erotic encounters between Hollywood stars and other celebrities. One represented the purification of the body, the other its debasement. One was officially distributed, the other circulated under the counter or in the back allies. Velez manages to carve out a space for herself somewhere between the two—making fun of the conventions of the glamour photograph and, at the same time, never escaping the raw sexuality of the Tijuana Bibles.

In my own previous work on film comedy, I had suggested that female comic performance allowed women a chance to transgress traditional gender roles.[21] However, I had found it impossible to discuss Velez within the terms set forth in my dissertation. If she is remembered today, it is almost entirely through a gross and disturbing representation of her death found in Kenneth Anger's *Hollywood Babylon*. Her films are almost totally forgotten. Unlike many other female clowns who presented themselves as desperate and unattractive, Velez was a beautiful and sexy woman who was excluded from mainstream femininity almost entirely on the basis of her race: she was unable to escape the stigma of being "non-white" in a culture still governed by a logic of white supremacy. Stereotypes about Mexico and Mexicans were used to contain and dismiss the transgressiveness of her comic performances on screen and to explain away her disruptive behaviors off camera. José Esteban Muñoz coined the phrase "disidentifications" to refer to moments when queer and/or minority performers exaggerate and deconstruct stereotypes and spaces "where the discourses of essentialism and constructivism short circuit."[22] It is tempting to read Velez's persona as similarly playing with and making fun of racial stereotypes—a predecessor of postmodernist performance art. Yet, as we read the competing descriptions of her death, we realize that hunger to escape from these stereotypes literally haunted her to her grave.

3 | Death-Defying Heroes

Media scholars draw an important distinction between mass culture and popular culture. Mass culture is mass-produced for a mass audience. Popular culture is what happens to those cultural artifacts at the site of consumption, as we draw upon them as resources in our everyday life. Many scholars have focused on how the same mass-produced artifacts generate different meanings for different consumers. Less has been said about the ways our relationships to those artifacts change over time, and the ways that what they mean to us shifts at different moments in our lives. This essay is an autoethnography of my relationship to superhero comics. What I have to say here is shaped by my experience of grief over the death of my mother six months ago. I had checked her into the hospital complaining of indigestion, only to discover what turned out to be a tumor in her kidney already so advanced it was no longer possible to operate. All we could do was keep her comfortable and wait for the inevitable.

I bought the comics on the way to the hospice. They were selected hastily, and even then, I felt guilty about the time it took. I was looking for something banal, familiar, and comforting at a time when my world was turning upside down. I read them intermittently as I and the other family members set on deathwatch, the experience of the stories becoming interwoven with old family memories and the process of letting go of my mother. Retreating from the emotional drama that surrounded me, I found myself staring into the panic-stricken eyes of a young Bruce Wayne, kneeling over the freshly murdered bodies of his parents. I have visited that moment many times before, but this time, our common plight touched me deeply.

A year ago or a year from now, I would have written a very different essay, but for the moment I am trying to work through what comics might have to say to me about death, aging, and mortality.

I am hardly the first to draw such connections. In his essay "The Myth of Superman," Umberto Eco describes the monstrous quality of the superhero who is not "consumed" by time, who never grows older, who is always cycling through the same kinds of experiences, never moving any closer to death. Eco approaches this question formally; describing how the iterative structure of comics creates its own kind of temporality, which he contrasts with the always already completed action of myth or the unique events of the novelistic: "He possesses the characteristics of timeless myth but is accepted only because his activities take place in our human and everyday world of time." The fan boy in me wants to point out all of the exceptions and qualifications to Eco's claim, starting with the fact that a whole generation of revisionist comics have sought to reintroduce death and aging into the superhero universe. The images of aging Batman and Superman duking it out in Frank Miller's *Dark Knight Return* comes immediately to mind, but most of these books came after Eco's essay was published and might well have been responding to his argument. Regardless, Eco understates the importance of continuity and, thus, of specific series history; to comics readers the same events may unfold again and again, but there is something distinctive about each issue, and mastering those distinctions is part of what separates comics fans from more casual readers. From time to time, the franchises build up such complex histories that they need catastrophic events—such as the Crisis of Infinite Earths—to wipe the slate clean again and allow a fresh start. Yet, such reservations aside, Eco's formal analysis hits on some core psychological truth that I want to explore on an autobiographical level.

One could understand the reading of comics as entering into a psychological space that similarly denies death and mortality, that encourages a nostalgic return to origins. Most of our stereotypes about comics fans start from the idea of arrested development, that is, that the fans have somehow sought to pull themselves out of life processes and to enjoy the same kind of iterative existence as the guys and gals in tights. Yet, I want to suggest that we cannot escape or forestall such dreaded feelings altogether, and that in their own way, both as texts and as artifacts, comics become reflective objects that help us think about our own irreversible flow toward death. In short, this is an essay about what it means to consume and be consumed by superheroes.

I am frequently so tired after the demands of my job that when I crawl into bed at night, I fall asleep too fast if I try to read prose. I move through novels at such a sluggish pace that I lose interest well before I reach the conclusion. I had found that I could maintain consciousness, however blurry my perceptions, long enough to make it through an issue of a comic. There is something energizing in the shift between text and images and in the larger-than-life stories so many comics tell. The repeated formulas of the superhero saga mean that each issue is in a sense predigested, but the most interesting contemporary writers—Brian Michael Bendis, Mark Waid, Greg Rucka, Ed Brubaker, Geoff Johns—bring a distinctive perspective or unique voice to those characters, offering me what I need to sustain my interest in these familiar characters over time.

Comics are the site of enormous diversity, innovation, and experimentation, and many of the titles I am reading this month weren't even being published a year ago; but a healthy portion of the books I buy were those I read as a kid. Nowhere else in popular culture can you find that same degree of continuity. *Star Trek*, currently the longest-running franchise on American television, goes back to the mid-1960s. The James Bond movies, currently the longest-running franchise in American cinema, go back to the early 1960s. Superman, Batman, Wonder Woman, and Captain America have been more or less in continuous publication since the 1930s or early 1940s—always fighting for truth, justice, and the American way, despite generations of readers and writers growing up, growing old, and, yes, dying in their company. There are, to be sure, enormous variations in the way these characters get interpreted across those various generations, dramatic shifts in styles, successive waves of revisionism, various stabs at relevance or topicality, which mean that the comics are never in a literal sense timeless. Yet, you can go away for decades on end, find your way back to a DC comic, and get reintroduced to the protagonists more or less where you left them. It is often this hope of rekindling something we once felt that draws us aging comic fans back to these titles. It is almost as if we would lose something important in ourselves if watching Batman stalk across a darkened alley or Spider-Man swing from building to building no longer made our hearts beat a little faster.

When I remember my personal history of comics, so much of what I remember are iterative events, the routine patterns that surround comics consumption, rather than specific storylines or particular life experiences.

Curiously enough, my earliest memories of comics tie me back to my mother. When, as a fourth or fifth grader, I would stay in bed with a fever, my mother would go to the local druggist in search of Coca-Cola syrup, which according to southern folklore, was supposed to have remarkable curative powers. In this era before specialty shops and comics "subs," she would return carrying an armload of comics, selected from a large spinning rack at the center of the store. She bought more or less what she could find, so sometimes she would return with a selection of kids comics (*Baby Huey*, *Donald Duck*, or perhaps *Archie*), other times with issues of *Classics Illustrated*, and still other times with DC superheroes. I came to associate comics with the sound of my mother's voice singing me to sleep or her hands feeling my forehead. And I suspect that's why I return to them now at moments of stress.

It is hard to remember when superheroes first entered my life. I suspect it must have been 1966, the year that *Batman* first appeared on television. I was seven or eight. The series rapidly became an obsession among the neighborhood kids. One of my aunts had given me a recording of the theme music, which my playmates and I played at full volume, bouncing up and down on the bed, biffing and powing each other, and tumbling backward into the pillows. Mother had given me an old leotard, sewed a cape and cowl, and cut me a batarang out of plywood. We didn't always understand what we saw. Once we heard an announcement for a forthcoming appearance of King Tut and thought the announcer had said King Duck, and so we spent a week battling it out in the backyard with web-footed foes before discovering that there was this Ancient Egyptian guy. Who knew? My father would peer out from behind his newspaper, expressing mock horror to have discovered that Batman and Robin had died that very day—frozen to death in a giant snow cone or in some other death trap. And every time, I would fall for his joke, bursting into tears, since I could never make up my mind which side of the dividing line between fantasy and reality *Batman* stood. I suspect he bred in me both an intense desire to be able to read the paper myself and some lingering suspicion that the journalists were pulling my leg.

Some of the boys in the neighborhood formed a superhero club. I remember us swearing an oath of loyalty over a stack of comics in my treehouse. We each chose the persona of one of the members of DC's Justice League. The guy who lived across the street was unnaturally big and strong for his age and was quickly cast as Superman. The kid next door was small, wiry, and fast on his feet, and he became the Flash. I had tired of Batman by this point and aligned myself with the Green Lantern for reasons long forgotten. We each spent our weekly allowance on comics and would pass them around. I have reread some of the stories of the era, only to be disappointed. We had fleshed out their personalities through our play, and most of what I recalled so fondly wasn't to be found on the printed page. A few contemporary writers add some of that clubhouse camaraderie into their books, and for a few moments I feel as if I were back with the old gang, drinking Kool-Aid and trying to second-guess the Joker's perplexing secret code, which almost always turned out to be something you could read if you held your comic up to the mirror.

Most of those kids have disappeared from my life and rarely reenter my thoughts. One of them (Superman) tracked me down on the Internet; we got together recently. We talked in big breathless gulps about boyhood days and then suddenly, silence fell over us. We looked at each other blankly as if we were suddenly confronting not the boys we were but the middle-aged men we had become, and we ended the evening early. Neither of us has called the other since. But, we both still read comics.

As I sit down to write this, I am haunted by a curious memory—one of the few memories of comics that centers on a unique event rather than a pattern of repeated experiences. It is early summer and I am sprawled out on the floor of my family's cabin in the north Georgia mountains coloring a picture of Batman as my mother watches television across the room. I have spent most of the day thrashing about in the water pretending to be Aquaman and am now awaiting bed, when a news report interrupts the show my mother is watching to tell us that Robert F. Kennedy has been shot. Why are my memories of my mother's tears over Bobby's death so firmly linked to my memories of superhero coloring books and fantasy play? Is it because at such a moment—which would have come when I was in sixth grade—I suddenly realized that a line separated the silly plots of the campy television series from the harsh realities of adult life? What had it meant to me as a boy to see my mother crying and not know how to comfort her?

You could say that what drew me to comics the week my mother died was nostalgia—which Susan Stewart describes as a desperate hunger to return to a time and place that never really existed, a utopian fantasy through which our current longings get mapped onto the past. Comics were comfort food, like the southern cooked vegetables my mother used to fix for me when I came home for holidays. Yet, these comics offered me little comfort. I hurt every place my mother had ever touched me and I found myself unable to separate out the comics from the memories they evoked. If comics brought me back to boyhood, then they brought me closer to an age when my mother's love had been the most powerful force in my life.

It is silly to try to explain why I read comics that week. I had been reading comics every week for some years running. I returned to comics sometime in my mid-thirties—searching for something I couldn't name at the time. A few years later, when I was diagnosed with gout, and suddenly faced the realization that I was not indestructible and inexhaustible, I found myself drawn passionately back into the world of the Flash and the Green Lantern. My recognition of my own approaching mortality drew me into the death-defying world of the superheroes, who, unlike me, never grew older, never had bodies that ached. The comics function for me as the reverse of Dorian Gray's portrait—they remain the same while my body ages and decays. And as such, they help me to reflect on the differences between who I am now and who I was when I first read them.

Again, it's not quite that simple because comics kept coming in and out of my life. To tell the story that way would be to skip over my various attempts to get my own son engaged with comics, all doomed to failure; or the way the release of the Batman films rekindled my passion for that character for a while; or my periodic raids on the comic shops to examine some title that a student brought to my attention. True that there are huge gaps in my knowledge of any given character—and whole series that came and went without my awareness—but I never really left comics. It just took me a while to admit that I wasn't wandering into the shop now and again to see what was new; I was going there every week and coming away with bags full.

I wasn't ready to come out as a comics fan. Even though my own work had debunked many stereotypes about science fiction fans, there was a side of me that still believed the clichés about middle-aged comic book readers. That stigma kept me from going down to the local comic shops and setting up my own subs folder, even though doing so would get me a significant discount on my purchases. It also prevented me from bagging, or even organizing, my comics, even though doing so was the only way to combat the clutter of having that many random issues lying around our apartment.

If I have an origin story for my passion for superheroes, I also have an origin story for my fear of becoming a comics fan. And it begins in Tom's smelly basement when I was in seventh grade and had decided I was too old for comics and ready to move on to more mature reading matter, like *Mad* or *Famous Monsters of Filmland*. Tom was a somewhat pudgy kid who lived down the street from my grandmother, and we became friends initially out of geographic accident and emotional necessity—his house was a place to go when I wanted to escape being cooped up with someone who was constantly complaining about her aging and ailing body.

Tom had just moved to Atlanta from Michigan. He read almost exclusively Marvel comics at a time when all of my other friends were committed to DC. (Tom had the last laugh since history has vindicated his tastes over ours.) We would sit in his basement and rummage through this huge mound of yellowing comics, reading late into the night by flashlight, as his two cocker spaniels snorted somewhere in the dark void around us. Every so often when we would explore his basement, we would come upon the fossilized dog turds that gave the space its pungent odor. And to this day, when I go into the dank, dark subterranean shops where comics are mostly sold, I think about Tom's basement and wonder what my foot is going to land on if I linger too long over a box of back issues.

One day in seventh grade, as we were flipping through *Incredible Hulk* comics, he told me that he thought he was gay. The next day, I blurted it out around a picnic table on a school field trip to a bunch of the other guys; and from that moment on, our friendship began to unravel until we were punching each other on the playground and getting sent to the principal's office for squirting each other with milk. I was racked with guilt about betraying his secret identity, even though I wasn't ready to come to grips with what that secret really meant—and in any case, it turned out to be a false alarm. Somehow, in a few short years, the nature of friendship had gotten much more complicated.

When I was an undergraduate, those comic-geek stereotypes got reinforced through encounters with two friends who were both comics collectors, both guilt-ridden Catholics, and both named Mark. One of the Marks was a square-jawed fellow who wanted to be Clark Kent—not Superman, just Clark Kent. What he wanted, above all else, was to be as normal as possible, to hold at bay anything unpredictable or uncontrollable. He wasn't just dull—he was desperately dull. Somehow, for him, memorizing as many facts as he could from superhero concordances was one of the ways he could bring his corner of the galaxy more fully under his control. Years later, when I began to collect comics seriously, my wife bought me some reference books at a used book sale. When we examined them more closely, we discovered Mark's name scrawled on the inside front cover. I am not sure what surprised me the most—that Mark had finally gotten rid of those books or that my interest had grown to the point that I saw a value in owning them. Was I becoming the guy I dreaded in college?

The other Mark took me to his apartment one time and showed me an entire room full of steel boxes, containing thousands of individually bagged comics backed with acid-free cardboard, and gave me a speech about how his comics would be safe and secure long after he was dead. Years later, I visited Mark in Brooklyn and sure enough, he still had all of those boxes of comics and many more. By that time, however, I wanted nothing more than to sit up all night asking him for recommendations or flipping through back issues. The mausoleum had become a library.

I fear that I have reduced Tom and the two Marks into fan boy clichés—not ready to confront the challenges of adult life, obsessed with trivia, determined to preserve their comics at all costs, and vaguely distasteful. And for a long time, those associations colored my memories and fed my own anxiety about admitting that comics were such an important part of my life. Those stereotypes are powerful forces shaping the ways we express and act upon our tastes. Yet, I have come to realize that Tom had shown better taste in comics than I did; Mark 1's encyclopedias were useful in sorting through more than forty years of encrusted DC continuity; and, as for Mark 2, collecting comics wasn't terribly different from collecting any other kind of book.

But there is a key difference. Unlike, say, leather-bound books, comics were not made to last. They were printed on cheap paper with bad ink on the assumption that they would be read and discarded. No one ever thought that people would still be reading them decades later, any more than one imagined holding onto to old newspapers. Superheroes may be invincible, but comics rot. What makes old comics valuable for collectors is that so many of them have been destroyed. Every mom who threw away her son's comics increased the fortunes of those who were lucky enough to hold onto theirs. Many fans spend their entire lives—and much of their incomes—trying to recover the issues they had once discarded so casually. And so, fans become preoccupied with the challenges of preserving their collections, with forestalling their ultimate destruction.

To her credit, my mother never threw away my comics. She took them up to the lake house and left them in a drawer. Over the years, they were literally read to death. Young visitors would paw through them with peanut butter–covered fingers. Mice, emboldened by the long months when the cabin was unoccupied, would rip them apart seeking material for their nests. The staples came undone and pages would come off when you tried to read them one last time. The humidity meant that the pages got more and more waterlogged and mildewed. The sun bleached the lurid covers if you left them lying on a window ledge too long. And in the end, not a single one of the superhero books made it past my adolescent years. The *Classics Illustrated* comics were more expensive than the rest—and came with the aura of high culture—so mom treated them as sacred and eternal, not unlike the way she dealt with *National Geographic* magazines. Interestingly enough, they are the only comics from my childhood that I still possess. Despite my horror in recalling how many Jack Kirby books got ripped up when a Boy Scout troop got rained in one weekend at our cabin, I still tend to loan out my comics to my students rather than worrying about keeping them in pristine condition. I have refused to take that last step into fan boy culture. For the moment, I am more interested in reading and sharing comics than in keeping them out of harm's way. I know nothing lasts forever and you are better off really enjoying the things you love while you can.

These are simply some of the memories that passed through my head as I sat on my deathwatch. I had pushed aside *Batman*, not ready to face young Bruce's angst, and turned instead to *Spider-Man*, only to discover that this particular storyline dealt with the memories stirred up by the anniversary of Uncle Ben's death. Eco is right: Superheroes don't move closer to death; they move further away from it. Yet, death still defines the cycles of their lives. It seemed that almost every one of the comics I brought to the hospice dealt—at least in part—with childhood trauma and loss. If comics provide youthful fantasies of empowerment and autonomy, they do so by severing the ties between the superheroes and their parents. Batman takes shape in Bruce Wayne's mind as he vows vengeance over his parents' tombstones. Superman's parents send him away from a dying planet. Peter Parker, not yet aware that with great power comes great responsibility, is too self-centered to stop a crook that runs across his path, allowing him to escape and kill his Uncle Ben. What separated the villains from the heroes wasn't the experience of loss, but what they did after that loss, how it shaped their sense of themselves and their place in the world. Some were strengthened by loss, others deformed.

Most of the literature of childhood has at its heart a kind of emotional violence: we expose children through fiction to the very forces from which we seek to shelter them in real life. Whether in comics or in traditional children's literature, the most powerful theme is almost inevitably the death of or separation from one's parents. Literature helps us to cope with those fears at one level removed. Comic books help us to confront those separation anxieties by depicting their protagonists as moving beyond their initial vulnerabilities and gaining some control over their lives after such losses.

It isn't that these events occur one time in the distant past; they crop up again and again in comics, because these images of death and mourning define the character's identities. And this cycling through the moments of death rings psychologically true. In the months that followed my mother's death, I found myself returning, almost involuntarily, to memories of her final days, the way that a tongue seeks out and presses against a loose tooth—to see if it still hurts. I came away with a new understanding of why the superheroes hold onto their grief, their rage, their anguish, and draw upon it as a source of strength. At one point in my life, I read those stories to learn what it was like to have the power and autonomy of adulthood. Now, I read them to see how you confronted death and came out the other side, how mourning forces you to reassess who you are and what your goals are and what you owe to the people who brought you into the world. My mother's death made no sense to me; I felt only the injustice of seeing her die so much younger than I had expected; I saw only my longing to be able to communicate with her. The comics didn't take away that pain; they helped me to make meaning of it. Some parts of what I read touched places in me that were too raw to endure. The reality of my mother's death had resensitized me to fantasy violence, making it hard to pull back from what the protagonists were feeling. Yet, at the same time, reading those books helped me to realize the common human experience of loss and recovery.

Comics are made to rot and decay. They are such a vital part of our developing imaginations that we try to preserve them forever, but despite our best efforts, they slip through our fingers. The comics of our childhood are impossible to recover. Even if you hold onto your comics, the stories on the page are not the same ones you remember, because our memories are so colored by the contexts within which we encountered them, and especially by the ways we reworked them in our imagination and our backyard play. Eco's claim that superheroes are not "consumed" by death helps to explain why we imagine them as a point of return to bygone days. Yet, even though we change and they don't, we find something new and different each time we come back to these stories. In this case, the death-defying superheroes helped me to model a process of letting go.

4

Never Trust a Snake
WWF Wrestling as Masculine Melodrama

See, your problem is that you're looking at this as a *wrestling* battle—two guys getting into the ring together to see who's the better
athlete. But it goes so much deeper than that. Yes, wrestling's involved. Yes, we're going to pound each other's flesh, slam each
other's bodies and hurt each other really bad. But there's more at
stake than just wrestling, my man. There's a morality play. Randy
Savage thinks he represents the light of righteousness. But, you
know, it takes an awful lot of light to illuminate a dark kingdom.[1]

—Jake "The Snake" Roberts

There are people who think that wrestling is an ignoble sport.
Wrestling is not a sport, it is a spectacle, and it is no more ignoble
to attend a wrestled performance of Suffering than a performance
of the sorrows of Arnolphe or Andromaque.[2]

—Roland Barthes

Like World Wrestling Federation (WWF) superstar Jake "The
Snake" Roberts, Roland Barthes saw wrestling as a "morality play," a curious hybrid of sports and theater. For Barthes, wrestling was at once a
"spectacle of excess," evoking the pleasure of grandiloquent gestures and
violent contact, and a lower form of tragedy, where issues of morality,
ethics, and politics were staged. Wrestling enthusiasts have no interest in
seeing a fair fight but rather hope for a satisfying restaging of the ageless
struggle between the "perfect bastard" and the suffering hero.[3] What
wrestling offers its spectators, Barthes tells us, is a story of treachery and
revenge, "the intolerable spectacle of powerlessness," and the exhilara-
tion of the hero's victorious return from near-collapse. Wrestling, like
conventional melodrama, externalizes emotion, mapping it onto the combatants' bodies and transforming their physical competition into a search

for moral order. Restraint or subtlety has little place in such a world. Everything that matters must be displayed, publicly, unambiguously, and unmercilessly.

Barthes's account focuses entirely upon the one-on-one match as an isolated event within which each gesture must be instantly legible apart from any larger context of expectations and associations: "One must always understand everything on the spot."[4] Barthes could not have predicted how this focus upon the discrete event or the isolated gesture would be transformed through the narrative mechanisms of television. On television, where wrestling comes with a cast of continuing characters, no single match is self-enclosed; rather, personal conflicts unfold across a number of fights, interviews, and enacted encounters. Television wrestling offers its viewers complexly plotted, ongoing narratives of professional ambition, personal suffering, friendship and alliance, betrayal, and reversal of fortune. Matches still offer their share of acrobatic spectacle, snake handling, fire eating, and colorful costumes. They are, as such, immediately accessible to the casual viewer, yet they reward the informed spectator for whom each body slam and double-arm suplex bears specific narrative consequences. A demand for closure is satisfied at the level of individual events, but those matches are always contained within a larger narrative trajectory which is itself fluid and open.

The WWF broadcast provides us with multiple sources of identification, multiple protagonists locked in their own moral struggles against the forces of evil. The proliferation of champion titles—the WWF World Champion belt, the Million Dollar belt, the Tag Team champion belt, the Intercontinental champion belt—allows for multiple lines of narrative development, each centering around its own cluster of affiliations and antagonisms. The resolution of one title competition at a major event does little to stabilize the program universe, since there are always more belts to be won and lost, and in any case, each match can always be followed by a rematch that reopens old issues. Outcomes may be inconclusive because of count-outs or disqualifications, requiring future rematches. Accidents may result in surprising shifts in moral and paradigmatic alignment. Good guys betray their comrades and form uneasy alliances with the forces of evil; rule-breakers undergo redemption after suffering crushing defeats.

The economic rationale for this constant "build-up" and deferral of narrative interests is obvious. The WWF knows how to use its five weekly television series and its glossy monthly magazine to ensure subscription to its four annual pay-per-view specials.[5] Enigmas are raised during the free broadcasts that will be resolved only for a paying audience. Much of the weekly broadcast consists of interviews with the wrestlers about their forthcoming bouts, staged scenes providing background on their antagonisms, and in-the-ring encounters between WWF stars and sparring partners that provide a backdrop for speculations about forthcoming plot developments. Read cynically, the broadcast consists purely of commercial exploitation. Yet this promotion also has important aesthetic consequences, heightening the melodramatic dimensions of the staged fights and transforming televised wrestling into a form of serial fiction for men.

Recent scholarship has focused on serial fiction as a particularly feminine form.[6] Television wrestling runs counter to such a sharply drawn distinction: its characteristic subject matter (the homosocial relations between men, the professional sphere rather than the domestic sphere, the focus on physical means to resolve conflicts) draws upon generic traditions that critics have identified as characteristically masculine; its mode of presentation (its seriality, its focus on multiple characters and their relationship, its refusal of closure, its appeal to viewer speculation and gossip) suggests genres often labeled feminine. These contradictions may reflect wrestling's uneasy status as masculine melodrama, a form particularly associated with feminine interests and targeted at female audiences.[7] Such a definition ignores the influence of melodrama on a broader range of genres, including some, such as the western or the social-problem drama, that focus on a masculine sphere of public action. Our inability to talk meaningfully about masculine melodrama stems from contemporary cultural taboos against masculine emotion. Men within our culture tend to avoid self-examination and to hide from sentiment, expressing disdain for the melodramatic. After all, we are told, "real men don't cry." Yet masculine avoidance of the public display of emotion does not mean that men lack feelings or that they do not need some outlet for expressing them. Patriarchy consequently constructs alternative means of releasing and managing masculine emotion while preserving the myth of the stoic male. A first step toward reconsidering the place of male affective experience may be to account for the persistence of melodramatic conventions within those forms of entertainment that "real men" do embrace—horror films, westerns, country songs, tabloid newspapers, television wrestling, and the like. By looking more closely at these forms of sanctioned emotional release for men, we may be able to locate some of the central contradictions within our contemporary constructions of masculinity.

This chapter will thus consider WWF wrestling as a melodramatic form addressed to a working-class male audience. Such a focus invites an inquiry into the complex interplay of affect, masculinity, and class, issues that surface in both the formal and the thematic features of televised wrestling, in its characteristic narrative structure(s), its audience address, its treatment of male bonding, and its appeal to populist imagery.

Playing with Our Feelings

Norbert Elias and Eric Dunning's path-breaking study *The Quest for Excitement: Sports and Leisure in the Civilizing Process* invites us to reconsider the affective dimensions of athletic competition. According to their account, modern civilization demands restraint on instinctive and affective experience, what they call the "civilizing process" of repression and sublimation. Elias has spent much of his intellectual life tracing the gradual process by which Western civilization has intensified its demands for bodily and emotional control, rejecting the emotional volatility and bodily abandon that characterized Europe during the Middle Ages:

> Social survival and success in these [contemporary] societies depend . . . on a reliable armour, not too strong and not too weak, of individual self-restraint. In such societies, there is only comparatively limited scope for the show of strong feelings, of strong antipathies towards and dislike of other people, let alone of hot anger, wild hatred or the urge to hit someone over the head.[8]

Such feelings do not disappear, but they are contained by social expectations:

> To see grown-up men and women be shaken by tears and abandon themselves to their bitter sorrow in public . . . or beat each other savagely under the impact of their violent excitement [experiences more common during the Middle Ages] has ceased to be regarded as normal. It is usually a matter of embarrassment for the onlooker and often a matter of shame or regret for those who have allowed themselves to be carried away by their excitement.[9]

What is at stake here is not the intensity of feeling but our discomfort about its spectacular display. Emotion may be strongly felt, but it must be rendered invisible, private, personal; emotion must not be allowed to have a decisive impact upon social interactions. Emotional openness is read as a sign of vulnerability, while emotional restraint is the marker of social integration. Leaders are to master emotions rather than to be mastered by them. Yet, as Elias writes, "We do not stop feeling. We only prevent or delay our acting in accordance with it."[10] Elias traces the process by which this emotional control has moved from being outwardly imposed by rules of conduct to an internalized and largely unconscious aspect of our personalities. The totality of this restraint exacts its own social costs, creating psychic tensions that somehow must be redirected and released within socially approved limitations.

Sports, he argues, constitute one of many institutions society creates for the production and expression of affective excitement.[11] Sports must somehow reconcile two contradictory functions: "the pleasurable de-controlling of human feelings, the full evocation of an enjoyable excitement on the one hand and on the other the maintenance of a set of checks to keep the pleasantly de-controlled emotions under control."[12] These two functions are never fully resolved, resulting in occasional hooliganism as excitement outstrips social control. Yet the conventionality of sports and the removal of the real-world consequences of physical combat (in short, sport's status as adult play) facilitate a controlled and sanctioned release from ordinary affective restraints. The ability to resolve conflicts through a prespecified moment of arbitrary closure delimits the spectator's emotional experience. Perhaps most important, sports offer a shared emotional experience that reasserts the desirability of belonging to a community.

Elias and Dunning are sensitive to the class implications of this argument: the "civilizing process" began at the center of "court society" with the aristocracy and spread outward to merchants wishing access to the realms of social and economic power and to the servants who must become unintrusive participants in their masters' lives. Elias and Dunning argue that these class distinctions still surface in the very different forms of emotional display tolerated at the legitimate theater (which provides a space for working-class excitement): the theater audience is to "be moved without moving," to restrain emotional display until the conclusion, when it may be indicated through their applause; for the sports audience, however, "motion and emotion are intimately linked," and emotional display is immediate and uncensored.[13] These same distinctions separate upper-class sports (tennis, polo, golf), which allow minimal emotional expression, from lower-class sports (boxing, wrestling, soccer), which demand more overt affective display. Of course, such spectacles also allow the possibility for upper- or middle-class patrons to "slum it," to adopt working-class attitudes and sensibilities while engaging with the earthy spectacle of the wrestling match. They can play at being working-class (with working-class norms experienced as a remasculinization of yuppie minds and bodies), and can imagine themselves as down-to-earth, with the people, safe in the knowledge that they can go back to the office the next morning without too much embarrassment at what is a ritualized release of repressed emotions.

Oddly absent from their account is any acknowledgment of the gender-specificity of the rules governing emotional display. Social conventions have traditionally restricted the public expression of sorrow or affection by men and of anger or laughter by women. Men stereotypically learn to translate their softer feelings into physical aggressiveness, while women convert their rage into the shedding of tears. Such a culture provides gender-specific spaces for emotional release that are consistent with dominant constructions of masculinity and femininity—melodrama (and its various manifestations in soap opera or romance) for women, sports for men. Elias and Dunning's emphasis upon the affective dimensions of sports allows us to more accurately (albeit schematically) map the similarities and differences between sports and melodrama. Melodrama links female affect to domesticity, sentimentality, and vulnerability, while sports link male affect to physical prowess, competition, and mastery. Melodrama explores the concerns of the private sphere, sports those of the public. Melodrama announces its fictional status, while sports claim for themselves the status of reality. Melodrama allows for the shedding of tears, while sports solicit shouts, cheers, and boos. Crying, a characteristically feminine form of emotional display, embodies internalized emotion; tears are quiet and passive. Shouting, the preferred outlet for male affect, embodies externalized emotion; it is aggressive and noisy. Women cry from a position of emotional (and often social) vulnerability; men shout from a position of physical and social strength (however illusory).

WWF wrestling, as a form that bridges the gap between sport and melodrama, allows for the spectacle of male physical prowess (a display that is greeted by shouts and boos) but also for the exploration of the emotional and moral life of its combatants. WWF wrestling focuses on both the public and the private, links nonfictional forms with fictional content, and embeds the competitive dimensions of sports within a larger narrative framework that emphasizes the personal consequences of that competition. The "sports entertainment" of WWF wrestling adopts the narrative and thematic structures implicit within traditional sports and heightens them to ensure the maximum emotional impact. At the same time, WWF wrestling adopts the personal, social, and moral conflicts that characterized nineteenth-century theatrical melodrama and enacts them in terms of physical combat between male athletes. In doing so, it fore-grounds aspects of masculine mythology that have a particular significance for its predominantly working-class male audience—the experience of vulnerability, the possibilities of male trust and intimacy, and the populist myth of the national community.

Remaking Sports

Elias and Dunning offer a vivid description of the dramaturgy of the ideal soccer match: "a prolonged battle on the football field between teams which are well matched in skill and strength . . . a game which sways to and fro, in which the teams are so evenly matched that first one, then the other scores." The emotional consequences of the close and heated action are viscerally felt by the spectators. Each subsequent play intensifies their response, "until the tension reaches a point where it can just be borne and contained without getting out of hand." A decisive climax rewards this active engagement with "the happiness of triumph and jubilation."[14] The writers emphasize many traits that football shares with melodrama—the clear opposition between characters, the sharp alignment of audience identification, abrupt shifts in fortune, and an emotionally satisfying resolution. Yet there is an important difference: While melodrama guarantees emotional release through its conformity to tried-and-true generic structures, actual athletic competition, unlike staged wrestling, is unrehearsed and unscripted. Matches such as the ones Elias and Dunning describe are relatively rare, since so much is left to chance. Where the actual competition lacks narrative interest, that gap must be filled by sports commentary that evokes and intensifies the audience's investment. However, as Barthes notes, wrestling is not a sport but rather a form of popular theater, and as such, the events are staged to ensure maximum emotional impact, structured around a consistent reversal of fortunes and a satisfying climax. There is something at stake in every match—something more than who possesses the title belts.

As a consequence, wrestling heightens the emotional experience offered by traditional sports and directs it toward a specific vision of the social and moral order. Peter Brooks argues that melodrama provides a postsacred society with a means of mapping its basic moral and ethical beliefs, of making the world morally legible.[15] Similarly, wrestling, Barthes argues, takes as its central problematic the restoration of moral order, the creation of a just society from a world where the powerful rule. Within the World Wrestling Federation, this battle for a higher justice is staged through the contest for the title belts. Like traditional melodrama, wrestling operates within a dualistic universe: each participant is either a good guy or a villain, a "fan favorite" or a "rule-breaker." Good guys rarely fight good guys, bad guys rarely fight bad guys. A championship is sometimes unjustly granted to rule-breakers, but ultimately it belongs to the virtuous. WWF wrestling offers its viewers a story of justice perverted and restored, innocence misrecognized and recognized, strength used and abused.

Might Makes Right

Within traditional sports, competition is impersonal, the product of prescribed rules that assign competitors on the basis of their standing or on some prespecified form of rotation. Rivalries do, of course, arise within this system and are the stuff of the daily sports page, but many games do not carry this added affective significance. Within the WWF, however, all competition depends upon intense rivalry. Each fight requires the creation of a social and moral opposition and often stems from a personal grievance. Irwin R. Schyster (IRS) falsely accuses the Big Boss Man's mother of tax evasion and threatens to throw her in jail. Sid Justice betrays Hulk Hogan's friendship, turning his back on his tag-team partner in the middle of a major match and allowing Hulk to be beaten to a pulp by his opponents, Ric Flair and the Undertaker. Fisticuffs break out between Brett Hart and his brother, "Rocket," during a special "Family Feud" match that awakens long-simmering sibling rivalries. Such offenses require retribution within a world that sees trial by combat as the preferred means of resolving all disputes. Someone has to "pay" for these outrages, and the exacting of payment will occur in the squared ring.

The core myth of WWF wrestling is a fascistic one: ultimately, might makes right; moral authority is linked directly to the possession of physical strength, while evil operates through stealth or craftiness (mental rather than physical sources of power). The appeal of such a myth to a working-class audience should be obvious. In the realm of their everyday experience, strength often gets subordinated into alienated labor. Powerful bodies become the means of their economic exploitation rather than a resource for bettering their lot. In WWF wrestling, physical strength reemerges as a tool for personal empowerment, a means of striking back against personal and moral injustices.

A central concern within wrestling, then, is how physical strength can ensure triumph over one's abusers, how one can rise from defeat and regain dignity through hand-to-hand combat. Bad guys cheat to win. They manipulate the system and step outside the rules. They use deception, misdirection, subterfuge, and trickery. Rarely do they win fairly. They smuggle weapons into the ring to attack their opponents while their managers distract the referees. They unwrap the turnbuckle pads and slam their foes' heads into metal posts. They adopt choke holds to suffocate them or zap them with cattle prods. "Million Dollar Man" Ted Dibiase purposefully focuses his force upon "Rowdy" Roddy Piper's wounded knee, doing everything he can to injure him permanently. Such atrocities require rematches to ensure justice; the underdog heroes return next month and, through sheer determination and willpower, battle their antagonists into submission.

Such plots allow for the serialization of the WWF narrative, forestalling its resolution, intensifying its emotional impact. Yet at the same time, the individual match must be made narratively satisfying on its own terms, and so, in practice, such injustices do not stand. Even though the match is over and its official outcome determined, the hero shoves the referee aside and, with renewed energy, bests his opponent in a fair (if nonbinding) fight. Whatever the outcome, most fights end with the protagonist standing proudly in the center of the ring, while his badly beaten antagonist retreats shamefully to his dressing room. Justice triumphs both in the long run and in the short run. For the casual viewer, it is the immediate presentation of triumphant innocence that matters, that satisfactorily resolves the drama. Yet for the WWF fan, what matters is the ultimate pursuit of justice as it unfolds through the complexly intertwined stories of the many different wrestlers.

Body Doubles

Melodramatic wrestling allows working-class men to confront their own feelings of vulnerability, their own frustrations at a world that promises them patriarchal authority but is experienced through relations of economic subordination. Gender identities are most rigidly policed in working-class male culture; unable to act *as* men, they are forced to act *like* men, with a failure to assume the proper role the source of added humiliation. WWF wrestling offers a utopian alternative to this situation, allowing a movement from victimization toward mastery. Such a scenario requires both the creation and the constant rearticulation of moral distinctions. Morality is defined, first and foremost, through personal antagonism. As Christine Gledhill has written of traditional melodrama, "Innocence and villainy construct each other: while the villain is necessary to the production and revelation of innocence, innocence defines the boundaries of the forbidden which the villain breaks."[16] In the most aesthetically pleasing and emotionally gripping matches, these personal antagonisms reflect much deeper mythological oppositions—the struggles between rich and poor, white and black, urban and rural, America and the world. Each character stands for something, draws symbolic meaning by borrowing stereotypes already in broader circulation. An important role played by color commentary is to inscribe and reinscribe the basic mythic opposition at play within a given match. Here, the moral dualism of masculine melodrama finds its voice through the exchanges between two announcers, one ("Mean" Jean Okerlund) articulating the protagonist's virtues, the other (Bobby "The Brain" Heenan) justifying the rulebreaker's transgressions.

Wrestlers are often cast as doppelgangers, similar yet morally opposite figures. Consider, for example, how *WWF Magazine* characterizes a contest between the evil Mountie and the heroic Big Boss Man: "In conflict are Big Boss Man's and the Mountie's personal philosophies: the enforcement of the law vs. taking law into one's own hands, the nightstick vs. the cattle prod, weakening a foe with the spike slam vs. disabling him with the nerve-crushing carotid control technique."[17] The Canadian Mountie stands on one page, dressed in his bright red uniform, clutching an open pair of handcuffs with a look of quiet earnestness. At this moment the two opponents seem to be made for each other, as if no other possible contest could bear so much meaning, though the Big Boss Man and the Mountie will pair off against other challengers in the next major event.

The most successful wrestlers are those who provoke immediate emotional commitments (either positive or negative) and are open to constant rearticulation, who can be fit into a number of different conflicts and retain semiotic value. Hulk Hogan may stand as the defender of freedom in his feud with Sgt. Slaughter, as innocence betrayed by an ambitious friend in his contest against Sid Justice, and as an aging athlete confronting and overcoming the threat of death in his battle with the Undertaker. Big Boss Man may defend the interests of the economically depressed against the Repo Man, make the streets safe from the Nasty Boys, and assert honest law enforcement in the face of the Mountie's bad example.

The introduction of new characters requires their careful integration into the WWF's moral universe before their first match can be fought. We need to know where they will stand in relation to the other protagonists and antagonists. The arrival of Tatanka on the WWF roster was preceded by a series of segments showing the Native American hero visiting the tribal elders, undergoing rites of initiation, explaining the meaning of his haircut, makeup, costume, and war shout. His ridicule by the fashion-minded Rick "The Model" Martel introduced his first antagonism and ensured the viewer's recognition of his essential goodness.

Much of the weekly broadcasts centers on the manufacturing of these moral distinctions and the creation of these basic antagonisms. A classic example might be the breakup of the Rockers. A series of accidents and minor disagreements sparked a public showdown on Brutus "The Barber" Beefcake's Barber Shop, a special program segment. Shawn Michaels appeared at the interview, dressed in black leather and wearing sunglasses (already adopting iconography signaling his shift toward the dark side). After a pretense of reconciliation and a series of clips reviewing their past together, Michaels shoved his partner, Marty Jannetty, through the barber-shop window, amid Brutus's impotent protests.[18] The decision to feature the two team members as independent combatants required the creation of moral difference, while the disintegration of their partnership fit perfectly within the program's familiar doppelganger structure. *WWF Magazine* portrayed the events in terms of the biblical story of Cain and Abel, as the rivalry of two "brothers":

> [The Rockers] were as close as brothers. They did everything together, in and out of the ring. But Michaels grew jealous of Jannetty and became impatient to succeed. While Jannetty was content to bide his time, work to steadily improve with the knowledge that championships don't come

easily in the WWF, Michaels decided he wanted it all now—and all for himself.[19]

If an earlier profile had questioned whether the two had "separate identities," this reporter has no trouble making moral distinctions between the patient Jannetty and the impatient Michaels, the self-sacrificing Jannetty and the self-centered Michaels. Subsequent broadcasts would link Michaels professionally and romantically with Sensational Sherri, a woman whose seductive charms have been the downfall of many WWF champs. As a manager, Sherri is noted for her habit of smuggling foreign objects to ringside in her purse and interfering in the matches to ensure her man's victory. Sherri, who had previously been romantically involved with "Million Dollar Man" Ted Dibiase, announced that she would use her "Teddy Bear's" money to back Michael's solo career, linking his betrayal of his partner to her own greedy and adulterous impulses. All of these plot twists differentiate Jannetty and Michaels, aligning spectator identification with the morally superior partner. Michaels's paramount moral failing is his all-consuming ambition, his desire to dominate rather than work alongside his long-time partner.

The Rockers' story points to the contradictory status of personal advancement within the WWF narrative: these stories hinge upon fantasies of upward mobility, yet ambition is just as often regarded in negative terms, as ultimately corrupting. Such a view of ambition reflects the experience of people who have worked hard all of their lives without much advancement and therefore remain profoundly suspicious of those on top. Wrestling speaks to those who recognize that upward mobility often has little to do with personal merit and a lot to do with a willingness to stomp on those who get in your way. Virtue, in the WWF moral universe, is often defined by a willingness to temper ambition through personal loyalties, through affiliation with others, while vice comes from putting self-interest ahead of everything else. This distrust of self-gain was vividly illustrated during a bout between "Rowdy" Roddy Piper and Bret "The Hitman" Hart at the 1992 Wrestlemania. This competition uncharacteristically centered on two good guys. As a result, most viewers suspected that one fighter would ultimately be driven to base conduct by personal desire for the Intercontinental championship belt. Such speculations were encouraged by ambiguous signs from the combatants during "buildup" interviews and exploited during the match through a number of gestures that indicate moral indecision: Rowdy stood ready to club Hart with an illegal foreign object; the camera cut repeatedly to close-ups of his face as he struggled with his conscience before casting the object aside and continuing a fair fight. In the end, however, the two long-time friends embraced each other as Piper congratulated Hart on a more or less fairly won fight. The program situated this bout as a sharp contrast to the feud between Hulk Hogan and Sid Justice, the major attraction at this pay-per-view event. Their budding friendship had been totally destroyed by Justice's overriding desire to dominate the WWF: "I'm gonna crack the head of somebody big in the WWF. . . . No longer is this Farmboy from Arkansas gonna take a back seat to anybody."[20] Rowdy and Hart value their friendship over their ambition; Justice lets nothing stand in the way of his quest for power.

Perfect Bastards

WWF wrestlers are not rounded characters; the spectacle has little room for the novelistic, and here the form may push the melodramatic imagination to its logical extremes. WWF wrestlers experience no internal conflicts that might blur their moral distinctiveness. Rather, they often display the "un-dividedness" that Robert Heilman sees as a defining aspect of nineteenth-century melodramatic characters:

> [The melodramatic character displays] oneness of feeling as a competitor, crusader, aggressor; as defender, counterattacker, fighter for survival; he may be assertive or compelled, questing or resistant, obsessed or desperate; he may triumph or lose, be victor or victim, exert pressure or be pressed. Always he is undivided, unperplexed by alternatives, untorn by divergent impulses; all of his strength or weakness faces in one direction.[21]

The WWF athletes sketch their moral failings in broad profile: The Mountie pounds on his chest and roars, "I am the Mountie," convinced that no one can contest his superiority, yet as soon as the match gets rough, he slides under the ropes and tries to hide behind his scrawny manager. The Million Dollar Man shoves hundred-dollar bills into the mouths of his defeated opponents, while Sherri paints her face with gilded dollar signs to mark her possession by the highest bidder. "Ravishing" Rick Rude wears pictures of his opponents on his arse, relishing in his own vulgarity. Virtue similarly displays itself without fear of misrecognition. "Hacksaw" Jim Duggan clutches an American flag in one hand and a two-by-four in the other.

The need for a constant recombination of a fixed number of characters requires occasional shifts in moral allegiances (as occurred with the breakup of the Rockers). Characters may undergo redemption and seduction, but these shifts typically occur quickly and without much ambiguity. There is rarely any lingering doubt or moral fence-straddling. Such characters are good one week and evil the next. Jake "The Snake" Roberts, a long-time hero—albeit one who enjoys his distance from the other protagonists—uncharacteristically offered to help the Ultimate Warrior prepare for his fight against the Undertaker. Their grim preparations unfolded over several weeks, with Jake forcing the Warrior to undergo progressively more twisted rituals—locking him into a coffin, burying him alive—until finally Jake shoved him into a room full of venomous snakes. Bitten by Jake's cobra, Lucifer, the Ultimate Warrior staggered toward his friends, who simply brushed him aside. As the camera pulled back to show the Undertaker standing side by side with Jake, the turncoat laughed, "Never trust a snake." From that moment forward Jake was portrayed as totally evil, Barthes's perfect bastard. Jake attacks "Macho Man" Randy Savage's bride, Elizabeth, on their wedding day and terrorizes the couple every chance he gets.

The program provides no motivation for such outrages, though commentary in the broadcasts and in the pages of wrestling magazines constantly invites such speculation: "What makes Jake hate Savage and his bride so fiercely? Why does he get his jollies—as he admits—from tormenting her?" What Peter Brooks said about the villains of traditional melodrama holds equally well here: "Evil in the world of melodrama does not need justification; it exists, simply. . . . And the less it is adequately motivated the more this evil appears simply volitional, the product of pure will."[22] Jake is more evil because he is a snake; it's in his character and nothing can change him, even though in the past he was just as essentially good as he is now totally demented. We know Jake is evil and without redemption because he tells us so, over and over:

> I'm not really sure I have any soul at all. . . . Once I get involved in something—no matter how demented, no matter how treacherous, no matter how far off the mark it is from normal standards—I never back down. I just keep on going, deeper and deeper into the blackness, far

past the point where any sensible person would dare venture. You see, a person with a conscience—a person with a soul—would be frightened by the sordid world I frequent. But Jake the Snake isn't scared at all. To tell you the truth, I can't get enough of it.[23]

Jake recognizes and acknowledges his villainy; he names it publicly and unrepentantly.

Peter Brooks sees such a process of "self-nomination" as an essential feature of the melodramatic imagination: "Nothing is spared because nothing is left unsaid; the characters stand on stage and utter the unspeakable, give voice to their deepest feelings, dramatize through their heightened and polarized words and gestures the whole lesson of their relationship."[24] The soliloquy, that stock device of the traditional melodrama, is alive and well in WWF wrestling. Wrestlers look directly into the audience and shove their fists toward the camera; they proclaim their personal credos and describe their sufferings. Tag-team partners repeat their dedication to each other and their plans to dominate their challengers. Villains profess their evil intentions and vow to perform various types of mayhem upon their opponents. Their rhetoric is excessively metaphoric, transforming every fight into a life-and-death struggle. Much as nineteenth-century theatrical melodrama used denotative music to define the characters' moral stances, the wrestlers' entries into the arena are preceded by theme songs that encapsulate their personalities. Hulk's song describes him as "a real American hero" who "fights for the rights of every man." The Million Dollar Man's jingle proclaims his compelling interest in "money, money, money," while Jake's song repeats "trust me, trust me, trust me."

Operating within a world of absolutes, WWF wrestlers wear their hearts on their sleeves (or, in "Ravishing" Rick Rude's case, on the seat of their pants) and project their emotions from every inch of their bodies. Much as in classical theater and melodrama, external actions reveal internal states; moral disagreements demand physical expressions. As Brooks writes, "Emotions are given a full acting-out, a full representation before our eyes. . . . Nothing is understated, all is overstated."[25] The Million Dollar Man cowers, covering his face and retreating, crawling on hands and knees backward across the ring. Sherri shouts at the top of her ample lungs and pounds the floor with her high-heel shoe. "Rowdy" Roddy Piper gets his dander up and charges into the ring. With a burst of furious energy, he swings madly at his opponents, forcing them to scatter right and left. Roddy spits in the Million Dollar Man's eyes, flings his sweaty shirt in his face, or grabs Sherri, rips off her dress, throws her over his knee, and spanks her. Such characters embody the shameful spectacle of emotional display, acting as focal points for the audience's own expression of otherwise repressed affect.

Invincible Victims

Fans eagerly anticipate these excessive gestures as the most appropriate means of conveying the characters' moral attitudes. Through a process of simplification, the wrestler's body has been reduced to a series of iconic surfaces and stock attitudes. We know not only how the performer is apt to respond to a given situation but what bodily means will be adopted to express that response. Wrestlers perform less with their eyes and hands than with their arms and legs and with their deep, resounding voices. Earthquake's bass rumble and Roddy's fiery outburst, Ric Flair's vicious laughter and Macho Man's red-faced indignation are "too much" for the small screen, yet they articulate feelings that are too intense to be contained.

This process of simplification and exaggeration transforms the wrestlers into cartoonish figures who may slam each other's heads into iron steps, throw each other onto wooden floors, smash each other with steel chairs, land with their full weight on the other's prone stomach, and emerge without a scratch, ready to fight again. Moral conflict will continue unabated; no defeat can be final within a world where the characters are omnipotent. If traditional melodrama foregrounded long-suffering women's endurance of whatever injustices the world might throw against them, WWF wrestling centers around male victims who ultimately refuse to accept any more abuse and fight back against the aggressors.

Such a scenario allows men to acknowledge their own vulnerability, safe in the knowledge that their masculine potency will ultimately be restored and that they will be strong enough to overcome the forces that subordinate them. Hulk Hogan has perfected the image of the martyred hero who somehow captures victory from the closing jaws of defeat. Badly beaten in a fight, Hulk lies in a crumpled heap. The referee lifts his limp arms up, once, twice, ready to call the fight, when the crowd begins to clap and stomp. The mighty hero rises slowly, painfully to his feet, rejuvenated by the crowd's response. Blood streams through his blond hair and drips across his face, but he whips it aside with a broad swing of his mighty arms. Hulk turns to face his now-terrified assailant.

"Seeing Is Believing"

Such broad theatricality cuts against wrestling's tradition of pseudorealism; the programs' formats mimic the structures and visual style of nonfiction television, of sports coverage, news broadcasts, and talk shows. The fiction is, of course, that all of this fighting is authentic, spontaneous, unscripted. The WWF narrative preserves that illusion at all costs. There is no stepping outside the fiction, no acknowledgment of the production process or the act of authorship. When the performers are featured in *WWF Magazine*, they are profiled in character. Story segments are told in the form of late-breaking news reports or framed as interviews. The commentators are taken by surprise, interrupted by seemingly unplanned occurrences. During one broadcast, Jake the Snake captured Macho Man, dragging him into the ring. Jake tied him to the ropes and menaced him with a cobra, which sprang and bit him in the forearm. The camera was jostled from side to side by people racing to Macho's assistance and panned abruptly, trying to follow his hysterical wife as she ran in horror to the ringside. A reaction shot showed a child in the audience reduced to tears by this brutal spectacle. Yet, at the same time, the camera refused to show us an image "too shocking" for broadcast. Macho Man's arm and the snake's gaping mouth were censored, blocked by white bars. (A few weeks later, the "uncensored" footage was at last shown, during a prime-time broadcast, so that viewers could see "what really happened.") The plotlines are thus told through public moments where a camera could plausibly be present, though such moments are supposed to allow us insight into the characters' private motivations.

As Ric Flair often asserted during his brief stay in the WWF, "Pictures don't lie; seeing is believing," and yet it is precisely seeing and not believing that is a central pleasure in watching television wrestling. What audiences see is completely "unbelievable," as ring commentators frequently proclaim—unbelievable because these human bodies are unnaturally proportioned and monstrously large, because these figures who leap through the air seem to defy all natural laws, and, most important, because these characters participate within the corny and timeworn plots of the nineteenth-century melodrama. The pleasure comes in seeing what cannot be believed, yet is constantly asserted to us as undeniably true. Fans elbow each other in the ribs, "Look how fake," taking great pride in their ability to see through a deception that was never intended to convince.

Such campy self-acknowledgment may be part of what makes male spectators' affective engagement with this melodramatic form safe and acceptable within a traditionally masculine culture that otherwise backs away from overt emotional display. Whenever the emotions become too intense, there is always a way of pulling back, laughing at what might otherwise provoke tears. WWF wrestling, at another level, provokes authentic pain and rage, particularly when it embraces populist myths of economic exploitation and class solidarity, feeds a hunger for homosocial bonding, or speaks to utopian fantasies of empowerment. The gap between the campy and the earnest reception of wrestling may reflect the double role that Elias and Dunning ascribe to traditional sports: the need to allow for the decontrolling of powerful affects while regulating their expression and ensuring their ultimate containment. The melodramatic aspects are what trigger emotional release, while the campy aspects contain it within safe bounds. The plots of wrestling cut close to the bone, inciting racial and class antagonisms that rarely surface this overtly elsewhere in popular culture, while comic exaggeration ensures that such images can never fully be taken seriously.

Romance in the Ring

WWF wrestling's plots center on the classic materials of melodrama: "false accusation . . . innocence beleaguered, virtue triumphant, eternal fidelity, mysterious identity, lovers reconciled, fraudulence revealed, threats survived, enemies foiled."[26] The ongoing romance between Macho Man and Elizabeth bore all of the classic traces of the sentimental novel. The virginal Miss Elizabeth, who almost always dressed in lacy white, embodied womanly virtues. WWF fans were fascinated by her struggle to civilize her impassioned and often uncontrollable Macho Man, withstanding constant bouts of unreasoning jealousy, tempering his dirty tactics. As a profile of Miss Elizabeth explained, "She embodies the spirit of a grass-roots American wife. She cares for her man. She provides him with comfort in the midst of chaos. She provides him with a sense of unity when his world seems to be disintegrating. Elizabeth calmly handles these difficult situations with grace and tact."[27] WWF fans watched the course of their romance for years, as Macho rejected her, taking up with the sensuous and anything-but-virtuous Sherri, but he was reunited with Elizabeth following a devastating defeat in a career-ending match against the Ultimate Warrior. They followed her efforts to rebuild her Macho Man's self-confidence, his fumbling attempts to propose to her, and their spectacular pay-per-view wedding. They watched as the beloved couple were attacked during their wedding party by Jake and the Undertaker, as Macho begged the WWF management to reinstate him so that he could avenge. himself and his wife against this outrage, and as he finally returned to the ring and defeated the heartless Snake during a specially scheduled event. No sooner was this conflict resolved than Ric Flair produced incriminating photographs which he claimed showed that Elizabeth was his former lover. In a locker-room interview, Ric and Mr. Perfect smirkingly revealed the photographs as evidence that Elizabeth is "damaged goods," while the fumbling announcer struggled to protect Elizabeth's previously unquestioned virtue. Once again, this domestic crisis motivated a forthcoming bout, creating narrative interest as the all-but-inarticulate Macho Man defended his wife with his muscles.

More often, however, the masculine melodrama of WWF wrestling centers on the relationships between men, occupying a homosocial space that has little room for female intrusions. There are, after all, only two women in the WWF universe—the domestic angel, Elizabeth, and the scheming whore, Sherri. A more typical story involved Virgil, the Million Dollar Man's black bodyguard, who, after years of being subjected to his boss's humiliating whims, decided to strike back, challenging his onetime master to a fight for possession of his "Million Dollar Belt." Virgil was befriended by the feisty Scotsman "Rowdy" Roddy Piper, who taught him to stand tall and broad. The two men fought side by side to ensure the black man's dignity. The antagonism between Virgil and the Million Dollar Man provoked class warfare, while the friendship between Virgil and Roddy marked the uneasy courtship between men.

Here and elsewhere, WWF wrestling operates along the gap that separates our cultural ideal of male autonomy from the reality of alienation, themes that emerge most vividly within tag-team competition. The fighter, the omnipotent muscle machine, steps alone, with complete confidence, into the ring, ready to do battle with his opponent. As the fight progresses, he is beaten down, unable to manage without assistance. Struggling to the ropes, he must admit that he needs another man. His partner reaches out to him while he crawls along the floor, inching toward that embrace. The image of the two hands, barely touching, and the two men, working together to overcome their problems, seems rich with what Eve Sedgwick calls "male homosocial desire."[28] Because such a fantasy is played out involving men whose physical appearance exaggerates all of the secondary masculine characteristics, it frees male spectators from social taboos that prohibit the open exploration of male intimacy. In their own brutish language, the men express what it is like to need (and desire?) another man. Consider, for example, how *WWF Magazine* characterized the growing friendship between Jake the Snake and Andre the Giant:

> At a glance, Andre gives the impression of granite—unshakable, immutable and omnipotent. Inside, there is a different Andre. His massive size and power belie the fact that his spirit is as fragile as anyone's. And that spirit was more bruised than was his body. Like Andre, Jake projects a sense of detachment from the world of the average guy. Like Andre, Jake has an inner self that is more vulnerable than his outer shell.[29]

The story describes their first tentative overtures, their attempts to overcome old animosities, and their growing dependency on each other for physical and emotional support. As Jake explains:

> Andre was afraid of serpents. I was afraid of people—not of confronting people, but of getting close to them. We began to talk. Slow talk. Nothing talk. Getting to know one another. The talk got deeper. . . . I never asked for help from anybody. I never will. But Andre decided to help me; I won't turn him down. I guess we help one another. You might call it a meeting of the minds.[30]

Jake's language carefully, hesitantly negotiates between male ideals of individual autonomy ("I never asked for help") and an end to the isolation and loneliness such independence creates. Will Jake find this ideal friendship with a man who was once his bitter enemy, or is he simply leaving himself open to new injuries? These images of powerful men whose hulking bodies mask hidden pains speak to longing that the entire structure of patriarchy desperately denies.

Such a narrative explores the links that bind men and the barriers that separate them. Yet, at the same time, its recurring images of betrayed friendship and violated trust rationalize the refusal to let down barriers. Texas Tornado describes his relationship to his former tag-team partner: "I know the Warrior as well as any man in the World Wrestling Federation. . . . Of course, in wrestling, you never get too close with anybody because one day you might be facing him on the other side of the ring. Still, Warrior and I have traveled and trained together. We've shared things."[31] Wrestling operates within a carefully policed zone, a squared ring, that allows for the representation of intense homosocial desire but also erects strong barriers against too much risk and intimacy. The wrestlers "share things," but they are not allowed to get "too close."

Consider what happened when the Beverley Brothers met the Bushwhackers at a live WWF event at the Boston Gardens. The two brothers, clad in lavender tights, hugged each other before the match, and their Down-Under opponents, in their big boots and work clothes, turned upon them in a flash, "queer-baiting" and then "gay-bashing" the Beverley Brothers. I sat there with fear and loathing as I heard thousands of men, women, and children shouting, "Faggot, faggot, faggot." I was perplexed at how much such a representation could push so far and spark such an intense response. The chanting continued for five, ten minutes, as the Beverley Brothers protested, pouted, and finally submitted, unable to stand firm against their tormentors. This homophobic spectacle may have served the need of both performers and spectators to control potential readings of the Bushwhackers' own physically intimate relationship. The Bushwhackers, Butch and Luke, are constantly defined as polymorphously perverse and indiscriminately oral, licking the faces of innocent spectators or engaging in mutual face-wetting as a symbolic gesture of their mutual commitment. By defining the Beverley "Sisters" as "faggots," as outside of acceptable masculinity, the Bushwhackers created a space in which their own homosocial desire could be more freely expressed without danger of its calling into question their gender identity or sexual preference. This moment seems emblematic of the way wrestling operates more generally—creating a realm of male action that is primarily an excuse for the display of masculine emotion (and even homoerotic contact), while ensuring that nothing that occurs there can raise any questions about the participant's "manhood."[32]

Populist Pleasures

One key way that wrestling contains this homoerotic potential is through the displacement of issues of homosocial bonding onto a broader political and economic terrain. If, as feminism has historically claimed, the personal is the political, traditional masculinity has often acknowledged its personal vulnerabilities only through evoking more abstract political categories. Populist politics, no less than sports, has been a space of male emotional expression, where personal pains and sufferings can be openly acknowledged only through allegorical rhetoric and passionate oratory. Melodramatic wrestling's focus on the professional rather than the personal sphere facilitates this shift from the friendship ties between all working men. The erotics of male homosocial desire are sublimated into a hunger for the populist community, while images of economic exploitation are often charged with a male dread of penetration and submission.

Although rarely described in these terms, populism offers a melodramatic vision of political and economic relationships. Bruce Palmer argues that populism is characterized by its focus on a tangible reality of immediate experience rather than political abstraction, its emphasis on personal rather than impersonal causation, and its appeal to sentimentality rather than rationality (all traits commonly associated with the melodramatic). As he summarizes the basic axioms of the Southern populist movement, "what is most real and most important in the world was that which was most tangible, that which could be seen and touched. . . . People made things move and if some people were moved more than movers, it was because others, more powerful, moved them."[33] American populism sees virtue as originating from physical labor, as a trait possessed by those who are closest to the moment of production (and therefore embodied through manual strength), while moral transgression, particularly greed and ruthlessness, reflect alienation from the production process (often embodied as physical frailty and sniveling cowardice). Populism understands politics through the social relations between individuals rather than between groups, though individuals are understood in larger allegorical categories—the simple farmer versus the slick Wall Street lawyer, the factory worker versus the scheming boss, the small businessman versus the Washington bureaucrat, the American voter versus the party bosses. In this model, social changes come about through personal redemption rather than systemic change. A populist utopia would be a community within which individuals recognized their common interests and respected their mutual responsibilities. As Palmer explains, "The only decent society was one in which each person looked out for every other one, a society in which all people enjoyed equal rights and the benefits of their labor."[34] Such a movement made common cause between the workers and farmers (and, in its most progressive forms, between whites and blacks) in their mutual struggle for survival against the forces of capitalist expansion and technological change.

If populism draws on melodramatic rhetoric, it has also provided the core myths by which the masculine melodrama might concern itself with the struggles of the aristocracy and the bourgeois; American faith in a classless society translated these same conventions into narratives about scheming bankers and virtuous yeomen, stock figures within the populist vision. In that sense, melodramatic wrestling fits squarely within the larger tradition of masculine melodrama and populist politics. What is striking about the mythology of WWF wrestling is how explicitly its central conflicts evoke class antagonisms. Its villains offer vivid images of capitalist greed and conspicuous consumption. The Million Dollar Man wears a gold belt studded with diamonds and waves a huge wad of hundred-dollar bills. Magazine photographs and program segments show him driving expensive cars, eating in high-class restaurants, living in a penthouse apartment, or vacationing in his summer home at Palm Beach. What he can't grab with brute force, he buys: "Everybody has a price." In one notorious episode, he bribed Andre the Giant to turn over to him the sacred WWF championship belt; another time, he plotted a hostile takeover of the WWF. Similarly, Ric Flair brags constantly about his wealth and influence: "I'll pull up [to the match] in my stretch limousine with a bottle of Dom Perignon in one hand and a fine-looking woman holding my other. The only thing I'll be worried about is if the champagne stays cold enough."[35] "Mean" Gene Okerlund interviews him on his yacht, *Gypsy*, as he chuckles over his sexual humiliation of the Macho Man and brags about his wild parties. The Model enjoys a jet-setting lifestyle, displays the "finest in clothing," and tries to market his new line of male perfumes, "the scent of the 90s, Arrogance." Irwin R. Schyster constantly threatens to audit his opponents, while Repo Man promises to foreclose on their possessions: "What's mine is mine. What's yours is mine too! . . . I've got no mercy at all for cheats. Tough luck if you've lost your job. If you can't make the payment, I'll get your car. Walk to look for work, Sucker."[36]

The patriotic laborer ("Hacksaw" Jim Duggan), the virtuous farm boy (Hillbilly Jim), the small-town boy made good (Big Boss Man), the Horatio Alger character (Virgil, "Rowdy" Roddy Piper, Tito Santana) are stock figures within this morality play, much as they have been basic tropes in populist discourse for more than a century. WWF heroes hail from humble origins and can therefore act as appropriate champions within fantasies of economic empowerment and social justice. A profile introducing Sid Justice to *WWF Magazine* readers stressed his rural origins: "Sid Justice comes from the land. . . . Born and raised on a farm in Arkansas, imbued with the hardworking values of people who rise before dawn to till the earth and milk the cows. . . . A lifestyle that is the backbone of this country."[37] Justice developed his muscles tossing bales of hay onto his grandfather's truck, and his integrity reflects the simplicity of an agrarian upbringing: "Don't confuse simplicity with stupidity. A man who learned to make the land produce its fruits has smarts." Sid Justice understands the meaning of personal commitments and the value of simple virtues in a way that would be alien to "people who get their dinner out of a cellophane package from a super market."

Pride in where one comes from extends as well to a recognition of racial or ethnic identities. Tito Santana returns to Mexico to rediscover his roots and take lessons from a famous bullfighter, changing his name to El Matador. Tatanka emerges as the "leader of the New Indian Nation," demonstrating his pride in his "Native American heritage." He explains, "The tribes of all nations are embodied in me."[38] The creation of tag teams and other alliances cuts across traditional antagonisms to bring together diverse groups behind a common cause. Tag-team partners Texas Tornado and El Matador, the Anglo and the Mexicano, join forces in their shared struggle against economic injustice and brute power. "Rule-breakers" are often linked to racial prejudice. The "Brain" releases a steady stream of racial slurs and epithets; the Million Dollar Man visits the "neighborhoods" to make fun of the ramshackle shack where El Matador was raised or to ridicule the crime-ridden streets where Virgil spent his youth. What WWF wrestling enacts, then, are both contemporary class antagonisms (the working man against the Million Dollar Man, the boy from the barrio against the repo man, the farmer against the IRS) and the possibilities of a class solidarity that cuts across racial boundaries, a common community of the oppressed and the marginal.

The rule-breaker's willingness to jeer at honest values and humble ancestry, to hit the proletarian protagonists with economic threats, and to shove their own ill-gotten goods in their faces, intensifies the emotions surrounding their confrontations. These men are fighting for the dignity of all against these forces that keep us down, that profit from others' suffering and prosper in times of increased hardship. Big Boss Man defends his mother against false allegations leveled against her by the IRS: "My Mama never had a job in her life. All she did was take care of her children and raise food on the farm down in Georgia."[39] Virgil strikes back not only against the man who forced him to wipe the perspiration from his brow and pick the dirt from between his toes, but also against the conditions of economic subordination that made him dependent on that monster.

Coming to Blows

Such an evil must be isolated from the populist community; its origins must be identified and condemned because it represents a threat to mutual survival. This attempt to name and isolate corruption emerges in a particularly vivid fashion when Sgt. Slaughter discusses the Nasty Boys' delinquency:

> The Nasty Boys are un-American trash. You know, their hometown of Allentown is a very patriotic town. Its people have worked in the steel mills for years. Their hard work is evident in every skyscraper and building from coast to coast. Allentown's people have worked in the coal mines for years. Their hard work has kept America warm in the dead of winter. But the Nasty Boys don't come from the same Allentown I know. . . . They spit on hard-working Americans. They spit on patriotic people. And they spit on the symbol of this great land. Old Glory herself.[40]

Slaughter's rhetoric is classic populism, linking virtue and patriotism with labor, treating evil as a threat originating outside of the community that must be contained and vanished.

This process of defining the great American community involves defining outsiders as well as insiders, and it is not simply the rich and the powerful who are excluded. There is a strong strand of nativism in the WWF's populist vision. When we move from national to international politics, the basic moral opposition shifts from the powerless against the powerful to America and its allies (the United Kingdom, Australia, New Zealand, and Canada) against its enemies (especially the Arabs and Communists, and often the Japanese). The central match at the 1993 Survivor Series, for example, pitted the "All-Americans" against the "Foreign Fanatics" (a mix that involved not only predictable villains such as Japan's massive Yokozuna but also less predictable ones, such as Finland's Ludwig and the Montrealers). The appeal to racial stereotyping, which had its progressive dimensions in the creation of champions for various oppressed minorities, resurfaces here in a profound xenophobia. Arab wrestlers are ruthless, Asian wrestlers are fiendishly inscrutable or massive and immovable. While America is defined through its acceptance of diversity, foreign cultures are defined through their sameness, their conformity to a common image. America's foreign relations can be mapped through the changing alliances within the WWF: Nikolai Volkov, one of the two Bolsheviks, retired from view when the Cold War seemed on the verge of resolution but reemerged as a spokesman for the new Eastern Europe, redefined as a citizen of Lithuania. The WWF restaged the Gulf War through a series of "Bodybag" bouts between Hulk Hogan and Sgt. Slaughter. Slaughter, a former Marine drill sergeant, was brainwashed by Iraqi operatives Col. Mustafa and Gen. Adnan. Under their sinister tutelage, he seized the WWF championship belt through brutal means and vowed to turn the entire federation and its followers into "POWs." In a series of staged incidents, Slaughter burned an American flag and ridiculed basic national institutions. The turncoat leatherneck smugly pounded his chest while his turbaned sidekick babbled incessantly in something resembling Arabic. Hulk Hogan, the all-American hero, vowed that his muscles were more powerful than patriot missiles and that he could reclaim the belt in the name of God, family, and country. He dedicated his strength to protect the "Little Hulkamaniacs" whose mothers and fathers were serving in the Gulf. The blond-haired, blue-eyed Hulkster looked directly into the camera, flexing his pythons and biceps, and roared, "What ya gonna do, Sarge Slaughter, when the Red, White and Blue runs wild on you?" Hulk and "Hacksaw" Jim Duggan incited the crowd to chant "USA" and to jeer at the Iraqi national anthem. Here, the working-class heroes emerge as flag-waving patriots, fighting against "un-Americanism" at home and tyranny abroad.

Yet, however jingoistic this enactment became, WWF's melodramatic conventions exercised a counterpressure, bridging the gap between otherwise sharply delimited ideological categories. Humiliated by a crushing defeat, Slaughter pulled back from his foreign allies and began a pilgrimage to various national monuments, pleading with the audience, "I want my country back." Ultimately, in a moment of reconciliation with "Hacksaw" Jim Duggan, the audience was asked to forgive him for his transgressions and to accept him back into the community. Sarge kneeled and raised an American flag, Hacksaw embraced him, and the two men walked away together, arm in arm. That moment when one tired and physically wounded man accepted the embrace and assistance of another tired and physically wounded man contained tremendous emotional intensity. Here, male homosocial desire and populist rhetoric work together to rein in the nationalistic logic of the Gulf War narrative, to create a time and space where male vulnerability and mutual need may be publicly expressed. Here, the personal concerns that had been displaced onto populist politics reasserted their powerful demands upon the male combatants and spectators to ensure an emotional resolution to a story that, in the real world, refused satisfying closure. The story of a soulless turncoat and a ruthless tyrant evolved into the story of a fallen man's search for redemption and reunion, an autonomous male's hunger for companionship, and an invincible victim's quest for higher justice.

Such a moment can be described only as melodramatic, but what it offers is a peculiarly masculine form of melodrama. If traditional melodrama centers upon the moral struggle between the powerful and the vulnerable, masculine melodrama confronts the painful paradox that working-class men are powerful by virtue of their gender and vulnerable by virtue of their economic status. If traditional melodrama involves a play with affect, masculine melodrama confronts the barriers traditional masculinity erects around the overt expression of emotion. If traditional melodrama centers on the personal consequences of social change, masculine melodrama must confront traditional masculinity's tendency to displace personal needs and desires onto the public sphere. The populist imagery of melodramatic wrestling can be understood as one way of negotiating within these competing expectations, separating economic vulnerability from any permanent threat to male potency, translating emotional expression into rage against political injustice, turning tears into shouts, and displacing homosocial desire onto the larger social community. Populism may be what makes this powerful mixture of the masculine and the melodramatic popularly accessible, and what allows wrestling to become such a powerful release of repressed male emotion.

5

Exploiting Feminism in Stephanie Rothman's *Terminal Island*

> I think films are a compromised and corrupted art form, a combination of business and art. And I think filmmakers who treat it completely as a business fail. A business-oriented film is too blatant. It must have something more. To me, films that succeed are those that are slightly corrupted, that attempt to be both business and art, knowing they can never be a full work of art and should never be a full work of business.[1]
>
> —Roger Corman

Two women—one white and blonde, the other black and sporting an Afro—are harnessed to a plow, struggling to move forward through thick muck. Glistening sweat slides through their exposed cleavage and down their taunt, muscular thighs. Their expressions are at once determined and humbled. They are dressed in tight cut-off jeans, halter tops tied off at the midriff, no bras and no shoes. Behind them, a man snarls, driving his human "cows."

This disturbing image is the core icon in the advertisements for *Terminal Island*. In the same ad, we see a stereotypical image of the black "buck," his broad chest bare, crushing a black woman's head into the dirt with his foot, "Welcome to Terminal Island, Baby!" The promotional campaign for an exploitation film characteristically reduces the movie to its most sensationalistic images, images that make its desired audience want to see more. *Terminal Island* is being "exploited" as a film in which one can see beautiful women "put in their place" by powerful men.

Another image circulates around *Terminal Island*—the only photograph I have been able to find of its director, Stephanie Rothman. Rothman, an attractive young woman with flowing black hair, is directing an early scene set in a television studio control-room. Her look is passionate, her expressive hands stretch wide, as she delivers instructions to the actress who plays a documentary filmmaker in the movie. The actress bears more than a passing resemblance to Rothman herself.[2] As a result, the image takes on a reflexive quality—the woman director as artist producing an image of the woman director. *Omni* magazine captions the photograph: "*Terminal Island* is consistent with her other films in that it is about several men and women who unite, then live together as friends and lovers without sexual distinctions being made, or infighting and petty jealousies developing. Her ideal world is one of equality and harmony."[3] *Omni* identifies the elements in *Terminal Island* and the other Rothman films, such as *The Velvet Vampire* (1971), *Group Marriage* (1972), and *The Working Girls* (1973), that attracted feminist interest.

Omni's juxtaposition of the exploitation poster and the photograph of Rothman leaves unreconciled two contradictory accounts of the film's politics and its audience appeals. Images of women as chattel compete with images of women as artists. Appeals to fantasies of male control compete with appeals to fantasies of "equality and harmony." Any film that negotiates between these two competing discourses warrants closer consideration. Such films may help us to better understand the ideological fault-lines within the popular cinema.

As Christine Gledhill suggests, the political commitments of filmmakers often have to get "negotiated" through generic traditions for constructing stories, as well as marketing appeals that sell those stories to demographically desirable audiences. Such negotiations produce ideological contradictions within the texts being sold, contradictions that in turn get negotiated by viewers seeking certain kinds of pleasures from going to the movies. In Rothman's case, a further series of negotiations occurred among feminist critics: after an initial flurry of articles advancing her case as a feminist filmmaker, references to Rothman all but disappeared. A generation of critics schooled in Laura Mulvey's assault on "visual pleasure" found it difficult to resolve the ideological contradictions surrounding a feminist exploitation filmmaker. They stopped looking for signs of feminist resistance in such an unlikely place and recoiled with puritanical discomfort from her eroticized images. Rothman's *Terminal Island* suggests the complexity of the negotiations that occur between feminist politics and popular entertainment within the marginal commercial space of the exploitation cinema.

As more recent feminist critics have sought a more complex account of the pleasures of popular culture, a reconsideration of Rothman seems in order. Re-examining Rothman is of critical importance, since the issues she poses are closely related to those raised by a whole range of Hollywood films released in the 1990s—*Aliens, Blue Steel, Silence of the Lambs, Thelma and Louise,* and *A League of Their Own*—that similarly seek to insert feminist politics into commercial genres. Many of these films were either directed by veterans of the exploitation cinema or were strongly influenced by its legacy. To fully understand the complex ideological negotiations within these equally "corrupted" works, we need to reclaim both the progressive generic traditions upon which they build and the critical tools by which an earlier generation of feminist critics sought to interpret and evaluate those traditions. This essay examines what may be at stake for feminism in the exploitation cinema, using Rothman and *Terminal Island* as a point of entry.

Rothman "exploits" the progressive potential already embedded within the exploitation genres to get her liberal feminist messages to a larger viewing public; Roger Corman's New World Pictures "exploits" the topicality of feminism in the early 1970s and the volatile emotions that surround it to attract an audience of male and female filmgoers. Emerging in this context of negotiation and exploitation, *Terminal Island* will be analyzed as a "partially corrupted" film, one that resists placement in a simple ideological category but nevertheless shows the possibility of expressing politics of resistance within mainstream genres.

Rothman at New World

A graduate of the University of Southern California cinema program, Rothman was one of a number of "film school brats" hired by Roger Corman to make low-budget exploitation films.[4] Starting as a personal assistant to Corman, she became one of the core directors for New World Pictures and later co-founded her own production company, Dimension Pictures.[5] Her independently produced films largely follow the conventions of the exploitation genres at New World. Unlike many of the male directors who worked under Corman's production supervision, such as Francis Ford Coppola, Peter Bogdanovich, Martin Scorsese, Jonathan Demme, Ron Howard, John Sayles, James Cameron, Jonathan Kaplan, and Joe Dante, Rothman was never able to move into mainstream Hollywood filmmaking.[6] She left the movie industry following the collapse of Dimension Pictures and has not made films since.

Rothman was one of a number of women employed by Corman during the 1970s and 1980s, among them directors like Barbara Peeters and Amy Jones, producers like Barbara Boyle, Gale Anne Hurd, and Julie Corman, and scriptwriters like Rita Mae Brown. Corman offered them a chance to make movies at a time when the Hollywood establishment was still almost impenetrable for women. Corman's motives were far from altruistic.[7] Having nowhere else to go, these women would work long hours for little money, hoping to get the film credits needed to break into Hollywood.[8]

Corman offered his young directors a straightforward deal: he would finance their films, albeit on low budgets and two-week production schedules, and insure their distribution in theaters. The film's promotional campaigns, which depended on highly charged elements such as sex, drugs, violence, nudity, and countercultural politics, were developed before the script was. Films were to be made according to his formulas. Jonathan Kaplan, one of Rothman's contemporaries at New World, described the formula for the working-girl comedies, a subgenre centering around the professional and romantic exploits of school teachers, nurses, or stewardesses:

> There was a male sexual fantasy to be exploited, comedic subplot, action/violence, and a slightly left-of-center social subplot. Those were the four elements that were required in the nurse pictures. And then frontal nudity from the waist up and total nudity from behind and no pubic hair and get the title of the picture somewhere in the film and go to work, so that was essentially it.[9]

Within those terms, the filmmaker was free to experiment with alternative political perspectives or new formal techniques, as long as the picture came in on time and on budget.

At the same time, Corman's recruitment of women was consistent with his self-perception as a liberal, "socially conscious" independent producer willing to "take chances" that the majors rejected. Enthusiastically displaying May 1968 political posters on the wall of his office, Corman saw himself as providing a home for those with "leftist anti-war sympathies." New World solicited the market of disaffected youths who were rejecting the mainstream films of the period. Reworking tired mainstream genres through gender-reversals, New World's films characteristically focused on the actions of strong-willed and independent-minded women.

Corman articulated those ideological commitments in specifically economic terms:

> We discovered a youth market between fifteen and thirty years of age. . . . Certainly action and sex sold. Also, the liberal or left-of-center political viewpoint was a third element worth "exploiting" and it made me happy to put some social point of view in. It improved the films, too, because it added a coherence usually lacking on low-budget films.[10]

Rothman worked within—and, to some degree, against—the generic space Corman provided, both building upon the liberal potential already in place at New World and posing an internal critique of its own "exploitation" of women.

Exploitation Cinema as Counter-Cinema

Rothman's feminist politics, so visibly pushing the limits of the exploitation genres, made her an interesting test case for the women's "counter-cinema" discourse advanced by British feminist writers such as Pam Cook and Claire Johnston.[11] Rejecting the political and aesthetic pretensions of the art cinema—the collectively produced documentary or the political avant-garde film—these critics identified ways that women filmmakers had operated within the popular cinema, seizing its materials and reworking them to more fully accommodate the possibility of female desire and feminist politics. The commercial cinema could get images and messages into broad circulation, a possibility feminists ignored at their own peril; Johnston and Cook were uncomfortable with feminist strategies that marginalized women's voices and cut them off from mainstream audiences. As Johnston writes in the conclusion of "Women's Cinema as Counter-Cinema": "In order to counter our objectification in the cinema, our collective fantasies must be released: women's cinema must embody the working through of desire; such an objective demands the use of the entertainment film." While Laura Mulvey was calling for a rejection of pleasure as always already corrupted by masculine fantasies,[12] Johnston was advocating a fuller dialogue between the entertainment film and the political cinema: "Ideas derived from the entertainment film, then, should inform the political film, and political ideas should inform the entertainment cinema: a two-way process."[13]

If the commercial cinema required compromises, it might nevertheless be important to see how far women could go in appropriating its borrowed and tainted terms to speak in their own voices. Films by women directors like Rothman, Dorothy Arzner, and Ida Lupino were contradictory and often incoherent, since women lacked the power within the Hollywood system to fully express their own visions. However, these films were vitally important to feminists hoping to find a new cinematic language that might more fully express their ideological commitments. As Cook explains, "While they [Rothman's movies] cannot in any sense be described as feminist films, they work on the forms of the exploitation genres to produce contradictions, shifts in meaning which disturb the patriarchal myths of women on which the exploitation film itself rests."[14]

Cook's project was largely auteurist, building a case for a women director, Rothman, as part of a larger project of feminist historiography. At the same time, it points toward the emergence of a feminist genre theory that would soon shift its attention toward film noir and melodrama. The tension between authorship and genre is one of the most productive aspects of her essay "'Exploitation' Cinema and Feminism." Cook ends the essay by calling for closer attention to specific Rothman works that will help to resolve their relationship to "other films in the exploitation field." I maintain that tension here. Without devaluing Rothman's importance as a director, I want to situate her within a broader generic tradition, to show both the possibilities and the limitations feminists encounter working within the popular cinema.

Passive Victims, Heroic Resistors

One of the two films Rothman directed at Dimension, *Terminal Island* is set in a near-future society in which the United States Supreme Court has outlawed capital punishment. The State of California has voted to establish a penal colony on an island fifteen miles off its coast, where convicted murders will fend for themselves. As the ad campaign succinctly puts it, Terminal Island is "where we dump our human garbage!"

The film opens as a new prisoner, Carmen Sims (Ena Hartman), is brought onto the island. Carmen, an angry black woman, embodies pride, strength, and resistance to male control. The first time we see her, she is punching out the camera of a photographer who tries to take her picture. When she arrives on the island, she finds herself in the midst of a ruthlessly patriarchal culture ruled by Bobby Farr (Sean Kenney), a vicious psychopath. Bobby sees her as "the new bitch" and sends his right-hand man, Monk (Roger E. Mosley), to "break her in." Monk appraises her sexual capacity, concluding "you look like you could take on three or four right off." When she resists, growling, "I don't get down on my knees to nobody," he overpowers her and crushes her head into the ground: "Welcome to Terminal Island, Baby."

Despite her cries for help, the other women watch the scene with cold disinterest, having already been taught "their place." Even after this public humiliation, Carmen continues to resist Bobby's orders, saying "nobody's gonna run me." We watch her get slapped, beaten, and harnessed in front of the plow, yet she still refuses to bow and scrape. Alone with the other women, Carmen demands answers: "What kinda bastards have you got here anyway?"

"What kind do you want? We've got white bastards, black bastards . . ."

"Why are we penned in here like pigs?"

"Because we are too valuable to run loose. We're the property of every man on this island."

The language is crude agit-prop, yet it articulates the film's fundamental concerns: a struggle between men and women, the experience of being oppressed by a more powerful force, the reduction of women to domesticated beasts. The women pull the plows, muck in the dirt, prepare the meals, and service the camp's sexual needs. As Carmen grumbles while she dishes out food, "Great! I've got tits so I have to play Betty Crocker." Writing in *Omni*, Rothman describes the women as "doubly enslaved, forced to work like beasts of burden by day and sexually service the men at night, which sounds to me a lot like a job description for the position of traditional wife in any patriarchal society."[15]

These images seem profoundly ambivalent. They do not seem designed for women's pleasure, and they are often hard to watch. Separated from their narrative context, run as elements of pure spectacle, as in the ads or trailers for the film, these images of women being treated as chattel offer sadistic pleasure and erotic fascination, reflecting a masculine backlash against the growing prominence of the feminist debate in the early 1970s. Yet, placed in their narrative context, the same images invite melodramatic identification with the suffering women and their hunger for freedom and self-respect. For the most part, these women do not suffer quietly, and Rothman allows them to voice their anger over their treatment by the men. Their anger evokes, albeit in simplified terms, feminist categories of analysis: the subordination of women as property within economic and social exchanges between men, the linkage of biological traits ("tits") with socially assigned responsibilities ("playing Betty Crocker"), and the possibility of revenge or revolt. In a particularly vivid moment of rage, Carmen vows to "smash his balls until they turn into Jell-O," hardly words calculated to comfort the film's male audience members.

Such direct expressions of feminist rage were rare in mainstream American cinema in the early 1970s, a period when, as feminist historians and critics note, Hollywood dealt with its uncertainty about how to respond to changing gender roles by retreating from the representation of women altogether.[16] In the exploitation cinema, however, such an exclusion would be counterproductive. The erotic display of women was a central market appeal. No women, no "tits." At the same time, Corman's focus on the drive-in market meant soliciting couples through "date movies" rather than simply appealing to male grindhouse viewers. Cook clearly overstates her case when she asserts that exploitation films were "produced exclusively by men for a male market."[17] Rather, Corman's films needed to appeal to mixed audiences by offering differing points of entrance for male and female spectators. The New World films were structured around the actions, desires, goals, and interests of women, albeit women who were often constructed within the terms of previously male-centered genres.[18] *Terminal Island* wasn't *The Turning Point* (1977), but then, precisely because it operated as part of a "trash" culture, it could pose blunt questions that middlebrow films had to dodge.

Women were to be simultaneously the objects of erotic spectacle and the active subjects of melodramatic plots, a double function aptly summarized by the ad campaign for Barbara Peeters's *Bury Me an Angel* (1971): "She's the Beauty and the Beast." The accompanying images showed the film's "biker chick" protagonist, Dag Bandy, holding a shotgun, confronting a cop, kicking a male assailant in the mouth, and taking a nude swim in a lake. Dag is described as "red-hot passion and cold steel anger all rolled into one explosive six-foot frame—a howling, humping hellcat with a major score to settle."[19]

Caught between conflicting audience desires and expectations, the "positive-heroine figure" in New World films holds a contradictory status. On the one hand, as Cook suggests, this stereotype was "based on the idea of putting the woman in the man's place," with the female protagonist still defined through "male characteristics" and a mastery over "male language, male weapons." She is an embodiment of "male phantasies and obsessions," rather than speaking for "women's experiences and desires." In many cases, the "bitchiness" of the female protagonists was build-up for a patriarchal pleasure in their abuse and humiliation. At the same time, such dominatrix-like figures could trigger male masochism, a fantasy of being dominated and controlled by powerful women. Despite their obvious ties to masculine erotic fantasies, Cook sees a "polemical" possibility in the image of female revenge, of "turning the weapons of the enemy against him."[20] Such films do provide images of resistance to patriarchal authority, be they in the form of women taking up guns (as occurs in any number of films about female gangsters or women's prisons) or simply in turning aside sexist comments with quick wit (as occurs in the working women comedies associated with Rothman's early career.) Such films open a space for women to play with power, a space traditionally reserved for men, even if they do not allow women to fully reclaim and redefine that space on their own terms.

Female protagonists often break down under these contradictory and irreconcilable impulses, torn between the needs to fit within the framework of conventional genres and to articulate their particularity as women. Typical of the female protagonists in the New World films of the period, Dag's actions are motivated both in traditionally masculine terms ("revenge") and in feminine terms (defending her family):[21] She wants to gun down the man who shot her brother and, along the way, to protect and defend the two childlike men who have joined her on the adventure. Peeters's persistent focus on Dag's motivations, through angst-ridden dialogue and flashbacks, contrast sharply with the treatment of male "angels" in other films in the same series. Male bikers' interest in riding the open road is taken for granted. Even Peeters's attempts to situate Dag within a larger community of women pose questions about her motivations. *Bury Me an Angel* includes several scenes centering on the emotional anguish and domestic isolation of Dag's mother or on the spiritual wisdom of a friendly "witch," both warning her against revenge. Their inclusion pulls the film from motorcycle action toward domestic melodrama. Dag's encounters with these women question the validity of her actions and the "eye-for-an-eye" logic of the genre. At the same time, the language and images surrounding her violence eroticizes it; the logic of the film demands that we see not only her "naked fury" but her naked body, and that she ultimately shed her rage long enough to find love in the arms of a man. When the time comes, however, she breaks off lovemaking and bolts from his house, panicked by her loss of control, unwilling to allow anything to distract her from her narrative goals.[22] As the film progresses, she moves from victim to hero to erotic "beauty" to blood-thirsty "beast," never able to fully or comfortably reside in any role for long, since the film cannot fully resolve how it feels about her core goals.

Terminal Island adopts a different strategy for dealing with the contradictory expectations surrounding exploitation film heroines. Rothman's films characteristically center less on an individual protagonist than on a community of women. Each woman embodies an alternative stereotype—erotic spectacle, suffering victim, or empowered hero. Some of the women, such as the long-suffering Bunny (Barbara Leigh), are cast as pure victims, subjected to endless humiliation and abuse. In true melodramatic fashion, Bunny is mute to voice her protests. An oddly passive character, Bunny has been unable or unwilling to speak since the murder of her parents. She is framed as the ideal sufferer. Bobby uses her as "bait" to lure the guards, dispatched periodically to drop shipments of food on the shore. He ties Bunny spread-eagle between two stakes, ripping off the back of her shirt, and whipping her until bloody welts are visible on her bare flesh. Bobby casts Bunny as the ideal melodramatic spectacle of violated innocence, a spectacle "nobody will be able to resist." The other women maintain a more heroic posture; their sufferings are temporary, their strength never fully crushed, and in the end, they get their violent revenge. Carmen's character is associated with raw courage, uncontainable rage, and pride in her race and her gender. Lee (Marta Kristen) combines revolutionary politics with intellectual skills and knowledge. Joy (Phyllis Davis) knows how to use her earthy sexuality to her own ends.

Playing with Stereotypes

From the outset, Rothman acknowledges that the film is involved in a play with stereotypes. The prologue deals with a female director putting together a television documentary on Terminal Island. Her discussion of the elements required to tell a compelling narrative constitutes a reflexive commentary on the exploitation film genre itself. A male producer, standing in for Corman, advocates the economical re-use of found footage, suggesting that the "dummies" in the television audience "can't remember what they saw five minutes ago." The characters are first introduced as mug shots, as the producers look for appropriate figures for the news report. Each is identified according to his or her offense and fit within conventional understandings of popular crime: the punk (Bobby) who killed his partner after a successful robbery; the revolutionary intellectual (Lee) who accidentally killed the night watchman when she blew up a bank; the middle-class black man (A.J.) who killed a cop and the more streetwise black (Monk) who gets flipped past without a second look; the sweet young girl (Bunny) who murdered her parents; the "doper-biker-rapist" (Dylan); the beautiful woman who poisoned her husband (Joy); the tragic handsome doctor who may have been falsely accused (Milford); and the "maniac" and mass murderer (Teale). The producers peg Joy as offering sex appeal and Milford as "something for the bored housewife" before identifying the recently convicted Carmen as "our star."

If the documentary's narration describes the criminals as "all convicted of the same crime," murder, Rothman wants to draw distinctions between different kinds of murders and different kinds of characters. If she wants to depict a penal colony as a microcosm, she must create moral distinctions. Within this moral economy, all of the women are already read as innocents, while some of the men (A.J.) show the capacity for change and others (Bobby, Teale) are beyond all redemption. As the film progresses, the characters are never allowed to escape those stereotypical characterizations and achieve more complex motivations. As Richard Dyer suggests, "the role of stereotypes is to make visible the invisible, so that there is no danger of it creeping up on us unawares; and to make fast, firm and separate what is in reality fluid."[23] The making of a new myth—in this case, a feminist counter-myth that challenges the dominance of patriarchal values—depends as much on the creation of order through stereotyping as does the mythmaking process that holds the old order in place. The question concerns what stereotypes are evoked, whose interests they serve, and what conception of the world they shorthand.

Pam Cook sees this foregrounding of stereotypes as among the most "subversive" aspects of the exploitation cinema: "the overt manipulation of stereotypes and gender conventions allows us to see that language is at work; myths are revealed as ideological structures embedded in form itself."[24] Exploitation films were "potentially less offensive than mainstream Hollywood cinema" because they "offer the possibility of taking a critical distance." Rothman thus needs stereotypes as the most efficient means to morally identify her characters, and at the same time parodies the exploitation cinema's dependence upon such stereotypes.

The Women's Prison Genre

The dominant stereotypes in *Terminal Island* can be traced to the women's prison genre, one of the core New World formulas of the early 1970s. Starting with Jack Hill's *Big Doll House* in 1971, many of New World's biggest successes came in this genre, including *Women in Cages* (Gerry De Leon, 1972), *The Big Bird Cage* (Jack Hill, 1972) and *Caged Heat* (Jonathan Demme, 1974). These films spoke to fairly reactionary and voyeuristic fantasies (the image of semi-clad women being tortured, the staging of scenes in women's shower rooms, the casual lesbianism that emerges in single-gender settings.) At the same time, the genre allowed for the expression of feminist rage over rape and sexual domination and for the climactic images of women taking up arms to end their oppression.

As in *Terminal Island*, the films most often open with the arrival of a new prisoner, through whose eyes we observe the repressive institutions and the social practices of everyday resistance. Through this figure, the film initially maps out the different moral distinctions between the various women and their crimes. Stereotypically (and the films almost invariably follow stereotypes), the women in a prison film will include:

(a) the rebel or revolutionary woman whose fighting skills and leadership experience will help galvanize the women's resistance;

(b) the tormented victim who needs nurturing by the others and who will become the focus of the community's moral outrage against the authorities;

(c) the tough black "soul sister" who wants to remain aloof from the group but who will ultimately be forced to make a commitment; and

(d) the "normal" middle-class woman, whose crimes often go unspecified, so that her judgments will be viewed most sympathetically by the audience.

The four women in *Terminal Island* can be seen as fitting within this same set of stereotypes: Lee is the revolutionary, Bunny the victim, Carmen the tough soul sister (who also functions as a source of identification), and Joy the middle-class woman.

For the most part, the women's crimes in these films are committed against the patriarchal order—killing unfaithful husbands, using violence to stop a rape, or engaging in prostitution out of economic necessity.

There is a constant suggestion that their victims deserved what happened to them or that the female prisoners have been unjustly sentenced. In other cases, however, the women are hardened criminals, who know how to use violence to resist authority but who are unwilling initially to contribute to the group effort. The confession of crimes is closely related to the moral redemption of the characters, so that as we get to know why they are in jail, we come to see them as fellow victims and potential allies in the struggle against institutionalized oppression.

In prison, they face endless humiliations: in *Big Doll House*, the prisoners are subjected to body-cavity searches, get groped by the sleazy men who come to deliver them food, and are tortured by the sadistic warden; in *Caged Heat*, the prison authorities subject the unruly women to electroshock therapy and lobotomy, while the doctor fondles and photographs the drugged women's bodies. As one female prisoner grumbles in *Caged Heat*, "If I ever get out of this hole, I'm gonna write my life story: All men are shit." Her summary is largely accurate: the male prison authorities are frequently portrayed in grotesque fashion—porcine, sweaty, dirty, unshaven, sex-crazed, and stupid. In most cases, the authority in the prison resides in women, who are portrayed as sadistic lesbians or as sexually repressed and emotionally crippled. The contrast between these "fat pigs" and the "caged birds" makes the films "morally legible" in the classic melodramatic tradition.

The focus on multiple female protagonists allows a multiplication of abuses, a succession of melodramatic excesses, building toward the women's final revolt against the system and their attempt to escape from prison. In *Caged Heat*, for example, Pandora, the black soul sister, is unjustly punished for her possession of a pornographic photograph and locked away, nude, in solitary confinement for a week. Her close friend, Belle, devises a bold scheme to steal food from the prison staff's refrigerator and smuggle it to her. Later, when Belle gets caught and framed for murder, she is subjected to the whims of the crazed doctor, who both molests her and prepares to lobotomize her. Pandora devises a scheme to smuggle a knife into the clinic and help her escape. The two women, portrayed as passionate friends, shift between the roles of eroticized victim and heroic rescuer, suggesting the fluidity in character relations characteristic of the genre as a whole.

The women's prison films tell stories of female victimization, radicalization, and empowerment. For those familiar with the genre, the sequences of melodramatic torture and abuse are necessary build-up for the women's heroic resistance. The women in *The Big Doll House* initially try to work through the system, appealing to the idealistic young prison doctor for help. When he is unable to elevate their situation—and, in fact, inadvertently identifies the resistors to the sadistic warden—they must take matters in their own hands.[25]

When you consider the controversy surrounding *Thelma and Louise*'s representation of armed women locking a cop in a car, shooting a rapist, and blasting off the tires of a truck some two decades later, the radical potential of these films seems clear. Here, as in *Thelma and Louise*, female protagonists break out of legal institutions to challenge their treatment at the hands of patriarchal authorities. Their actions range from comic reversals, such as making the leering guards drop their pants (*Caged Heat*) or forcing a man to perform sexually at knife-point (*The Big Doll House*), to more overt acts of violence, such as shooting it out with machine guns.

At the same time, a series of displacements works to contain the films' most radical implications. First, the prison authorities are most often portrayed as women. If the dialogue situates the events in a larger framework of male abuse, we are drawn most directly toward acts of revenge against other women. Being in charge seems to have left these women emotional, and sometimes, physical cripples and to have warped their sexuality. A stock scene involves the female commandant's attempts to establish a romantic relationship with the male prison doctor, often with discomfort and embarrassment, if not overt humiliation. Second, the radical potential is contained by locating the action in the Third World, in contrast to male-prison films, which typically occur in an American context.[26] Rothman's film involves a similar displacement, situating it within a near-future society that closely resembles, yet is marked out as separate from, our own.

Utopian Communities

Fantasies of resisting or transforming the social order are not restricted to the women's prison genre. Corman's films are preoccupied with images of the apocalyptic destruction of old societies and the emergence of new social orders. Drawing on the work of E. R. Leach and Mircea Eliade, Paul Willemen argues for a recognition of Corman's "millenic vision," which he identifies as operating in films as generically diverse as *Teenage Cave Man* (1958), *House of Usher* (1960), *The Last Woman on Earth* (1960), and *The Trip* (1967).[27] As a director and producer, Corman has consistently examined the process of social degeneration and regeneration; his films almost always center upon alternative communities existing on the edges of the social mainstream. As the focus of Corman's work shifted to embrace the 1960s counterculture, both as subject matter and as audience demographic, this utopian impulse took on new importance. In Martin Scorsese's *Boxcar Bertha* (1972), produced by Corman, we are presented with two conceptions of the utopian community: the union of working men that David Carradine's character is trying to organize, and the outlaw band that forges together the fortunes of "a Bolshevik, a nigger, a New York Jew, and a whore."

The communities depicted in many of New World's productions of the early 1970s are almost obsessively multiracial, reflecting the identity politics of the civil rights era and their largely urban base. At the same time, targeting the interests of their drive-in audiences, the films frequently incorporate representations of the working-class American South. The result is an imaginary resolution to the racial conflicts of the period, as urban blacks and rural whites find a common ground in resisting forces of exploitation and oppression. While the economics of the blaxploitation market, which centered on inner-city theatres, pushed toward images of racial antagonism, the economics of New World's distribution encouraged a politics of reconciliation and racial interdependence. Following Corman's influence, Rothman also constructs utopian images of alternative communities: the circles of women friends in *The Student Nurses* and *The Working Women*, the beach bums in *It's a Bikini World*, and the radical social arrangements in *Group Marriage*.

Terminal Island represents a specifically feminist inflection of New World's "millenic vision," closely tied to the images of social transformation found in 1970s feminist utopian novels, such as Ursula K. Le Guin's *The Dispossessed*, Joanna Russ's *The Female Man*, or Marge Piercy's *Woman on the Edge of Time*. These novels, according to Peter Fitting, construct utopian societies based on "non-hierarchical and non-oppressive social and sexual relationships," contributing to feminist politics by helping us understand what a "qualitatively different society" might look like.[28] Such narratives differ significantly from the broader tradition of utopianism in science fiction, particularly in their focus on personal politics—the sexual, social, and economic relations between men and women—rather than (or in addition to) large-scale technological or political change. According to Fitting, these novels "depict society in process, straining to come into being and open to change."

Rothman describes her film in remarkably similar terms: "*Terminal Island* is not the story of a utopian community built on a bedrock of ideology, but of how a group of antisocial people rediscover their own social needs, needs for companionship and cooperation that exist within us all."[29] Its opening images—a series of man-in-the-street interviews responding to the Terminal Island "experiment"—invite us to understand the story in a broader political context. Again and again, the central question becomes what kind of society the prisoners will create for themselves. One person suggests, "Let them fight among themselves if that's what they want to do," while another proposes, more optimistically, "Maybe they can get together and make a better life for themselves." Rothman constructs two different answers to that question. The first one, the society that Bobby and his henchmen create, is profoundly dystopian, where the worst tendencies of traditional society emerge unchecked by any civilizing influences. The other, a tribe of outcasts and freedom fighters who have broken with Bobby and are struggling to survive on their own, seems equally optimistic, a utopian transformation of a repressive society.

Bobby's culture is authoritarian and the division of labor is rigidly structured: he gives the orders and the others obey. Those who disobey or challenge his authority are punished and usually killed. Bobby shares his plans with no one, not even Monk, his most loyal friend. He constantly feels threatened, needing to strike out with more and more ruthlessness until, by the end of the film, he has few loyal men left. Not surprisingly, he is afraid of the dark. Ruling by terror means that he lives in fear. The patriarchal domination of the women, then, fits within a larger critique of Bobby's authority as crushing and unproductive.

Midway through the film, Carmen and the other women are "liberated" by A.J. (Don Marshall) and his followers. At first, the women are suspicious of what is expected of them in the new community. Shortly after their arrival, one of the men asks A.J. whether he's going to just let the women "run around loose." Refusing to accept subservience to another group of men, Carmen grabs a knife and threatens A.J., who explains that he will need the full cooperation and participation of everyone if the group is going to survive. This "new society" is free, democratic, and equalitarian. The leadership structure is fluid, with everyone contributing to the group's plans, based on what they know. One group member knows how to brew mead; another how to make gunpowder; Carmen draws on her grandmother's voodoo magic to make poison darts. Together, the group will survive, not by fixing everyone into pre-scribed roles, but by liberating everyone to achieve their full potential. As Rothman explains, "Since they are so few, the nomads can't afford the wastefulness of strict sex role divisions. With more hands to share the work, and share it more equitably, life becomes easier for everyone."[30]

Terminal Island traces the group's "political education" and its victory over Bobby and his hordes. In the process, Rothman shows us stories of personal redemption through incorporation into the alternative commu-nity—Carmen lets down her defensiveness and distrust; Dylan (Clyde Ventura), the convicted rapist, must be taught how to respect women; the drugged-out doctor (Tom Selleck) kicks the habit; Bunny learns to talk again as she tries to communicate with her new "family."

The film's closing images suggest the fertile new life these characters have created for themselves. Joy is pregnant, eagerly anticipating a baby. Monk, blinded by the fire that killed Bobby, has been accepted as a full member of the clan. The doctor decides to stay with the group, even after he has been offered a chance at a new trial that could firmly establish his innocence. The closing image shows a new woman getting off a boat, inviting us to take stock of the transformations. "Welcome to Terminal Island."

Rothman's primary images are sexual. In Bobby's totalitarian society, women's sexuality is alienated labor. Monk comes into their tent at night and reads off a duty roster, assigning them to satisfy specified men. When Carmen protests that she is tired after a day's field work, Monk grunts, "All you got to do is lie back and take it. Nobody ever said that you got to stay awake." In A.J.'s more democratic society, sexual relations are freely chosen, and in this context, romance blossoms. Joy unleashes a playful sexuality that is full of laughter, while Carmen's clenched teeth give way to a smile, as she expresses tenderness to several men. Sponta-neous, playful, sensuous sex is seen as the hallmark of an equalitarian so-ciety, with pleasure freely given and accepted between independent men and women.

In that sense, *Terminal Island* is closely related to Rothman's *Group Marriage*. This farcical film proposes a radical reconstruction of family relations and traces the process by which the various characters overcome their jealousies and find happiness in communal relations. In *Group Mar-riage*'s final scene, the characters go before a justice of the peace—three grooms, three brides—all to be married to each other. In the spirit of social transformation through sexual liberation, they have included their gay neighbors as yet another couple formed outside the established order. As a country-and-western love ballad plays on the soundtrack, we watch them all being driven away in police cars, ready to stand trial for their alternative lifestyles.

Terminal Island's community seems all encompassing, accepting into its ranks anyone who will contribute actively to its survival and embrace its ideals of personal freedom and sexual equality. In *Group Marriage*, however, the limitations of this utopian community are more clearly stated. When the group runs a classified ad in an underground newspaper, searching for a new member, they are shocked and bemused by a succession of applicants clearly marked as comically inappropriate—a bisexual man, a dominatrix, a nudist, a voyeur, an underage girl, and a man with a pet sheep. More strikingly, as the social ties within the community strengthen, they find themselves unable to contain one of the original members, who insists on her rights to have sex with people outside their core group. Earlier in the film, Rothman parodies the arbitrariness of conventional sexual morality through the figures of the gay neighbors, who ironically express discomfort with the "disgusting," "perverse," and "unnatural" behavior of the polygamists. However, the film ends up setting equally arbitrary limits on acceptable and unacceptable forms of sexual expression.

Such limits point to the blind spots and contradictions within the liberal middle-class politics that Rothman embraces, blind spots that would become the central focus of debates within the feminist and queer communities in the coming decades. Rothman does question many of the double-standards that ascribe fixed social roles to men and women on the basis of their gender. Women are allowed more active roles in the struggles for social transformation; images of professional or professionally trained women abound in her comedies, where almost every woman seems to be a lawyer or an artist or training to become one. Men are similarly challenged to accept a softer, tenderer form of sexuality. Yet, the stratification of her couples according to race and the introduction of limitations on community membership based on sexuality pose the issue of whom her feminism speaks for. More broadly, one must ask what kinds of utopian politics it is possible to express within exploitation film genres. There is, after all, a central paradox about using genres based on the exploitation of sexual differences to articulate a politics designed to end that exploitation.

Transforming Erotic Spectacle

So far, in focusing on issues of narrative and characterization, we can see that the conventions of exploitation film genres foreground women as active agents and construct narratives of exploitation and resistance, social oppression and social transformation. Yet, people don't typically go to drive-in to watch a story. They go to see moments of spectacle, particularly erotic and violent spectacle, which are the chief elements marketed through newspaper ads, trailers, movie posters, and, nowadays, the video and CD-ROM boxes for these titles. The danger and potential of spectacle is that it does not depend upon narrative. If "sometimes a cigar is just a cigar," a bare breast is always a bare breast and is always subject to erotic fascination. Yet, feminist critics in Mulvey's tradition sometimes assumed that this erotic fascination was open to simple ideological analysis and was necessarily complicit with the patriarchal order. Increasingly, we have come to see spectacle as more polyvalent, as holding radically divergent potentials for pleasure and fantasy. Such work may help us to reassess the erotic politics of these films. Rothman and the other New World directors were fully compliant with audience and producer demands to present a certain number of naked female bodies on the screen. At the same time, they adopted a variety of strategies to subvert or disclose the politics of erotic spectacle.[31]

Nude scenes are frequently the most reflexive moments in these films. In *Terminal Island*, Rothman links our desire to see female nudity to the most oppressive and hypocritical aspects of traditional patriarchy. Bobby orders the mute Bunny to undress and she complies, facilitating a soft-focus display of her nude body glowing in the candlelight. However, as we watch her undress, we are also listening to Bobby's taunting words, "Of course, if you don't want to, just say no." Through this running monologue, the film poses questions about the possibility of sexual consent within a male-dominated culture. We become progressively uncomfortable with the forced display of Bunny's body as we are unable to separate the audience's demands and Bobby's. He both speaks the spectator's desires and renders them base and hypocritical.

Something similar occurs in Rothman's *Working Girls*. A destitute young woman orders a big meal at a restaurant, consumes it, and then announces to the leering manager that she is unable to pay. The cigar-chomping man suggests, not so subtly, that she might be able to work off her debts through sexual favors after closing hours. Calling his bluff, she proceeds to undress in the middle of the crowded restaurant ("Why wait? Now or never") until the flustered man orders her to leave. If Bunny's passive compliance creates viewer discomfort in *Terminal Island*, the woman's overeager compliance in *Working Girls* can be read as an act of defiance, taking charge of the conditions of display and using them to her own ends.

Later in *Working Girls*, a young woman taking small jobs to work her way through law school gets bullied into trying out as a stripper. The film works to deglamorize stripping. As the older stripper who trains her explains, "When I perform, my mind's somewhere else. Tonight, I thought of a new way to arrange my patio furniture." As she is performing, she recalls her friend's advice that she overcome her nervousness by imagining the audience naked. Her nudity is accompanied with the absurd image of a room full of fat men sitting around naked. Again, the presence of a diagetic stand-in for the male film audience creates discomfort and embarrassment over the presentation of the eroticized female body. We are invited to share the uncomfortable experience of becoming a spectacle.

Rothman also adopts more aggressive or confrontational approaches, linking images of female nudity with images calculated to produce male anxiety and disgust. In *Terminal Island*, for example, an extended sequence deals with Joy's revenge on Dylan for his attempted rape. She learns that "royal jelly," a form of beeswax, can be used to attract agitated swarms of bees. She conspires to have Dylan stumble upon her while she is bathing naked in the lake, allowing for one of the film's few soft-core sequences. She seduces him, getting him to undress and spreading his cock with the royal jelly, which she promises will make it especially "tasty." The seduction sequence, with its exaggerated eroticism, ends with the image of the bees stinging Dylan's bare ass while he races away in pain and the others laugh.

To call such devices distanciation is to deny them their own emotive power.[32] We do not so much adopt a critical distance from such images as feel assaulted by them; they kick us in the groin, where our arousal had resided only moments before, and it is through the juxtaposition of these two rather different genital sensations that Rothman sends a clear, if not especially subtle, message to her male viewers. To say that these competing discourses of pleasure and pain, or of a male privilege to look and a feminist critique of the patriarchal exploitation of women, overpower the conventional erotic possibilities of these images would be equally false. Clearly, there are some men who get off on these movies, and the generic framework of the exploitation film may allow them to look past devices designed to problematize our relationship to these images. Yet, such images point to a struggle over meaning, a conflicting set of desires and expectations, which are characteristic of feminist attempts to operate within the genre.

Rothman's films are not, in any simple sense, antisexual or puritanical. They offer plentiful images of a "free," "natural," "spontaneous" sexuality that allows men and women to take pleasure through mutual arousal and satisfaction. Participants in the feminine sexual revolution of the early 1970s, Rothman's female protagonists are sexually active and often comfortable having sex with a variety of men. Broadening the range of available erotic representations, Rothman's films include soft-porn shots of male nudity. These images are sometimes treated as comic (as in *Working Girls*, where a man walks nude out of the bedroom holding a piece of fruit and asks the gaping woman, "Haven't you ever seen a banana before?) or as highly eroticized (as in the slow-motion shots of a muscular lifeguard jogging nude on the beach, his penis bouncing up and down in the bottom edge of the frame). As Rothman explains: "I'm very tired of the whole tradition in western art in which women are always presented nude and men aren't. I'm not going to dress women and undress men—that would be a form of tortured vengeance. But I am certainly going to undress men, and the result is probably a more healthy environment because one group of people presenting another in a vulnerable, weaker, more servile position is always distorted."[33] Rothman's female characters openly assert their own sexual appetites, be they the woman in *Group Marriage* who programs the computer at the rent-a-car place where she works to keep up with the details of her love life or the artist in *Working Girls* who always seems to have a naked male model on hand even though her paintings are non-representational.

In balancing the representation of male and female nudes, Rothman rejects conventional structures of objectification and exploitation in favor of reciprocal sexual attraction. Her films embody progressive attitudes toward human sexuality that are consistent with her liberal feminism. Sex has consequences in the exploitation cinema of Stephanie Rothman, be it the debates about abortion in *The Student Nurses* or the images of social transformation in *Terminal Island*. Women have historically had to pay the price for sexual freedom, so a feminist eroticism requires a recognition of both the costs and the benefits of sex. Her films reject the alienated sexuality of prostitution and sexual exploitation; her women don't want to "just lie back and take it," as Monk describes their sexual services in *Terminal Island*, nor do they want to have to focus on patio furniture, as the stripper advises in *Working Girls*. Sex is not to be treated as part of a system of economic exchange, but rather to be part of the regeneration of the social order.

The transformative potential of erotic imagery is suggested by another scene from *Working Girls*. The manager of the strip club complains that the sexual revolution and the casual acceptance of public nudity are cutting into his business: "Who's gonna pay to see Katrina strip when the whole family can picnic on the beach and see the same thing for nothing." The student explains, "People aren't ashamed of their body anymore," to which the caustic manager explains, "Good for them—bad for me." Rothman suggests that the emergence of healthier, mutually accepting attitudes toward sexuality, and the creation of a utopian community based on the interdependence of men and women, will result in an end of exploitation, and with it the death of the exploitation film genres. Working within the exploitation film tradition, Rothman wants to transform its imagery, to instruct its audiences in new ways of taking pleasure in sexual looking and of thinking about the desirability of the human body. Her fascination with the possibility of feminist eroticism points toward the more overtly pornographic films of Candida Royalle and Annie Sprinkle, which have been embraced by contemporary feminists as holding radical possibilities for women.

Conclusions

Rothman's politics are nowhere more utopian than when they deal with the erotic material that is at the heart of the exploitation film, and this may explain why she chose to continue to work within these genres, even when she gained control over the mode of production at Dimension Pictures, the studio she co-founded with her writer-producer husband Charles Swartz. Rothman's engagement with the exploitation genres was a tactical one; she agreed to follow certain formulas and produce certain images in order to gain access to systems of production, distribution, and exhibition. Working within the popular cinema, she could reach a broader audience than could a political avant-garde filmmaker; *Terminal Island* can be found at my local Blockbuster, while Lizzie Borden's *Born in Flames* cannot. The exploitation cinema demanded that she work with certain exploitable elements, yet she found ways to redefine those images to speak to alternative pleasures and politics. At the same time, the exploitation cinema holds progressive potentials, facilitating stories with strong female protagonists, stories of exploitation and resistance, victimization and empowerment. Rothman borrowed these stories from Roger Corman and from the broader generic history of New World and sought to render them meaningful to women. She could not fully control the promotion and reception of her films, nor could she prevent those images and stories from being used in a reactionary fashion. Yet, for these very reasons, their radical potential takes on new importance. The people who go to see *Born in Flames* probably already have a solid commitment to feminism; the people who go to see *Terminal Island* probably do not. If most of her feminist politics falls on deaf ears, some of it probably gets heard, and in being heard, creates an opening for change where none existed before.

The vexing complexities of this situation may account for why Pam Cook's persistent attempts to claim Rothman for feminism have not had the impact of her similar arguments ·on behalf of Dorothy Arzner. Arzner's oppositional and marginal position as a lesbian woman operating within the classical Hollywood system could be taken for granted. Arzner's radical difference, her disruption of the codes of classical cinema and her exposure of the mechanisms of female spectacle, can be read against a shared understanding of the classical Hollywood cinema as allowing only limited space for female expression. Rothman's "counter-cinema," on the other hand, occurs against the backdrop of a producer (Corman) and studio (New World) already associated with leftist politics and within genres already seen as outside dominant film practice. The exploitation cinema, paradoxically, displayed the most reactionary and patriarchal tendencies of the commercial cinema and, at the same time, an already partially realized radical potential. Rothman can be seen, then, as working both within and in opposition to the exploitation film, a complex set of "negotiations" that allows no simple labeling of her films. Her cinema is "partially corrupt." This is its curse as well as the source of its power.

6

"You Don't Say That in English!"
The Scandal of Lupe Velez

In a church, I am a saint. In a public place, I am a lady. In my own home, I am a devil. . . . My house is where I can do as I please, scream and yell and dance and fall on the floor if I like. I am myself when I am in my home.[1]

—Lupe Velez

The following is one of the many stories Hollywood told about Lupe Velez. This version appeared in *New Movie* magazine in 1932 and begins when Lupe is twelve years old:

> Even at that tender age, Lupe had sex appeal and no race is as quick to recognize this quality as the Mexican. The house was surrounded by boys of all ages, who whistled in various keys. For Lupe those young swains were simply a means to an end. She had an absorbing curiosity about motion picture stars and she discovered, young as she was, that her kisses were marketable. She would bestow a chaste salute on a masculine cheek in exchange for a picture of a star or a colored ribbon to wind in her dark braids. Thus, men became to her tools to gain the things she wanted, and the house was besieged with them. Her more placid sister, Josephine, carried notes between Lupe and the boys, and Lupe's keen little ears soon learned the different whistles of the young lovers.[2]

This remarkable story links together the origins of Lupe's transgressive female sexuality (her willingness to use men as "tools" for her own ends) with the origins of her desire for film stardom. Lupe, the young Mexican girl, desires glamour photographs of Hollywood stars and is willing to trade her sexual favors to get them, to exchange bronze flesh for silvery images.

Underlying this story is a perverse suggestion of child sexuality. Another variant on the story places its starting date even earlier, claiming that Lupe seduced her first lover at the age seven, offering "all of my best kisses" for "the boy who could get me the most pictures of the women who play in the movies," but she was quick to add, in her characteristically broken English, "That is all I have ever sell is my kisses. And kisses—bah, what do kisses matter."[3] That such a denial was thought necessary tells us something of the rumors that dogged Velez throughout her career.

The specter of prostitution surrounded Lupe Velez, often surfacing in more blunt and explicit terms, as in screenwriter Budd Schulberg's autobiography *Moving Pictures*: "Lupe's mother had been a walker of the streets. . . . Lupe herself had made her theatrical debut in the raunchy burlesque houses of the city. Stagedoor Juanitos panted for her favors and Mama Velez would sell her for the evening to the highest bidder. Her price soared to thousands of pesos."[4] Schulberg's memoir makes explicit something that the Hollywood press of the 1930s only hinted—that Lupe Velez was a woman who sold her body for money. Lupe's mother becomes both whore and pimp in this narrative, while Velez becomes the "goods" for trade.

More often, Lupe was characterized as a woman who knew how to use her body to get what she wanted. One fan magazine writer rhapsodized: "I have never seen a body so completely under control. I haven't asked Lupe to wiggle her ears but everything else she can move at will."[5] The Hollywood press consistently portrayed Velez as a woman who took great pleasure in her body. Lupe was quoted as saying, "I do not like to see any one mans too often. The same face over and over. Pretty soon his nose comes to look like the nose of a dog to Lupe."[6] Velez often flaunted her disregard for public opinion and conventional morality, asserting that "people like to talk and I want to give them something to talk about."[7]

If Velez is remembered today, it is not through her on-screen performances (since her career was characterized by marginal roles in major films and major roles in B-movie programmers) but because of the scandal that surrounded her life and death. She gave people "something to talk about" decades after her last film disappeared into obscurity. Kenneth Anger devotes an entire chapter to Velez in his underground classic *Hollywood Babylon*, referring to her in the book's typically purple prose as "the gyrating cunt-flashing Hollywood party girl."[8] Reversing the terms of the prostitution rumors, Anger hints that Lupe, in her "later years" (i.e., at 35), was reduced to buying sexual favors from "professional older-dame pleasers, studs on the take whose gig was gigolo."[9] The only biography currently in print is entitled *Lupe Velez and Her Lovers* and manages to link her romantically and sexually with a who's who of Hollywood in the 1920s and 1930s, everyone from Gary Cooper and Errol Flynn to Red Skelton, from Johnny Weissmuller to black boxing champ Jack Johnson. Risky encounters with Lupe Velez are a stock element in star biographies and autobiographies, including Edward G. Robinson's description of playing opposite her in *Where East Is West* (1930): "Sex was her game and she played it on stage and off the stage. I could deal with the rubbing and roving hands. . . . But I managed to elude her. Because she was a hot tomato and I was not a rock, it was not easy."[10] Velez was even more blunt in her assessment of the sexual prowess of her leading men, suggesting that Gary Cooper "has the biggest organ in Hollywood but not the ass to push it in well."[11] To understand Velez's screen persona, we must, I am afraid, wallow pretty deeply in the muck of Hollywood scandal, though what this essay hopes to address is why those scandals surrounded her and how they relate to the broader tradition of "unruly women" in Hollywood comedy. Some of what we are going to talk about is tasteless, but then, taste is precisely the issue we are exploring here.

In her own time, Velez became famous for her flamboyant personality, with writers finding it difficult to separate her on-screen comic performances from her histrionic activities at Hollywood parties. She was sometimes accused of performing herself badly, of becoming a failed version of her own press copy.[12] More often, she was praised for being herself, "simply Lupe." Velez was, from the start, surrounded by a culture of scandal, which seems to have been actively constructed by the studio system to add allure to her vehicles, and the scandals were restaged, often literally and explicitly, as slapstick in films, such as *The Half-Naked Truth* (1932), *Hollywood Party* (1934), and *Mexican Spitfire* (1940). Velez might be read as a prototype for contemporary female stars, from Madonna to Annie Sprinkle, who have proclaimed their pleasure in their bodies—a pro-sex activist before her time, doomed to suffer the rejection of a more puritanical age.[13] Velez offers a particularly vivid enactment of the myth of the "unruly woman" that Katherine Rowe finds at the heart of female comic performance, a woman who, in Mary Russo's suggestive terms, wants to "make a spectacle of herself," rather than allow the Hollywood system to manufacture her as an erotic spectacle for the male gaze.[14]

Cultural historian Natalie Zemon Davis first introduced the concept of the "woman on top" to considerations of comic representation of gender relations, and her work has been foundational for subsequent accounts of this figure. Its influence can be traced from ancient representations of Phyllis riding Aristotle or terra cotta statues of ancient hags, through such Early Modern figures as the Wife of Bath and Shakespeare's Katrina in *Taming of the Shrew,* to contemporary comic stars such as Roseanne Barr. Davis tells us, "The female sex was thought the disorderly one par excellence in early modern Europe. . . . Her womb was like a hungry animal; when not amply fed by sexual intercourse or reproduction, it was likely to wander about her body, overpowering her speech and senses. . . . The lower ruled the higher within the woman, then, and if she were given her way, she would want to rule over those above her outside."[15] As described by Davis, the "woman on top" is sometimes conceptualized as a virago, who possesses an uncontrollable temperament that leads her to berate and nag men, and sometimes as sexually insatiable and promiscuous, though the concept of the "wandering womb" bridged the two.

Velez managed to be figured both as a violent shrew and as a slut, becoming simultaneously an object of male dread and male desire, a woman of fearful and unpredictable disposition and of insatiable sexual appetites. As one movie magazine profile explained, "Lupe's antics have been the despair and joy of Hollywood for a long time. Those who seek to win her affections in private life find the courtship a hazardous business, for it is impossible to tell when Lupe, the doe-like maiden, may become Lupe, the angry miniature cyclone."[16] Kenneth Anger offers a vivid description of the hazards of loving Lupe through this depiction of her relations with Johnny Weissmuller: "The love-hate madness of their intense passion often left Lupe marks on Weissmuller's godlike torso, strawberry hickeys on that Thor throat, annular bites on his perfect pecks, eloquent scratches on his ivory back."[17] Lupe, we are told, made love like an animal, was given to frequent jealous rages, and just as often felt an uncontrollable urge to seduce other men. She comes close to the image of the "wandering womb" when she discusses her flirtatious impulses: "Whenever I see a man, there is something in here which must make me winkle my eyes at him. I cannot help myself anymore than you can help yourself from breathing. Sometimes I say I will never flirt again. I sit around. I grow sick. When I cannot flirt with some mens, I get a fever."[18]

Unlike other contemporary female clowns, such as Winnie Lightner or Charlotte Greenwood, Velez did not position herself as a spectacle of "failed femininity," nor did she construct her image as grotesque, graceless, and gawky.[19] Rather, she flaunted her sexual attractiveness as central to her comic persona. She was rendered funny because of an excess of sexual energy, not because of a lack of physical attractiveness. Unlike other sexually charged comic performers, such as Mae West, who foregrounded the process of "feminine masquerade" as a central aspect of their comedy, Velez sought little ironic distance.[20] Velez could never be described as a female "drag queen," as West has been. Instead, her on-screen persona was a "natural" extension of her "spontaneous" and uninhibited off-screen personality.

Recent feminist criticism has done a wonderful service in rescuing female comic stars and texts from obscurity and acknowledging that comedy may be a powerful vehicle for expressing feminine opposition to gender stereotypes, for challenging the conventional construction of women's desires and sexuality, and for promoting a more active and empowered vision of femininity that cannot easily be contained within the domestic sphere. Rowe, for example, speaks of comic representations of "unruly women" as allowing women to become "subjects of a laughter that expresses anger, resistance, solidarity and joy."[21] Such work has made comedy as central to the development of contemporary feminist cultural theory as melodrama was for an earlier generation. However, it is possible to overstate the case for female comic resistance, especially when gender and sexual identities are understood in isolation from racial identities, an issue that is only starting to get the critical attention it needs. As Davis notes, the "woman on top" was always an ambivalent figure, reconfirming stereotypes even as it questioned them, allowing for female agency but at the cost of rendering it laughable, allowing women to speak while designating what they said meaningless. The question always becomes who's laughing now and why.

The reintroduction of race into this discussion further complicates any easy ideological reading of the "unruly woman" as a trope of screen comedy. Reassessing her own earlier work, Pamela Robertson stresses the way Mae West's campy and transgressive performances depend upon her ability to claim "authenticity" through her appropriations from black culture, while denying her black co-stars the right to speak up or act up to the same degree.[22] West shines, in Robertson's account, because she has darkened the other women around her. Michael Rogin's book *Blackface, White Noise* poses another challenge to what he sees as a postmodern celebration of the fluid identities in early sound comedy. Rogin rejects the idea that the layering of racial identities in the performances of Eddie Cantor, Fanny Brice, or Hugh Herbert might be read as breaking down racial and cultural stereotypes.[23] Rogin reminds us that not all performers enjoyed this same freedom to play with—or escape from—their fixed identities, suggesting that blacks wearing blackface were reduced to racial stereotypes, even as Jews wearing blackface might claim a space for themselves within the American mainstream. Thus, the ability to flirt with "darkness" was a freedom enjoyed only by those who could maintain a strong claim on whiteness.

Race operates in a somewhat different way in relation to Lupe Velez, the "Mexican Spitfire," who was constantly linked through star discourse to her "south of the border" origins. Velez enjoyed tremendous freedom to transgress the sexual and gender norms of American culture, precisely because her transgressions could be ascribed to particular racist myths of a "primitive," violent, "untamed," and unpredictable Mexican character. Consider, for example, how one movie magazine profile dealt with the issue of her cursing: "As most of her so-called profanity is translated literally from the Spanish, where Dios and other sacred words are tossed lightly about, it doesn't seem to mean much."[24] What might have been read as a refusal to conform to social expectations was instead repositioned as a natural consequence of her racial otherness. In the 1930s, white women didn't curse, but Mexican women, apparently, did, but "it doesn't seem to mean much" because her cursing itself conform to norms within her native culture. Despite, or perhaps even because of, persistent themes and images of inter-racial romance in Velez's screen vehicles, Lupe was constructed—on screen and off —as "non-white."

Velez's status as "non-white" is particularly complex because, as Richard Dyer notes, whiteness often has ambiguous borders: it "creates a category of maybe, sometimes whites, people who may be let into whiteness under particular historical circumstances. The Irish, Mexicans, Jews and people of mixed race provide striking instances: often excluded, sometimes indeed being assimilated into the category of whiteness, and at others treated as a 'buffer' between the white and the black or indigenous."[25] One early profile of Velez positions her alongside Myrna Loy, who is characterized as "the screen's foremost oriental siren," as two "misbehaving ladies."[26] Once she achieved stardom, Loy's yellow-face make-up quickly washed off, but Lupe couldn't scrub the brown-face from her skin. Dolores del Rio, a Mexican actress who was Velez's contemporary, was able to move from exotic roles that were heavily coded in terms of her race, toward acceptance in racially neutral roles as a romantic leading lady, in effect, becoming "white" on screen. Despite the fact that she was often compared to Del Rio early in her career, Velez remained trapped on the other side of the color barrier, and, as a consequence, remained more a comic than a romantic star. To understand the "scandal" surrounding Lupe Velez, then, we need to consider not only how she "transgressed" gender norms but also how she conformed to racial stereotypes, not only how she refused to "act like a lady" but also how, as a "nonwhite woman," she was excluded from being considered a "lady."

"It Would Be So Dull If We Were All Garbos": *The Politics of Glamour*

In his classic essay "The Face of Garbo," Roland Barthes examines the fascination and allure of Hollywood glamour photography. Garbo's face, he suggests, becomes the "absolute mask," less a real human face than "an archetype of the human face," which is "offered to one's gaze as a sort of Platonic Idea of the human creature."[27] Barthes emphasizes the ways in which the conventions of the glamour photograph produce an unattainable beauty, making Garbo's physical features visible but, at the same time, positioning her on a level the audience could never reach. The glamour photograph is an abstraction, a perfecting of the human form, at the cost of removing it from the realm of human experience. The glamour photograph involves an erasure of the corporeal body, even as it makes the physical surfaces of the body glowingly visible. The female body is, as the language of the period suggested, "glorified," becoming soft, shining flesh, which seemingly lacks an interior, which is streamlined and polished to perfection.

A dramatically different image of many of these same stars emerged in the so-called Tijuana Bibles, cheaply reproduced sex comics, often depicting the exploits of Hollywood actors and actresses, which circulated in great numbers in the 1930s and 1940s. Historian Robert Gluckson estimates that in 1939 alone, more than three hundred different titles were produced and marketed as an underground literature existing in the shadows of the Hollywood entertainment system.[28] According to R.C. Harvey, who has pulled together and republished several collections of these truly tasteless works, "the little booklets were drawn in attics, printed in garages on cantankerous machinery, and distributed surreptitiously from the back pockets of shady vendors in alleyways and in dimly lit rooms. Since the traffic was wholly underground, no one was likely to keep records."[29] Typically only eight pages long, the Tijuana Bibles offered little more than raw sex, sometimes between two screen stars (such as William Powell and Myrna Loy, or Errol Flynn and Maureen O'Hara), more often between a beautiful leading lady and some nameless schlub who could satisfy her desires far more fully than the Hollywood glamour boys. For example, in *Hot Panties*, Ginger Rogers expresses her boredom with "these so called men here in Hollywood" and takes to the road, where she finds satisfaction through making love with a bellhop who stumbles upon her naked gropings with a dildo.[30] In *Bigger Yet*, after expressing a desire to discover the relationship between the size of a man's mouth and that of his organ, Claudette Colbert has a go at the boy who delivers her groceries (who is drawn remarkably like comic actor Joe E. Brown).[31] Nothing is sacred in this realm, so we get to see Popeye and Wimpy take turns on Olive Oyl, Snow White have a tumble with Dopey, and Batman and Robin give each other head while complaining that they really need to have a Batgirl. Tijuana Bibles strip Hollywood's screen goddesses not only of their clothes but also of the aura of glamour, making us forcefully aware of the bodies underneath. Hollywood becomes a "pornocopia" where erotic desire is everything and must be satisfied at all costs. Sex is sloppy business in this realm, with saliva and sperm drawn dripping, spurting, and flying from every slurping orifice, yet there is nothing grotesque about the depiction of the female bodies—no sagging breasts, no bulging thighs—which are still depicted as erotically desirable. What has changed is not the conception of beauty but the relationship of that physical attractiveness to the spectator. What was once unreachably high has been brought low and within reach; what was once disembodied has been restored as all body; what was rendered invisible within the conventions of the Hollywood glamour photograph has been visualized in anatomically correct detail in the Tijuana comics.

As their name suggests, the Tijuana Bibles occupy a space "south of the border" or "below the belt" from Hollywood, reflecting the ways that, as Peter Stallybrass and Allon White have suggested, cultural categories, bodily categories, and geographic categories get mapped onto each other.[32] For many in southern California, Tijuana was closely associated with cheap and unpoliced prostitution, offering what Anglos could not obtain so readily closer to home. The concept of the Tijuana Bible frames

Mexico as the carnivalesque and grotesque alternative to Hollywood, with Tijuana understood here less as physical space than as a cultural mode or, better yet, a state of erotic frenzy.

The contrast between the Hollywood glamour photograph and the Tijuana Bible, between Garbo's face and Ginger's "lips," would seem to closely parallel the distinction Mikhail Bakhtin has made between classical and grotesque conceptions of the body. The glamour photograph performs many of the same formal operations that rendered the classical body "isolated, alone, fenced off from all other bodies." In Bakhtin's words, "All signs of its unfinished character, of its growth and proliferation were eliminated; its protuberances and offshoots were removed, its convexities (signs of new sprouts and buds) smoothed out, its apertures closed. The ever unfinished nature of the body was hidden, kept secret; conception, pregnancy, childbirth, death throes, were almost never shown."[33] The classical Garbo wants to be alone. The grotesque Ginger wants company. The images of Ginger Rogers's body in *Hot Panties* could not be more different from this "platonic ideal": she is falling out of her clothes from the first panel, her nipples are visible through the fabric, her genitals emerge as a set of dense spiraling lines and sharp gashes, hot clouds of smoke radiate from her crotch, and she becomes the subject of a succession of insertions. She is all protuberances and openings. Her star image, as we might all agree, is "degraded" by the fantasies the Tijuana Bibles project onto it, all the more so because of Rogers's conservative reputation. As Bakhtin writes, "The essential principle of grotesque realism is degradation, that is, the lowering of all that is high, spiritual, ideal, abstract; it is a transfer to the material level, to the sphere of Earth and body in their indissoluble unity." Degradation means a stress on those operations and properties that all bodies have in common over those that are unique. Degradation, Bakhtin argues, means "coming down to Earth," and in doing so, it often involves making public what was once private, making social what was once personal, and breaking down the boundaries between the body and the rest of the world. Often, the Tijuana Bibles are very explicit about offering us images of the stars not available in their films. Powell protests to Loy, "I'm sick of being married to you in the movies without getting anything."[34] Errol Flynn complains that he plays Robin Hood but "all I get to shoot is arrows."[35] Our desires are projected onto the stars, who want to satisfy urges that are evoked but not satiated by the screen representations of glamour and romance. The classical Hollywood cinema seemed to be all about sex, and yet the Production Code made it impossible for sex to be represented directly, and so it developed a language of suggestion and equivocation, a language that teases more than it "puts out," a language that substitutes dancing for lovemaking and cigarette smoke for bodily fluids.

The culture of scandal and gossip that has always surrounded the Hollywood system performs a similar function, allowing us a peak at what gets hidden behind the glamour. This "degradation" function explains why gossip is so often preoccupied with the themes of "conception, pregnancy, childbirth, death throes," which are "hidden, kept secret" within representations of the classical body. Such themes represented the reassertion of the "material body" into discussions of ethereal stars, and thus also represented a process that rendered the unattainable ideal more accessible to the audience. This idea that the Tijuana Bibles and the scandal sheets represent the grotesque of the classical cinema is certainly consistent with Bakhtin's assertions that, in Mary Russo's words, "the grotesque goes underground in the course of the nineteenth century, becoming increasingly hidden and dispersed—a private and 'nocturnal' category."[36] These grotesque conceptions of the body shadow the Hollywood glamour system, occupying a space of ill-repute, sold in the back allies, printed in ink that comes off on your hands, yet essential to the system's creation and dispersal of erotic desire. This myth of the scandalous and uninhibited body may have been a necessary fiction, even for those who worked within the studio system, as the screenwriter and director Garson Kanin suggests in his memoir, *Hollywood*. Kanin describes a brothel called "Mae's" that was frequented by film industry employees and film actors, where the prostitutes were fashioned to resemble Myrna Loy, Carole Lombard, Ginger Rogers, Claudette Colbert, and other leading ladies.[37] The "stars" at Mae's were kept apprised of the latest "gossip, rumors, innuendos" so that they could more fully embody their customers' fantasies. Kanin suggests that actors went there to release tensions that built up during the production day, and thus, as in the Tijuana Bibles, satisfy the fantasies hinted at but never delivered by their films.

Glamour, which involves the erasure of the body and the isolation of the star from the public, has no place in the grotesque, except to be degraded. Beauty may be another question. Bakhtin's descriptions of the grotesque body often conjure up images of bodies that are grossly overweight or sagging from age, but Mary Russo's *The Female Grotesque* also makes a case for considering bodies that push against other norms of feminine appearance and conduct as falling into the cultural category of the

grotesque, even if they are otherwise physically attractive. Her example is
Amelia Earhart, who was figured as "tall, slim, and aerodynamic like the
planes beside which she modeled" yet also often depicted as "boyish" and
asexual, as outside the norms of traditional femininity, and therefore, in
a larger sense, grotesque.[38] The female figures in the Tijuana Bibles are
grotesque in a similar sense—not in their appearance (at least as we traditionally understand the term), but in the ways that the openings and
protuberances of their bodies become the central focus of our attention
and interest, in that their desires and appetites are openly displayed, in
that they refuse to keep their proper distance. In short, Ginger in *Hot
Panties* is grotesque because she is "in heat" and "out of control."

Lupe Velez's "out of control" persona follows a similar pattern. Her
excessive female sexuality cannot be easily rendered laughable because
she cannot be discounted as grotesquely unattractive, yet it pushes well
beyond the classical conceptions of the body and sexuality that dominate
the Hollywood glamour system. Far from unattainable, Velez, according
to one 1932 *Vanity Fair* profile, enjoyed "distributing her wiles among
the male members of the cast—a while here and a while there."[39] Far
from regulated and disciplined, the same writer suggests that Velez "acts
in general as if she had just downed six seidels of tequila." Velez emphatically refused to conform to the norms of decorum associated with
the Hollywood system. She protested to one interviewer who reported
that an unnamed actress had said she was "no lady": "What the hell?
How can they tell? To act like everyone else, is that what they call a lady?
Then, I am not a lady."[40] In another interview, she contrasted herself with
Garbo: "I couldn't be like Garbo. But it would be so dull if we were all
Garbos! People like her because she's quiet and so beautiful. They like me
because I have pep!"[41] She told one fan magazine that her mother was
constantly begging her for money, jewels, and other material goods: "She
carried me for nine months and now she wants rent."[42] And she emphatically refused to accept any attempts by men to regulate her behavior: "A
husband might try to stop me. If he did, I would kill him. I am un-
afraid."[43]

Despite the romantic stories of her girlhood fascination with pictures
of Hollywood stars, Velez's publicity pictures were often framed as parodies of the codes and conventions of the glamour photograph. One photograph, picturing her sprawled on a diving board, sticking her tongue
out at the camera, bears the caption: "You've seen this yourself—the
unimaginative stars who pose on diving-boards as if they intended to do

something aquatic—when they haven't even removed high-healed slippers! Lupe's divorce [from Weissmuller] is now final and she was making this face at Mr. [Clayton] Moore. It may be her way of looking 'lovesick.'"[44] Velez seemed to take enormous pleasure in finding new ways to shock or bemuse glamour photographers and the readers of the glossy fan magazines. She smoked a pipe. She was photographed with her pet chihuahua biting her on the nose. She adopted a graceless and contorted posture trying to lift her leg to her breasts. A series of portraits depict her as sulking, glaring, snarling, and making aggressive gestures at the camera. *Screen Guide* framed one particularly grotesque set of photographs in terms of Velez's open antagonism to other screen stars: "GLAMOUR GIRLS TAKE ANOTHER BEATING! Annoyed glamour girls are almost constantly in a fret over the fact that Lupe Velez pokes fun at them in hilarious poses—which *Screen Guide* photographs and prints. They retaliate by looking down their noses, saying they don't think she is so funny. But the funny part is that the poses are basically true."[45] Posing for such pictures was her way of thumbing her nose at the Hollywood establishment. Sometimes the photographs even give us a whiff of her own earthy sense of humor, as when, following her divorce from Weissmuller, she was photographed on a lawn chair, her legs spread wide and the funny pages open between them to *Jungle Jim* (a strip widely perceived as a "rip off" of Edgar Rice Burroughs's character). The magazine's caption asks, "Where can she find another Tarzan? It is sad, si, si?"[46]

"Glamour girls" took a beating through her performances, as well. Velez was notorious for standing up at Hollywood parties and launching into vicious parodies of other screen actresses, especially those she regarded as rivals, such as Delores del Rio, or those she felt had "stolen" one of "her men." When she suspected Gary Cooper of having an affair with Marlene Dietrich during the filming of *Morocco*, she staged an outrageously off-color impersonation of Dietrich before half of the movietown big shots. When, at various points, Velez toured in vaudeville or appeared in stage revues, these parodies of Hollywood stars formed her act, translating antics that had been scandalous off-stage into performances that drew praise and laughter from audiences. One movie magazine spread features a series of mocking photographs where Velez suggests her ability to mimic Gloria Swanson, Dolores del Rio, Fanny Brice, and her other contemporaries.[47] Some of her caricatures are captured on film in the Wheeler and Woolsey vehicle *High Flyers* (1937), where she impersonates Del Rio, Simone Simon, and Shirley Temple in quick succession. As Del Rio, she arches her neck, wrapping a shawl over her head, and presses her teeth against her lips as she sings. As Simon, she adopts a more demure demeanor, lisping and simpering incomprehensibly. As Temple, she is perkier and more outgoing, though there remains something profoundly silly about her singing "On the Good Ship Lollypop" through a thick Mexican accent. Her frontal assault on her screen rivals seems contagious, since later in the same film Robert Woolsey dresses in Latin American attire and sings "I am a Gaucho," a number that parodies the team's long-time competition with the Marx Brothers. Lupe sings, "We girls don't know Harpo or Chico. We all love Gaucho." Bert Wheeler first blackens his upper lip to mimic Charles Chaplin and later blackens his whole face and struts like Eddie Cantor. These spoofs provide the comic highpoints of an otherwise tepid comedy, the last to team Wheeler and Woolsey, and completed shortly before Wheeler's death.

If the classical conception of the body that dominates glamour photography stresses the screen goddess's unattainable beauty, Velez's body was consistently depicted as all too easily attainable—for a price. Apart from the rumors that she once worked as a prostitute and a stripper, she is often depicted as flashing guests at her Hollywood parties, flinging her dress high above her head as she dances, to reveal that she wore no underwear.

Her film roles often capitalize on these same traits, casting her as a prostitute or fallen woman (*Lady of the Pavements*, *Where East Is East*, *Resurrection*, *Kongo*) or a stripper (*Half-Naked Truth*, *Hot Pepper*, *The Morals of Marcus*), as a woman who loves two men at once (*The Storm*, *The Broken Wing*) or as the destroyer of good men's innocence (*Palooka*). A notable exception is the *Mexican Spitfire* series, for which Velez is best remembered, and in which she played a good, faithful wife, despite farcical situations and innuendos by her rival, Elizabeth, that suggest she may be breaking her marriage vows. Velez's screen vehicles seem to obsessively restage her real-world scandals, most overtly in *Hollywood Party*, which casts her as the Jungle Girl, opens with a spoof of a Tarzan movie, describes her break-up with Schnarzan star Jimmy Durante, and documents her frustrated attempts to crash a big Hollywood party, all evoking public knowledge of her on-again, off-again relationship with Weissmuller. Echoing many of her off-screen lovers, Durante protests, "You don't belong at these parties. You get too rough. You get too involved."

Courting Lupe was, according to *New Movie*, like "flirting with dynamite."[48] Gary Cooper gave her two eagles, which she jokingly called her "love birds," suggesting that they both understood the predatory nature of her attractions. Velez took great pleasure in shocking the bashful Cooper with her exhibitionist impulses, and indeed, in outraging many who worried that a return of the sex scandals of the 1920s might taint the film industry at a time when Hollywood was courting the Catholic Legion of Decency. Perhaps this discomfort explains why Velez, along with fellow Mexican-Americans Dolores del Rio and Ramon Novarro, were accused of being "communists" by Sacramento District Attorney Neil McAllister in 1934, representing one of the first volleys in the decades' long attempt to link Hollywood with "un-American activities." Defending her, Weissmuller protested, "Why Lupe doesn't even know what communism means."[49] Lupe was not red; she was just red-hot.

"Paprika on Chile Con Carne": The Girl from Mexico

That McAllister's charges against Lupe lumped her together with Del Rio and Novarro (stars of fundamentally different status, not to mention ideological commitments) is deeply suggestive of the racial politics that was never far beneath the surface in Hollywood in the 1930s. By definition, the three studio stars were "un-American." They were Mexicans, and none of them could, in the end, escape the taint of being born "south of the border."

The Mexican cultural critic Carlos Monsiváis describes Dolores del Rio in language remarkably similar to Barthes's paean to Garbo: "A dazzling face. Timeless—not because it is immune to the devastation of age but, rather, for the radiant effect it still has on those who contemplate it. A figure boldly kept, accomplished in the slow sinuosity of its movements, in the care of its magnificent skin, in the way it incorporates elegance into facial movement, a stillness that denies languor, and in the Indian cheekbones that maintain both tension and imperial repose. The gift—we call it being photogenic—of knowingly administering one's looks for the camera, and keeping a wardrobe in which fashion pays homage to perfect features. A woman, the possessor of a face, who in the preservation of her beauty finds the meaning of her artistic life."[50] Only one detail in this description—Monsiváis's reference to her "Indian cheekbones"—serves to separate del Rio from Garbo, but that one detail makes visible how much Barthes's essay on Garbo is really a celebration of her whiteness.

Barthes speaks of Garbo's face as possessing the "snowy thickness of a mask"; he suggests she looks as if her features had been "set in plaster." He writes, "Amid all this snow at once fragile and compact, the eyes alone, black like strange soft flesh, but not in the least expressive, are two faintly tremulous wounds. In spite of its extreme beauty, this face, not drawn but sculpted in something smooth and friable, that is, at once perfect and ephemeral, comes to resemble the flour-white complexion of Charlie Chaplin, the dark vegetation of his eyes." She is described as "descended from a heaven where all things are formed and perfected in the clearest light." Far from a celebration of Garbo as a "universal" beauty who transcends culture, Barthes's essay positions her as the embodiment of all that is desirable and precious about white women—their purity, their cleanliness, their illumination, their "perfect" features.[51]

Richard Dyer's *White* provides a detailed account of the ways in which the technical parameters and lighting conventions surrounding glamour photography—and Hollywood cinematography more generally—took shape around the presumption of a white subject, with the goal of accurately reproducing the "normal" range of white skin tones as the primary objective. Filming and photographing "non-white" skin was taken as a special problem, requiring adjustments and extra efforts; and, of course, in a culture like Hollywood, where few "non-whites" achieved any degree of stardom, there was rarely a need to take that "special care" to make sure that non-white skin was reproduced with that same aura of glamour.[52] Photographed according to those conventions, glamour became something that white people—especially white women—possessed and darker people lacked. Dyer writes, "White women thus carry—or, in many narratives, betray—the hopes, achievements, and character of the race. They guarantee its reproduction, even while not succeeding to its highest heights. Yet their very whiteness, their refinement, makes of sexuality a disturbance of their racial purity."[53] If whiteness is associated with purity and cleanliness, and sex in our culture is often described as "dirty," then this celebration of the white woman must surround her with an aura of glamour that protects her from sexual contamination. By this same logic, it becomes clear why an entertainment system that fed upon the creation of an erotic allure needed the presence of women who are "sometimes" or ambiguously white, who occupy the racial borderlands between whiteness and blackness. If they were black women, they would be closed off to white men's desires, at least within the public discourse of screen entertainment. If they were white women, they might become too clean to become the focus for nasty little fantasies and sleazy gossip. As a Mexican, Lupe Velez was neither white nor black, neither prohibited nor sanctified, and that made her a potent signifier for the grotesque conception of female sexuality that the classical narrative sought both to evoke and to contain.

Monsiváis notes the ways that the "authenticity" of Del Rio often lent credibility and concreteness to Hollywood's orientalist fantasies: "As played by Del Rio, the unusual (read 'foreign') beauty is possessed by an uncontrollable psyche, the emotions of a native frightened by the gods of the volcano, or a Hispanic whose sophistication stops at her clothes."[54] On screen, Velez proved to be equally versatile in her ability to stage exotic (and erotic) otherness, playing a Greek peasant girl in *Stand and Deliver*, a Parisian courtesan in *Lady of the Pavements* (1929), a half-cast Indochinese girl in *Where East Is East* (1929), the daughter of Morgan the pirate in *Hell Harbor* (1930), a French-Canadian in *The Storm* (1930), a Russian peasant in *Resurrection* (1931), an Indian maiden in *The Squaw Man* (1931), and a mulatto in *Kongo* (1932). On screen, she could play anything except Anglo-Saxon.

Off screen, she remained, inescapably, unmistakably, Mexican, as suggested by the range of nicknames applied to her in her film career: "Mexican Wildcat," "Mexican Spitfire," "Mexican T.N.T." Such phrases suggest her "wildness," often through explicit analogy to animals. Much of the comedy in *Mexican Spitfire's Blessed Event* (1943) turns on her husband's mistaken (and improbable) belief that she has born him a child, when in fact it is her pet jaguar who has given birth. Either way, the gags suggest, the offspring will be a wildcat. Most often, such phrases evoke images of exotic "spices" that stand out against the blandness of American cuisine: "Hot Tamale," "Human Pepper Pot," "a Little Mexican Dish of Hot Chili," one of the "Tabasco Twins of the Silver Screen," "Paprika on Chile Con Carne." In short, Lupe was a spicy dish, good enough to eat, but she would burn the American tongue.

Her star biographies pile on the ethnic signifiers, making her a literal embodiment of twentieth-century Mexican culture: "Lupe is a native of San Luis Obispo, a historic Mexican pueblo, the daughter of an opera singer and a colonel in the Mexican army. This she can authenticate with a series of documents as long as your arm."[55] An article about her new mansion, titled "Mexican Fire," notes that she, "after the fashion of her own country," had an outside hearth built on her patio, so that she could "make herself feel that her own temperature is normal."[56] Another fanzine tells us that "Little Mexican Lupe is black-haired, black-eyed, slender, small and untamed. Lupe comes from Mexico—from the seething, turbulent Mexico of incessant warfare."[57]

Often, the fanzine writers would describe various attempts, largely unsuccessful, to assimilate Velez into our American ways: "Lupe was just a crude, little soubrette who knew nothing of subtle make-up until Max Factor instructed her. Lupe Velez has changed her manner of dress and make-up, but her Americanization ended there."[58] Her co-stars were even more blunt, often describing her as "dirty" or "unwashed." Velez might be dressed in better clothes, pampered with Hollywood luxury, and powdered by Max Factor, but she could never become fully white, could never become a "lady." Read within this racist and nationalistic discourse, her transgressive behavior and flamboyant mannerisms could be understood as "proof" of the distance separating white and nonwhite women, as evidence of a violent and primitive temperament that could never be assimilated into American culture.

Velez is linked to the natural wonders that captured the American imagination, with publicity photographers posing her with monkeys, tropical birds, and wildcats, suggesting that she had only recently emerged from the jungles. *Photoplay*'s Ruth Biery situated her spontaneous Mexican temperament against the calculations of other Hollywood stars, describing her as "the most natural, the most primitive, the most unaffected offspring of an affected generation,"[59] phrases that reflect a larger cultural movement—embodied in modernism's interest in pre-Columbian art—that sought in the Mexican soul qualities which supposedly had been corrupted in modern American culture. Lupe was not a product of modernity but a force of nature, whose temper tantrums were "an act as natural as the one nature puts on when it has two clouds collide to produce lightening and thunder . . . an act as natural, to Lupe, as nature's rains or droughts or river currents."[60] Her biographer, Floyd Conner, begins his book by noting that she was born the same day that a hurricane devastated her town: "The violent weather was an appropriate introduction to the world for the woman who would become known as the 'Mexican hurricane.'"[61]

This theme of her "untamed" nature most fully surfaced in discussions of her entanglements with Johnny Weissmuller, a match made in some publicity agent's heaven. As Walt Morton notes, the film versions of

Tarzan shift from the "naked nobleman" of the books to emphasize his status as a barely human savage—a man of actions, not of words. Weiss-muller's films, in particular, were structured around the spectacle of male bodily display: "His only apparel is a thong waistband and buckskin loin-cloth, considerably more revealing than the costumes worn by previous Tarzans, many of whom wore an over-the-shoulder leopard-skin tunic. . . . Attention centered on Tarzan's appearance (sleekly muscled, 'natural') but not what he says ('Hungawa!')."[62] Velez jokingly suggested that she spoke English so poorly because "I was married to a guy who can only say, 'Me Tarzan, You Jane.'"[63]

As this joke suggests, Velez was famous for her own mangled syntax, which was often mimicked by fan magazine prose, to exaggerate and poke fun at her Hispanic accent: "Dees Fiery-y-y Tempestous-s-s Lupee-e-e, she geeve *Six Lessons from Madame La Zonga*. But eef she geeve only wone leetle lesson (whether eets lofe or la conga) you'd had to ad-meet you 'learn' well. For Lupee-e-e is wone gran-n teacher."[64] Much of the comedy in her films involves plays on her accent or malapropisms that suggest an inability to master English. Promising to keep a secret in *High Flyers*, she explains, "I will say nothing to somebody." When Uncle Matt describes himself as footloose in *Mexican Spitfire*, she ex-claims, "I have a loose foot too." Later, in a more awkward situation, she explains, "I am just a gallstone around your neck." In *Mexican Spitfire Out West* (1940), she advises Uncle Matt to "keep a stiff upper mouth." Other jokes stem from her cursing in Spanish. After a long tirade in Spanish, a friend asks Carmelita, "What does this mean in Eng-lish?" She shrugs and explains, "Oh, you don't say that in English." In *Hollywood Party*, her cursing gets translated into English as "dirty such and such, so and so, this and that." But, for most of what she wants to say, Velez doesn't need words. Her broad gestures and sharp tone con-vey her anger and frustration even to those who can't understand Span-ish, and her swinging hips and seductive gestures are charged with "an-imal spirits" that transcend national borders.

Similarly, Weissmuller's physicality made him an appropriate match for Velez. The opening sequence of *Hollywood Party* parodies this rela-tionship. In a mock preview for *Schnarzan the Conqueror*, "the mighty monarch of the mudlands," Schnarzan (Durante), his chest padded with fake muscles and covered with tufts of fake hair, wrestles a stuffed lion, while Velez, dressed in a skirt that looks like it was made of the black-and-white fur of lion-tail macaques, squeals with excitement. Later, as they are hanging together from a tree branch, Schnarzan proclaims, "Can't you see, jungle woman, that I'm human even if I have a touch of the King Kong." When she scoffs at his proclamations ("Human, ha! Don't make me laugh"), he asserts, "Underneath this lion skin beats a heart seeped in sentiment." "Bah," she sputters, "I'll bet you say that to all the animal women." The razzed hero pushes down the tree in an exaggerated display of his virility. Elsewhere in the film, Velez plays the woman jilted by Durante, "that pelican face," who would stop at nothing to wreck his party. In one especially heated scene, she shouts in Spanish into a telephone that keeps rattling even after Durante hangs it up. She stomps on his picture until his image has torn clothing and a black eye.

Film fans no doubt speculated that this portrayal contained more than a little truth about her relationship to Weissmuller, which was rumored to have been equally combative. She was said to have given him boxing gloves as a wedding gift.[65] Lupe entertained fan magazine readers with her vivid blow-by-blow accounts of their arguments and her tactics for winning him back again: "If I scream at him and tell him that I am right, he will never give in. The only way I can win an argument with Johnny is to act like I am very hurt and pretend to cry. Then I make him ashamed and he is so sorry he says I am right."[66] If Velez embodied a wild and untamed feminine sexuality, Weissmuller personified a wild and untamed masculine sexuality, making them an explosive combination. As one profile suggests, "Lupe Velez's primitive nature finds its answer in Johnny Weissmuller, an athlete whose nerves are insulated by hawserlike muscles, kept in condition by much swimming."[67] The movie magazines had often speculated how any man could withstand Lupe's lovemaking, but the muscular Weissmuller was portrayed as the one man for the job. A thin line separates romance from hand-to-hand combat in the world of Lupe Velez.

The American romanticization of a primitive Mexican sensibility, though couched as a criticism of urban knowingness and modern alienation, was nevertheless a thinly veiled celebration of American cultural superiority, a call for the economic exploitation of our sister country. As James Oles writes, "Mexico is personified as an innocent woman who lives in a land of Spanish traditions and religious ceremonies. This gendering of Mexico in feminine terms found visual resonance in widely varied forms, ranging from the photographs of elegant señoritas commonly depicted in the pages of *National Geographic*, to sensual travel posters, postcards and Hollywood films. As female, Mexico could be easily dominated by the artistic or economic forces of the North."[68] If Mexico was depicted as feminine in the American imagination, popular memories of the still-recent Mexican Revolution left many perceiving it as an "unruly woman" of fierce temperament and violent manners, one who would as soon scratch your eyes as kiss your lips. Americans had been both fascinated and frightened to witness a full-fledged revolution occurring just beyond the Rio Grande, and this experience led to much more ambivalent feelings toward Mexico in the 1920s and 1930s. Star biographies link Lupe Velez directly with the violence and bloodshed of the revolution. Her father, we are told, was Colonel Jacob Villalobos, known as "El Gallo" (the Rooster), an important officer in Porfirio Díaz's army during the struggle to put down Pancho Villa. She would recall riding with her father on military inspections and witnessing the massacre of partisans.[69] As Monsiváis notes, Dolores del Rio was also touched by the revolution; she came from a rich banking family that was part of the "Mexican aristocracy," and as a small girl she had been taken to sit on the lap of the President of the Republic.[70] One of her uncles was murdered by the revolutionaries, and Del Rio and her family fled from Pancho Villa, who had taken possession of their bank and family home. The class differences between Del Rio and Velez contributed to the resentment and rivalry that Lupe felt toward the other Mexican-born actress, since the lower-class Velez felt she was always denied the recognition and respect that had come easily for Del Rio.

Comic portrayals of Lupe's temper would seem to be part of this larger discourse about Latin violence, a translation of the political upheaval into the figure of the unruly woman. Jean Franco traces a long tradition of disorderly women in Mexican literature and culture, starting with the female mystics in seventeenth-century New Spain, who smeared their bodies with menstrual blood, spoke in tongues, and writhed in religious ecstasy, finding a voice through their hysteria denied them elsewhere in the culture. Far from demanding their silence, the Church fathers forced them to confess and dutifully recorded their often erotically charged visions. This image of a grotesque female spirituality existed alongside myths of extraordinary female purity, such as the Virgin of Guadalupe (after whom Lupe Velez was named), whom Franco characterizes as one of the central symbols of Mexican nationalism: "a Virgin who is not represented as a mother but rather as the woman of the Apocalypse, crushing the serpent and in possession of the heavens from which she protects her chosen people."[71]

These two contrasting constructions of Mexican femininity—the wild woman and the virgin—structure *The Gaucho* (1927), one of Velez's earliest films. In the film's opening moments, a peasant woman (Geraine Greear, better known as Joan Barclay) has a vision of the Virgin Mary (Mary Pickford) on the wall beside a spring, and the site becomes a shrine where the poor of the countryside come to be blessed. When we encounter Greear's character later in the film, she has assumed many of the aspects of the saintly virgin; surrounded by radiating light, she places her hands on the sick and the desperate and offers them hope. Velez, on the other hand, is cast as the wild woman, who seems, at first, to be the perfect mate for the equally unruly El Gaucho (Douglas Fairbanks), the local bandit who has his own popular following among "the people."

When we first see Velez, she is mooning over a wanted poster for El Gaucho, and when he enters her village, she throws herself at him, swooning in his arms. However, when another woman pursues a prior claim on his affections, she seethes with jealous rage, suggesting that she is something more than a star-struck maiden. She throws crockery at her rival and then pushes back the crowd, preparing to dance before her man. He tosses his whip, encircling her, and then ties the two of them together as they dance the tango—their bodies joined at the hips, but their hands at their sides. He tries to kiss her but she shoves him away, beating him on his chest. In another scene, which opens with Velez gnawing on a chicken leg, El Gaucho insists that she pack up and leave with him at once, and she refuses, waving her knife and insisting on finishing her meal. An impatient Gaucho ties a team of horses to the house where she sits and pulls it behind him, as they both laugh. At first, they seem evenly matched, with the acrobatic Fairbanks holding his own against the histrionic Velez, and their scenes together are charged with a playful yet earthy energy. He tells her at one point, "I love you as an Eagle loves the wings upon which it soars." She bites him on the hand when he tries to make love to her and he bites her back, giving as well as he takes.

However, when Fairbanks encounters the Virgin of the Spring, the once profane and openly atheistic bandit is dazzled by her beauty, purity, and spirituality and undergoes a religious conversion. Richard Dyer notes that whiteness is often associated with translucent light: "Idealized white women are bathed in and permeated by light. It streams through them and falls on to them from above. In short, they glow. They glow rather than shine. The light within or from above appears to suffuse the body. Shine, on the other hand, is light bouncing back on the surface of the skin.

It is the mirror effect of sweat, itself connoting physicality, the emissions of the body and unladylike labor, in the sense of both work and parturition. . . . Dark skin too, when it does not absorb the light, may bounce it back."[72] The casting of the film reflects the same ideology: Pickford and Greear, the figures of saintliness in the film, are both white. They are both portrayed in relation to illumination. Pickford always appears surrounded by glowing white light, a heavenly messenger. Early on, Fairbanks notes that Greear's eyes have "caught the moonbeams," and later he tells her, "You're like a beautiful sunset—something I can't embrace," a creature of whiteness and light, against whom the darkness of Velez's character will be contrasted. Greear, Fairbanks proclaims, is "not of this earth." Though they both come from common origins, the saintly Greear has become a lady, while the film pokes fun at Velez's aspirations to rise above her class. Despite being dressed in lace and finery, Lupe chomps on an apple, eats with her elbows on the table, and takes great relish when El Gaucho sentences a man who beat his wife to harsh punishment. Greear, on the other hand, is consistently portrayed with grace and dignity that transcend her dress. The core conflict in the film stems around whether Fairbanks will stay with the dark, wild, and uncivilized woman, who fits him so comfortably, or the saintly white woman whom he has placed upon a pedestal. Though Fairbanks applies dark makeup to give himself a swarthy complexion appropriate to the character of a Mexican bandit, we know that he is white, just beneath the surface, thus predetermining his final rejection of Velez for Greear, his repudiation of the disorderly woman in favor of the saintly one.

"I Laugh; I Get Mad; I Cry": Emotional Excess

Describing the reason that the stardom of both Del Rio and Velez ended at the very moment when the "good neighbor" policy made the Hollywood screen more accommodating to Latin American actresses such as Carmen Miranda, Ana M. Lopez notes that Del Rio was "not ethnic enough" and Velez was "too 'Latin'" to fit within "Hollywood's new, ostensibly friendly, and temperate regime."[73] Yet, one wonders why Velez remained "too 'Latin," while Del Rio could pass for white. It isn't a matter of skin color per se. Velez's complexion is no darker than a good many leading ladies of the period, even if her recalcitrant accent might have given her away. Her exclusion from whiteness, was more a matter of taste and temperament than of skin color. White women displayed a refinement of manners, a regulation of emotions, and a control over their bodies that Velez refused to adopt. John F. Kasson's *Rudeness and Civility*, drawing on the work of Norbert Elias, traces the process by which Americans, in the late nineteenth century, sought to temper the robust and rustic manners of their frontier past and embrace the more restrained etiquette associated with Victorian English and European high culture. Both men and women were brought under "public scrutiny" to see if they could maintain the self-restraint and dignity expected of the middle and upper classes, with the greatest burden born by white middle-class women, who were consistently expected not only to police their own behavior but also to discipline others in their families. Kasson writes, "Embarrassment could act as a powerful instrument of social regulation, guarding privileged social pathways and taking the place to some degree in a modern industrial society of older codes of social deference. . . . Rudeness in this culture constituted a kind of social obscenity, a violation of the codes of civility in such a way as to make public that which should remain private, to single out for special attention that which should remain inconspicuous, or else to cast public actions, conduct and individual actors in an unworthy or degrading fashion."[74]

One of the reasons that slapstick was experienced as so subversive and "vulgar" from the perspective of the middle classes was that it invited us to take pleasure in witnessing the breakdown of this whole cultural system, the destruction of dignity, the loss of bodily control, the acting out of emotions that were expected to be suppressed. Laughter itself, Kasson notes, was often perceived as undignified and socially inappropriate, and, if carried to excess, "might topple the carefully constructed public persona that the individual had erected."[75] Yet, comedy was also a way of reinforcing the values of proper manners and bodily control, rendering those who clung to more primitive ways as comic rustics and those who could not regulate their tempers as laughable spectacles. The "pie in the face" became a signifier of the emotional volatility of contemporary culture, suggesting a world of well-behaved people who would shove pastry up each others snouts if their dignified facade was penetrated by someone else's rude actions. Often, as well, this comedy staged inappropriate and transgressive behavior between those of the lower orders and their social betters, focusing on tramps and cops, immigrants and aristocrats, at a time when, Kasson suggests, manners were perceived as an important marker of upward mobility and social betterment.

Compared to the restraint and decorum associated with white bourgeois ladyhood, Lupe Velez was like a bull in a china shop. She often flaunted her lower-class tastes and origins, hosting parties that featured cock fights and stag films. She conducted a public feud with Gary Cooper's mother, who felt Lupe was too "vulgar" and "tasteless" for her son. She was an enthusiastic fan of wrestling matches and boxing bouts, where she would verbally abuse the combatants and generally make a spectacle of herself. Budd Schulberg reports, "How many times had we seen the tempestuous Lupe in the front row at the Hollywood Legion Stadium, pounding on the blood-stained canvas of the ring and screaming profane Mexican incantations at brown-skinned countrymen who were failing to live up to her high standards of conduct?"[76] Schulberg describes a particularly bloody match, where one boxer's eye was reduced to a pulp, as Velez screamed for him to fight harder, while Schulberg himself passed out from nausea.[77] Schulberg's story casts not only the bloody boxing match, but Velez's intense pleasure in the spectacle, as a violation of his own white and refined sensibilities. The white man faints; the "non-white" woman craves more blood. Not surprisingly, Velez's passion for boxing also found its way into her films, such as *Palooka* (1934), in which she plays a nightclub singer who floats from one boxing champ to the next, luring them into a wild nightlife that destroys their ability to fight. Here, the camera records her intense engagement with the ring action, as she shouts when she is unhappy with her champs, though the Production Code only allows an expurgated version of her actions and language to reach the screen. At one point, when she keeps leaping out of her chair in response to the action, a man protests: "Hey, keep your seat, Lady." She retorts, "I'll do what I want with my seat," and he responds curtly, "Well, then, keep it out of my face."

Lupe, as Durante reminds us in *Hollywood Party*, plays "too rough," gets "too involved," and as a result, she can't be admitted to more refined company. *Hollywood Party* contains the scene that showcases Velez's comic talents perhaps more fully than any other moment in her career. Having finally gotten into Durante's mansion, she demands a drink at the bar, only to be told that Durante has prohibited the bartender to serve her. She explodes, pounding the counter with her fist, and kicking off her shoes in rage, as Laurel and Hardy watch with perplexed expressions. Oliver Hardy picks up her shoe and hands it to her, starting a slow-paced and hysterically funny series of ritual humiliations. She takes the shoe and hits him in the head with it. Lupe takes off Hardy's shoe and dumps a raw egg into it; Hardy dumps another raw egg into the palm of her out-stretched hand, but she responds by pouring it into his pocket and wiping her hand on his coat. Planning to strike back, Hardy takes an egg in each hand, but she punctures them, plop, plop, with the high heal of her shoe. She stuffs an egg down the front of his pants and slaps it with her hand. He writhes with a mixture of discomfort and (it is suggested) pleasure as the yolk oozes down his pants leg. Hardy puts an egg on her chair and she sits down on it, squirming uncomfortably. And then they all break down laughing, their animosity vanishing in their pleasure in playing with each other.

Lupe looks sexy and yes, even glamorous in this sequence, clad in an eloquent gown with a low-cut backline and cutaway patches on each hip that reveal her glistening flesh. She is restrained, embracing Edgar Kennedy's "slow burn" response to Laurel and Hardy's antics, a restraint that comes unexpectedly after a thunderstorm of curses and screams. She maintains a surprising level of dignity, even when she has eggs dripping from her hands, and it is this dignity that makes the indignities they perform on each other howlingly funny. But in the end it is perhaps her reputation for angry outbursts that makes this scene so funny, giving its quietude the uneasy sensation of watching someone kick a jug of nitroglycerin until it blows up in his face. We keep watching wondering when she is going to lose it and unleash on Laurel and Hardy the fierce temper we have already seen her direct against Durante. Even when she is describing what she plans to do to Durante when they meet again, she gives mild-mannered Charles Butterworth a serious thrashing. But with Laurel and Hardy, she finds perfect comic timing by slowing down her reactions and holding in check her more aggressive impulses. Such moments of true comedy are rare in Velez's vehicles, which are often too fast-paced to allow us to experience individual gags or to appreciate the sheer pleasure Velez takes in her own performances.

Velez's "vulgarity" and her exclusion from whiteness constitute a central subtext running through her *Mexican Spitfire* films. Across a series of eight programmers, produced in the final years of her screen career, Lupe plays Carmelita, a spirited Mexican nightclub performer who has retired from the stage and married American ad executive Dennis (Donald Woods). His former fiancée, Elizabeth Price (Linda Hayes), still hangs around in the background, scheming to break up their marriage and reclaim her "rightful" place at his side, and she seizes every opportunity to embarrass Carmelita or spark an argument with her. Promising to take her to buy some "decent clothes" so that she can dress more appropriately for her new role as a corporate wife, Elizabeth takes her bar-hopping instead and then condemns her for her "disgusting" drunkenness. Dennis's Aunt Della (Elisabeth Risdon) shares her disappointment in Dennis's bride, protesting that the "Mexican wildcat," as she often calls Carmelita, has "no right to be his wife" and hoping she will soon return to Mexico, "where she belongs." Della is clearly scandalized by their mixed-race marriage and especially by the displacement of a white woman by a nonwhite one. In gag after gag, Elizabeth's WASP-ish background is contrasted with Velez's Latin origins, though often in ways that suggests WASPs have their own kind of sting. In *Mexican Spitfire*, Della notes that "Elizabeth Price can trace her family back to the Pilgrims. She's real Plymouth Rock Stock." Uncle Matt (Leon Errol), who has taken a liking to Carmelita, wisecracks that Elizabeth is a "Rhode Island Red," changing the discourse about breeding into a reference to livestock. Elizabeth tricks Carmelita into barging into Dennis's office during an important business conference, pretending to be his secretary. Then, to avoid embarrassment (now displaced from concern about a multi-racial romance onto issues of class), Elizabeth offers to pose as Dennis's wife when a client, Lord Epping (also played by Leon Errol), comes to dinner. The white, well-bred Elizabeth will, according to Aunt Della, "lend dignity and culture to the occasion." The comedy hinges on the contrast between Elizabeth's snooty pretensions and Carmelita's down-to-earth innocence, with Carmelita finding one way after another to thwart and confound Elizabeth's schemes and retain her claims on Dennis's affections. Elizabeth almost gets her way at the end of *Mexican Spitfire*, when Dennis and Carmelita both believe that she has divorced him, only to discover that their "phony Mexican divorce" isn't worth the paper it is printed on. Rallying to the fight, Carmelita disrupts the wedding, waving a cape around as an angry Elizabeth charges her, resulting in a pastry-tossing cat fight that leaves all concerned dripping with icing. If the *Mexican Spitfire* series is very much about the cultural norms that exclude Lupe Velez from assimilating into American culture, it sides with her desires for acceptance and her unquestioned love for her husband over Elizabeth and Della's attempts to police racial and class boundaries.

Carmelita and Dennis's claims to belong to the white American aristocracy are rendered absurd by the character of Lord Epping, an absent-minded, often drunk, and always rude and intemperate British nobleman, whose advertising contracts form the fulcrum of each of the films. Dennis wants to sign the Epping account; Lupe wants to help but makes things farcically worse until the films' closing moments, when she and Uncle Matt find some way to restore order to the chaos. Often, the farce requires Uncle Matt to impersonate Lord Epping, allowing him an excuse to insult Elizabeth and get revenge on Della for meddling in Carmelita's marriage. When Aunt Della brags that Elizabeth has had "lots of experience mixing cocktails," Uncle Matt (as Lord Epping) scrutinizes her face and then says, "I can tell." Later, he asks an offended Aunt Della whether she does her own laundry and ironing. When he leaves the room, they both protest, "I was always under the impression that the British were exceptionally polite." However, the actual Lord Epping behaves no better. Burping and grumbling "hang that curry," so drunk he can barely walk, incapable of conducting his own affairs, Lord Epping offers us a debased image of the aristocrat, one more governed by his body than ruling over it, rendering the American's attempts to suck up to him totally absurd. In *Mexican Spitfire Out West*, Epping meets his match in an assertive secretary who is totally unimpressed by his British accent and mannerisms, telling him to "take that phony Boston accent down to the janitor. Maybe he can use it." If accents are what keep Lupe from gaining acceptance into white society, the film suggests, then accents deserve no great respect after all. As Dennis concludes in *Mexican Spitfire*, "There is only one Carmelita. I can get thousands of contracts."

The Final Farce

Lupe Velez seemed to resist attempts by writers and critics to fit her into stock feminine roles. One writer struggled to find the perfect comparison: "Lupe Velez! My mind played over the world's famous women whose charms had made men their victims. Which one did Lupe Velez resemble? Cleopatra? No! Cleo was too cold, too calculating in her captivations. Isadora Duncan? No! Isadora loved to suffer. Lupe loves only to be happy. Marie Antoinette. I hesitated. In some ways. Only Marie was selfish, Lupe is not selfish. Madame de Pompadour, Josephine, Bernhardt? I shook my head at each mental suggestion. Was she really a new type of woman?"[78] This exceptionality, this refusal to fit readily available categories, has made comic female stars such an attractive subject for feminist critics in recent years. The "unruly woman" refuses to remain in her proper place, to play her assigned role, to be domesticated, tamed, contained, mastered by a patriarchal culture. Yet, in other ways, Lupe Velez was anything but exceptional; she was trapped within a succession of racial and ethnic stereotypes. Here, considering race alongside gender complicates any simple celebration of Lupe's transgressiveness: there was always the hurtful suggestion that Mexican women are unfit, "dirty," sexually charged, temperamental, crude, and vulgar. One recalls Chicana feminist Gloria Anzaldua's powerful phrase, "Wild tongues can't be tamed, they can only be cut out."[79] And that's why Lupe remained the subject of scandal: she could never fit comfortably within the discourse of Hollywood glamour, despite her obvious charms and beauty.

The little girl who sold her kisses for glamour photographs always seemed too "non-white" to fit into Hollywood's inner circle. Schulberg quotes a dignified Mexican gentleman he met on a train, "Del Rio, si! Velez, no!" implying that even in Mexico, Velez was perceived as a national embarrassment.[80] The Lupe Velez story always threatens to spill over into such bad taste that it can't be told at all.

It is tempting to celebrate Lupe for pushing back against those racial stereotypes, and yet she never fully escaped their taint—even at the moment of her death. Velez, who had often startled Hollywood with talk of adopting a child, found herself pregnant, and the father, Harold Raymond, a twenty-seven-year-old bit player, refused to marry her. His rejection represented the final indignity for a woman who had once claimed that "she always geets her mans." A "good Catholic girl" despite her sexual transgressions, Velez found the idea of abortion unthinkable, and instead decided to take her own life—or rather, more accurately, to stage her own death. She had her hair and nails done, and had her room, which had been redecorated all in white, filled with flowers and illuminated with dozens of candles. Dressed in blue satin pajamas, and having taken a lethal dose of Seconal, she lay down beneath a large crucifix and folded her hands in prayer upon her breast. Kenneth Anger describes the scene: "Her bedroom was Our Lady of Guadalupe's Chapel on her Day of Days: flowers, candles everywhere—everything aglow."[81] Her friend Louella Parsons reported the death in the *Los Angeles Examiner*, just as Lupe would have hoped: "Lupe was never lovelier as she lay there, as if slumbering. . . . A faint smile, like secret dreams. . . . Looking like a child taking a nappy, like a good little girl." The scene as Velez staged it and Parsons described it represented the epitome of Hollywood glamour, evoking the purity and illumination associated with whiteness.

However, even at the moment of her death, as Anger claims, her grotesque body erupted. When her maid opened the door the next morning, she found not the image of glistening whiteness Velez had imagined, but a foul-smelling mess. Having consumed a huge Mexican meal and a good deal of alcohol, the sleeping pills hit Lupe's stomach badly. As Anger writes, "The bed was empty. The aroma of scented candles, the fragrance of tuberoses almost, but not quite masked a stench recalling that left by Skid-Row derelicts. Juanita traced the vomit trail from the bed, following the spotty track over to the orchid-tiled bathroom. There she found her mistress, Señorita Velez, head jammed down in the toilet bowl, drowned." What had been her last great chance at glamour had turned into a dirty farce. If Barthes treated the glamour photograph of Garbo's face as a kind of death mask, Anger offers an altogether more down-to-earth image of Velez's final moments, one rendered even more ugly by his repeated use of racial epithets. Here, again, Lupe remains "non-white" and locked out of the glistening kingdom of Hollywood. Tragically, Lupe is remembered today more for Anger's vivid account of her final indignities than for her film performances or even her star persona. This should be a brutal reminder of the limits of comic transgression.

PART III

Welcome to the Playground

So far, we have read popular culture as being governed by a logic of aesthetic intensification. We have also seen that the immediacy of popular culture can become the focus of anxiety or fear since it is often read as breaking down constraints that operate elsewhere in the culture. From both perspectives, the child consumer becomes a central figure in any discussion of popular culture.[1]

On the one hand, the child is often read as more open to emotional engagement than the adult consumer. The circus used to pitch itself to "children of all ages," as if the experience of entertainment represented a return to the pleasures of childhood. Think of all of the images that circulate in our culture of children staring in wide-eyed wonderment at fireworks displays, puppet shows, magic acts, and circus clowns. Often, the most emotionally charged elements of popular culture—for example, the larger-than-life heroics of superhero comics, the cute and colorful characters of Japanese anime and video games—are assumed to be aimed at children, even when they are not. Childhood is celebrated as a time of sensual discoveries and playful experimentation, as an age free from adult demands and responsibilities. And this is in part why childhood becomes the focus of such adult nostalgia.

At the same time, children are seen as particularly vulnerable to the seductions of popular culture. Often, moral regulation of media content is put forth in the name of protecting the child. Frederic Wertham's 1954 book *The Seduction of the Innocent* provided an early template for contemporary critics of mass culture and public amusements. Popular culture is accused of stirring up too many emotions, leaving children in a state of frenzied excitement. Then again, as writers like James R. Kincaid and Jacqueline S. Rose have suggested, such representations of the child are themselves the products of adult fantasies—erotic, nostalgic, utopian, and otherwise.[2]

We use the child to imagine a past, simplified beyond recognition, when we felt safe and secure; and we use the child to imagine ways of perfecting the future, ridding society of the contradictions or anxieties that riddle our own present-day experiences. Perhaps as importantly, we also use these fantasies about children to justify the adult exercise of control over children's lives. Images of children at risk produce amusement, titillation, and horror in equal measure. In vaudeville, the child star Buster Keaton would submit to intense physical treatment by his parents: he was tossed about the stage or hung by his feet, his hair used to mop up the sawdust; he was kicked and spanked, at a time when the culture more generally was preoccupied with reforming child labor and regulating child abuse. Kincaid has similarly shown the ways our contemporary media eroticizes children even as it claims to protect them from unwanted sexual attention. Loving parents send children to bed each night with their heads full of stories that center around trauma and loss, even as they tuck them in and promise that everything is going to be alright: fear is brought forth so that they can be reassured, often in rituals that reassert adult authority and control.

These tensions shape popular culture that is constructed for the child consumer. We never seem to be able to decide whether children's culture is culture that children enjoy consuming or culture that adults want their children to consume; we can never fully resolve the tension between entertainment and education.

The three essays in this section approach the concept of children's culture from three different vantage points. "Going Bonkers" might be seen as an extension of the focus in the previous section's on "body genres": *Pee-Wee's Playhouse* was most famous for encouraging children to play with their bodies—and, in the end, it was Pee-Wee Herman's own bodily play that led to his downfall when he was arrested and charged with public masturbation at a porno movie). The most ethnographic essay in this book, "Going Bonkers" is primarily concerned with deciphering children's own responses to *Pee-Wee's Playhouse*. This essay reflects my own fascination as a parent with this disreputable and yet much loved children's program. Play enters the account at two levels—first, in terms of children's own efforts to experiment with and manipulate the conditions of media consumption, and second, in terms of their fascination with the anomaly posed by Pee-Wee's adult status and childlike personality. Kindergarteners took great pleasure in watching Pee-Wee "go bonkers" even as they censored themselves and others who went "bonkers" at inappropriate times or in inappropriate contexts.

"Complete Freedom of Movement" continues this exploration of children's play—this time drawing more heavily on the work of cultural geographers and social historians to help contextualize developments in digital media. If "Going Bonkers" asked what play means to children, this essay is more interested in the investments adults make in the design of play-spaces for children. This essay responded to efforts by feminist entrepreneurs to develop computer and video games for girls. With Justine Cassell, I hosted a conference and later edited a book, *From Barbie to Mortal Kombat: Gender and Computer Games*, which brought together industry insiders who were designing games for girls and cultural critics who were concerned about how those games might perpetuate gender stereotypes.[3] Both groups saw shaping children's play as a way of defining what kinds of adults they would become.

Finally, "Her Suffering Aristocratic Majesty" focuses on the sentimentalization that runs through many of the most respected children's books. In this case, I read Eric Knight's *Lassie Come-Home* as occupying the intersection between two of the great sentimental myths of the early twentieth century—the loyalty of dogs and the innocence of children. The essay examines how the media franchise has negotiated moments when Lassie's ownership has to be transferred from one person to another. Knight used the story of a boy and his dog to comment on the economic forces that were breaking down traditional British working-class culture, raising questions about the relative value of children's sentimental attachment and adult's claims of legal ownership. What would it take to break the bonds between a boy and his dog? Running through the essay is Susan Stewart's claim that nostalgia represents a form of the utopian imagination, a longing for a world that never really existed. For nostalgia to operate, we must in fact forget aspects of the actual past and substitute a sentimental myth about how things might have been. In the essay's closing passages, I turn back to my own childhood to try to show the gap between the reality of dogs (including unpleasant aspects of their bodies) and our nostalgic memory of dogs (which often strips away the body in order to focus on an emotional or spiritual essence).

7

"Going Bonkers!"
Children, Play, and Pee-Wee

We've watched them gaping at the screen.
They loll and slop and lounge about,
and stare until their eyes pop out . . .
they sit and stare and stare and sit
until they're hypnotized by it,
until they're absolutely drunk
with all that shocking ghastly junk.[1]

—Roald Dahl

Roald Dahl's *Charlie and the Chocolate Factory*, a Dantesque vision of the faults and foibles of contemporary children, reserves special ire for the young television addict, Mike Teavee. When we first encounter Mike, he is so preoccupied with a television gunfight, "his eyes glued to the screen," eighteen cap guns assembled at his side, that he refuses to be distracted even by the news that he is the recipient of one of the much coveted Golden Tickets: "Didn't I tell you not to interrupt! This show's an absolute Whiz-banger! It's terrific! I watch it every day! I watch all of them every day, even the crummy ones, where there's no shooting!" (p. 39). Once inside the mysterious chocolate factory, where the punishment always fits the crime, the sensation-crazed youngster receives his just deserts: he is "televised." "A giant camera split[s him] up into millions of tiny little pieces which are so small that you can't see them, and these little pieces are shot out into the sky by electricity" (p. 134). In order to be projected through the medium he loves, Mike must be transformed, atomized and shrunk to fit within the cramped confines of the television world. Meanwhile, the moralistic Oompa-Loompas sing of the dire consequences of excessive viewing:

It rots the senses in the head!
It kills the imagination dead!
It clogs and clutters up the mind!
It makes the child so dull and blind
he can no longer understand
a fantasy, a fairyland!
His brain becomes as soft as cheese!
His powers of thinking rust and freeze!
He cannot think-he only sees (p. 146)

Dahl's nightmarish parable about a youngster physically confined within the television set that has already captured his imagination merely exaggerates the hyperbolic claims activists and empirical researchers make about the negative "effects" of television viewing on children. Such accounts reject, from the outset, any notion that children might exercise selective viewing strategies or that they may bring their own agenda to bear on television rather than remaining passive consumers of its preset curriculum. Befitting their roles as academic apologists for the media reformers, these researchers ask questions that already presume that what is to be investigated is the impact television has on children, and not the impact that children's viewing strategies might have on program-preferred meanings. Children are preconceived as victims, not users, of television, and their viewing habits are stripped of any social context, allowing the researchers, and the activists who feed upon their work, to rationalize their own efforts to exert greater control over children's playtime.

More recently, however, several scholars working within the Anglo-American Cultural Studies tradition have sounded a welcome note of discord to the monotonous chorus of professional Oompa-Loompas. Robert Hodge and David Tripp insist that we should begin from the assumption that youngsters find the shows they watch somehow meaningful and that we should pay closer attention to the process by which these television meanings are negotiated between young viewers, texts, and contexts. Hodge and Tripp effectively reverse the logic of existing media research. No longer is Mike Teavee perceived as being transformed by his encounters with television; rather, Mike fragments television content and reshapes it to respond to his own cultural, social, cognitive, and emotional needs:

Television sends out messages, which are interpreted and acted on by social agents responsible for their actions. . . . We need to know how television carries meanings; how different minds will interpret and use these meanings, particularly children's growing and developing minds; and how such meanings are likely to be enacted in the real world of the child viewer.[2]

This essay represents my own provisional response, both as a concerned father and as a media scholar, to those central questions. I do so by examining the ways in which a particular group of five Madison kindergarteners made sense of and found pleasure in a specific Saturday morning show, *Pee-Wee's Playhouse*. The nature of the meanings produced—and even, to some degree, the strategies for meaning production—are particular to the reception context, the broadcast material, and the specific socio-cultural experience of the individual child. But a "thick description"[3] of how a limited group responds to a favored show can illustrate how social factors shape the kinds of meanings produced and how children's characteristic viewing strategies reflect the process of making sense of program materials.

As a parent, I felt I might bring special insight to the discussion. While "kidspeak" proves highly resistant to adult interpretation—and, as we will see, works to create an autonomous space for children—my prior exposure to the rituals, slang, and norms of kindergarten society and my familiarity with most of the children's common cultural references helped me to recognize at least some of the complex connections underlying their fragmentary and often poorly articulated comments about the program content.[4] My own enthusiasm for *Pee-Wee's Playhouse* granted me freer interaction with the children than traditional media effects researchers, for whom all "kidvid" is treated as the "same stuff" without much regard to the particulars of program content.

In researching this essay, I sought to create a more natural environment than the traditional laboratory setting, one in which the children could interact more spontaneously with each other and the television program. Four of my son's classmates were invited to our apartment to participate in a "Pee-Wee Party."[5] While some activities (drawing, storytelling, etc.) were designed to provoke specific feedback about the program content, plenty of time was available for children to simply play with each other in an unstructured, often unnervingly chaotic fashion. The party setting provided a catalyst that intensified children's normal responses to program content, creating a situation where they would be more open to examination. It also allowed me to examine not simply how individual children reacted to program content but how those responses were used in their interaction with their social peers, how they provided content for play, jokes, and conversations, and how television meanings were integrated back into lived experience.

Watching Children Watch TV: Play as a Viewing Strategy

Q. What did you think of the way they watched the show? Did they, er, seem to be having a good time?

A. (long pause) Well, ah, most of the time. But, some of the time, they were going wild—bonkers! . . . They were hopping on the hoppity-hop and not watching the show! They were paying no attention to the show!

—Henry, 51/2 years old

Henry's distress over his playmates' conduct at our "Pee-Wee Party" echoes concerns many parents feel when they witness the frankly irreverent attitude young viewers display toward a particularly favored text. Although television viewing is obviously a source of pleasure for children, they rarely watch the screen with rapt attention and frequently dash from one activity to another with only occasional glances toward the screen.[6] At our "party," children dragged several of Henry's toys into the living room. A large stuffed He-Man doll was used alternately as a "seat belt," lying across the lap of several children, or as an imaginary playmate, addressed as a "naughty" child and even spanked, to the objection of some participants who felt he was not being "bad." One girl watched part of the episode through the eyes of a Man-at-Arms mask. One boy pushed a fire truck around on the floor. A Silverhawks doll, with a telescopic eye, was passed around the circle so that all could get a glance to look at the "tiny tiny tiny TV set" through its distorting lens. Kids grabbed at grapes or raced to the bathroom. To adult eyes, this mode of reception may appear haphazard. If, however, a parent attempts to recapture the set or worse, turn it off, he or she is apt to receive resounding protests. For the children involved the interaction is of immense importance, and the challenge facing the researcher is to account for the kinds of pleasures and meanings that could be produced in this context.

We might begin with a deceptively simple assertion: for children, watching television is a type of play. Those attempting to describe the cognitive activity of spectators frequently resort to the metaphor of a game played between viewer and text. David Bordwell writes, for instance, "The perceiver in effect bets on what he or she takes to be the most likely perceptual hypothesis."[7] Bordwell's game is goal-centered and rule-governed. Participants seek to reconstruct the event chain and the textual world, to make predictions about likely outcomes of story actions, and to learn whether or not they have guessed correctly, to achieve a sense of "unity" and "coherence" from the fragments of the text. In doing so, their projections are constrained, at least in part, by textual properties, by reading "rules" imposed upon them intrinsically by the work itself and extrinsically by their interpretive community. "Grown-ups" like to play games of this type; preschoolers rarely do. Bruno Bettelheim draws sharp distinctions between children's play and adult games:

> Generally speaking, play refers to the young child's activities characterized by freedom from all but personally imposed rules (which are changed at will), by free-wheeling fantasy involvement, and by the absence of any goals outside of the activity itself. Games, however, are usually competitive and are characterized by agreed-upon, often externally imposed, rules, by a requirement to use the implements of the activity in the manner for which they were intended and not as fancy suggests, and frequently by a goal or purpose outside the activity, such as winning the game. Children recognize early on that play is an opportunity for pure enjoyment, whereas games may involve considerable stress.[8]

For young children, watching television lacks the textual imperatives that confront adults. Their viewing is unstructured and exploratory. It is responsive only to self-imposed rules, and those are often temporary and provisional. Left to their own devices, children frequently display little interest in "following the plot" or locating the moral behind a particular episode, "games" that require skills which they have imperfectly mastered and that assume goals which they do not yet share. Rather, they watch to have "fun," a pleasure that is found more often in "sensation," and even incoherence, rather than in causality and unity. Spectacle displaces narrative as the dominant appeal of the text. A youngster who has a favorite film or program on videotape often fast-forwards past the slow expository passages on a second viewing to get to the "good parts," to find the place where Large Marge's eyes pop from her head or where Slimer smears the Ghostbusters with noxious green goo, displaying increasingly less interest in character motivation or causal logic.

This difference is readily apparent in the kinds of stories that children choose to create about their favorite television characters. Consider an excerpt from a bedtime storytelling session with my son:

> Once upon, er, next, he goes back to his place and then he goes to sleep and then at the crack of dawn, he wakes up and then plays with his toys and right when it's . . . Then when it's 6:30 he rushed to the TV set to watch He-Man and She-Ra. He likes to do the same things I do on Saturday morning. . . . And, then, after he watches the show, he goes out and wakes his dog, Speck, and asks him, "Should we have breakfast right now today?" and he goes, "Not right now," and then Pee-Wee says "Okay" and then he goes play with his toys some more and then after that, he takes a piece of paper and puts it in front of his paper ball and then he crumbles it up with that and then he says, he asks to his dog, "Should we have breakfast now?" and then his dog says, "Yes, let's" and then the breakfast song again from the movie . . . And then he takes his fortune and it says, "Leave the house today, Urgent.". . . [Whispers] He has some books and he has to take them back to the library and the library will be boiling up mad at him because he bringed the book back a hundred days later from the day he is supposed to.

I view this story as a transitional work between a childlike emphasis on "sensation" and an adult-like emphasis on linearity and causality. Henry has partially accepted more adult story structures but still chooses to pursue childish pleasures that draw him from narrative logic. While there is a kind of rough sequential patterning here ("and then"), borrowed from his own Saturday morning routine and from the opening of *Pee-Wee's Big Adventure*, there is only limited causal logic linking the various story events. We are well into it before Pee-Wee's narrative goal is firmly established: he needs to return some books to the library. But, even then, he is consistently sidetracked along the way to water the neighbor's lawn, to play with mechanical gadgets, to fight with the boy next door, etc:

> And then he can't get past Francis's house. Francis is out, outdoors and he is right where Pee-Wee is about to step he says [mimics], "Good morning Pee-Wee Herman," and he says, "It's my birthday and my fa-

ther says I can have anything I want and guess what I want?" and he says, "A new bank teller?" and he says, "No! Your bike!" and then Pee-Wee says, then Pee-Wee rolls down on the ground and goes HAHAHAHA! and then Francis says, "What's so funny, Pee-Wee?" and then Pee-Wee says, "It's not for sale" and then the people start arguing and it sounds like this: "I know you are but what am I"? "You're an idiot!" "I know you are but what am I?" . . . and then after that, he says he wouldn't sell his bike for all the money in the world and he says, "Well, I will just drive through galaxies and get money from two worlds," and then he says, "not even for that price." Pee-Wee says that and then he goes to the library. And he drops his books off in the inside of the thing and the library-man walks around and says [shouts], "Pee-Wee Herman! You stop that! You got this book here a hundred days late and you have to give us the money from two galaxies!" and Pee-Wee says, "I can't give you that price!" and then the librarian says, "You have to!" and Pee-Wee says, "It's not a deal, okay!" and the librarian says, "Okay, we'll get out this gun and kill you!" . . .

An adult telling this same story might have drawn the obvious connection between Francis's offer of money for the bike and the library's absurd demand that Pee-Wee pay them "all the money in two galaxies," thereby creating unity and closure within the work. Henry does not. Problems are not so much resolved as forgotten. Yet, what may sound to adult ears like digressions are really the heart of the tale, an important source of pleasure.

Although, as Hodge and Tripp note, children have generally absorbed adult viewing strategies by age twelve, these skills develop slowly and often under some duress: they depend upon social knowledge that must be learned over time; the very notion of rule-governed or goal-centered games requires a certain degree of cognitive and social development; the rules represent adult-imposed restraints upon the interpretive process that may repress or redirect the joy found in "pure" play with media content. Learning to play (or read) by the sanctioned rules may allow for the child's admission into adult society, but at the high cost of repressed spontaneity. All too often, such socialization is accompanied by feelings of inadequacy and anxiety.

Children's play is not ideologically innocent; it is the primary means by which they absorb the values of their society and master both their own bodies and other culturally significant materials.[9] By experimenting with various social roles, by toying with a variety of different rules for structuring experience, the child comes to explore the preferred meanings of his or her cultural community and to develop self-mastery. Such play may and often does reinforce parental values, but it also contains a countersocial potential: it may be used to express the child's feelings of outrage over the expectations imposed upon him or her by the social formation, over the pressure to conform to rules that constrain instinctual life and frustrate personal desire.

Over time, as the reality principle comes to restrain the pleasure principle, the "pure" enjoyment of childhood play becomes a kind of "guilty pleasure" that must be rationalized through the guise of some more purposeful or goal-centered activity. Consequently, parents often defend their children's television viewing through appeals to educational benefits or "pro-social" values. Asked to describe the qualities they regard as "desirable" in a program aimed at kindergarten-age children, all of my adult respondents emphasized education over entertainment:

> The show must have a point to it. It must educate her either with a situation she could encounter or something she would face at school.

> Programs that teach the child something as well as entertain.

> Any show where there is a moral at the end. Even the action/adventure cartoons (He-Man, She-Ra, etc.), have a lesson to teach.

> We have normal concerns about sex and violence and nonsensical shows.

Some openly acknowledged the contradiction between their goals and those of their children:

> I would like her to watch more educational type shows, but I also want her to enjoy it.

Others expressed discomfort over their child's indiscriminate pursuit of pleasure:

> He would overindulge in cartoons if I let him . . . but I limit what he can watch. He could watch cartoons for hours.

When parents watch television with their children, they frequently spend much of their time instructing them in the "rules," the "normal" interpretive strategies they use in making sense of narratives, encouraging the children to make predictions about the plot or to locate character motivations, directing wandering attention back toward the screen at moments that seem of especial importance in the unfolding story. But children watching television without adult interference make very different kinds of comments and adopt very different kinds of reading strategies. Their "fun" comes precisely from their unbounded play with program material. They may cluster together events across a limited time span and seem to respond quite emotionally to these two- or three-minute segments. But little attempt is made to integrate narrative material across the full span of the episode. Rather, the kids watch the show in short spurts, allowing their attention to wander to other things, until it is again drawn back toward full concentration during moments of intense spectacle or heightened sensation. In a social viewing situation such as I observed, their sudden and insistent outbursts cue each other to watch a particularly promising passage:

Bill: Dinosaurs! Dinosaurs!
Cassandra: The ants!
Henry: Yeah. That's the ant family.

Bill: A vacuum cleaner?!!
Henry: This is a silly family. I mean, see what the vacuum cleaners does. It just sucks up their carpet and it just gets everything sucked.
Bill: They really know how to clean up! They sucked the ball up! Maybe they'll suck themselves up!

Jackie: Hey, these cartoons look funny!

Regular viewers of *Pee-Wee's Playhouse* develop a strong sense of its formulaic structure that they rely on to determine which moments offer the greatest potential reward and which can be missed in good conscience:

Several: Watch the crazy fridge!
Henry: Yeah, look at his refridge. Something crazy is going to happen. It's a crazy refridge. I mean, see—why!!!

The remainder of this essay will offer a description of children at play with the materials of their cultural environment and with the roles they are invited to assume as socialized members of the kindergarten community. Such a viewing strategy is far more experiential than interpretive, far more interested in finding pleasure than in making meanings. But it does produce meanings, however atomistically, that are of vital importance to the children involved. These meanings are localized and transitory, reflecting an immediate response both to specific program content and to particular concerns of pre-school life. But, the meaning-production process described here—the resistance to adult dominance over their cultural space, the process of textual fragmentation and the accruing of associated meanings around the bits of program material, the translation of narrative content into images for drawings and jokes, the forging of intertextual links between seemingly disparate texts, the manipulation of modal relations to create proximity or distance from represented material, etc.—reflect children's characteristic ways of making sense of television texts.

TV "Ket": Childhood as (Candy) Counter-culture

You'll love it! It's really gross!

—Cassandra, 51/2 years old

The most fun we had writing the show was when we would come up with stuff we knew was going to kill the five-year-olds.

—Paul Reubens (a.k.a. Pee-Wee Herman)[10]

These youngsters, undergoing an awkward transition from the relative freedom of their pre-school lives into the institutional demands of kindergarten, generally found great pleasure in the unstructured activity of watching children's television: "Saturdays are really neat. I get up and I don't have school and then I watch what I want to watch" (Bill). But parental opposition to the kinds of sensation-centered programming preferred by children can transform gratification into an act of open defiance. Although it has attracted a cult following among some college students, many adults find *Pee-Wee's Playhouse* highly abrasive and experience discomfort over its flashing colors and screeching noises, over the androgyny and spasticity of its central figure, over the playhouse that *Rolling Stone* described as "the collision of *The Cabinet of Dr. Caligari* with a raspberry-and-lime Jell-O mold constructed by Disney technicians recovering from the Taiwan flu."[11] It is precisely the kind of "pointless" or "nonsensical" show that parents hate. Bill reported that his father "won't let me watch that crazy show." Kate, acknowledging that "it's kind funny-talking," said that her father does not like her to watch the show either, though she frequently views it anyway. My son responded that "finally, at last," they would be able to watch Pee-Wee at our party: "And your parents won't be able to do anything about it." Several of the children giggled appreciatively. For these children, part of the appeal of watching Pee-Wee at a friend's house was the opportunity to circumvent parental authority, to push toward greater control over their recreational life and thereby to assert a degree of autonomy from the adult-dominated world. These playful children are discovering the pleasures of resistance.

Alison James offers a similar version of a children's culture cast in opposition to adult norms and satisfying the growing youngster's need for personal autonomy.[12] Her examination of children's consumption of cheap confections (called "kets" in certain British children's slang, a term also used by adults to refer to "rubbish") suggests that youngsters' favorite sweets may provide entry into an "alternative" culture system, constructed from the "rubbish" and remnants of adult society, satisfying drives and desires basic to pre-pubescent sexuality while opposing parental efforts to bring those drives under control: "The eating of dirty, decaying 'kets' is condemned by adults and it is this very condemnation which allows the child to assume control over at least one of his orifices" (p. 306). This confectionary economy operates, consciously or unconsciously, to confuse adult categories and resist parental intrusion, placing the greatest value on precisely those things that "grown-ups" find worthless and undesirable:

> By confusing the adult order children create for themselves considerable room for movement within the limits imposed upon them by the adult society. This deflection of adult perception is crucial for both the maintenance and continuation of the child's culture and for the growth of the concept of the self of the individual child. (p. 295)

Children's candies adopt the names of things "grown-ups" find distasteful or of things that would not normally be consumed (candy cigarettes, bubble gum cigars, jelly worms, gummy mummies, etc.), assume unusual textures (rubbery, slimy, etc.) or synthetic flavors, provoke strong and sometimes unpleasant sensations (Pop Rocks that literally explode on the tongue), demand to be eaten in unsanitary ways (sucking, slurping, fingering, blowing), and come in flamboyant patterns or clashing color combinations that disturb our normal aesthetic sensibility. Such sugary delights seduce children into playing with their food, even though they recognize parental prohibitions against doing so. Semi-digested chewing gum is removed and stretched into saliva-coated sculptures. Slobbery suckers are passed from mouth to mouth as a kind of kiddie communion. Children take pleasure in confections that sizzle and crackle in their mouths and turn their tongues lurid purple: "Kets are not distanced from the body. . . . Hands become covered in 'ket' and the normal eating conventions, instilled by parents during early childhood, are flagrantly disregarded" (p. 304).

Such logic pervades the cultural world of contemporary children. Toys "R" Us stores have been transformed into junior galleries of the grotesque. Shelves are crammed with Mad Balls with protruding eyeballs, cans of mucus-like green slime, dolls with bad breath or ones that make "disgusting noises," Garbage Pail Kids bubble gum cards that crudely parody popular consumer goods and playfully represent various bodily functions, monster labs where would-be "mad scientists" can watch acid decay the flesh from the body of hideous toy monsters. Playground slang abounds with frank references to "fungus," "snot," and "poop." The cable children's channel Nickelodeon features scatological comedy programs like *Turkey Television* and *You Can't Do That on Television*, offering Monty Python–style humor for the youngsters. Their most successful program, *Double Dare*, invites kids to swim through vats of assorted goops and to fling goo at each other. *Finders Keepers*, another popular children's game show, has the young contestants trash a model house, with rooms like Granny's Kitchen and Dad's Den, in search of prizes.

James's analysis would suggest that children find these "gross" things appealing precisely because their parents find them so unappealing. Their meaning comes through opposition, through allowing youngsters to carve for themselves a cultural space "just for kids," to construct a society that is responsive to their whims and that allows them a momentary release from adult control.

Pee-Wee's Playhouse seems ideally constructed for these preschoolers' needs: a garishly colored, sensation-saturated, slickly packaged televisual "ket," something like Pop Rocks for the mind. Its fragmentary structure encourages a playful response from its fans while its abrasive edge keeps (at least some) parents from intruding into their play space and claiming it as their own or imposing strictures upon its use. If *Pee-Wee* actively offends some parents, so much the better, since it is through resistance to parental pressures that the kids are able to make the program truly their own. Like all good "kets," it lacks obvious nutritional value and resists transformation into an "educational" experience. "It's just fun, that's all!"

"A Place Where Anything Can Happen":
Domesticity, Disorder, and Desire

> There will be no more nappin', we're going to a place where anything can happen. We've given fair warnin' it's gonna be that kind of mornin' for getting wacky, for being snotty, for going cuckoo at Pee-Wee's Playhouse.
> —Pee-Wee's Playhouse theme song

Like "ket" or its American counterpart, "junk," such words as "fun," "neat," "bonkers," "crazy," "cuckoo," and "silly," which occur so frequently in children's conversation, are open to a broad range of significations. Their poly-vocality makes them particularly obscure to adult ears. They describe a wide variety of cultural experiences and qualities, but what many of these share is their displacement of adult-imposed rules, their disruption of the tidy realm of the schoolroom and the family dinner table, their transgressions of the cultural categories and social norms that order "grown-up" society. Having "fun" or acting "crazy" frequently represents a momentary release from the intense pressures of the socialization process, a brief resurrection of the infantile pleasures that are being sublimated in the name of maturity.

What makes *Pee-Wee's Playhouse* "fun" for these preschoolers, then, is the way that it operates as a kind of anti-kindergarten where playful "misbehavior" takes precedence over "good conduct," children are urged to "scream real loud" at the slightest provocation, making a mess is an acknowledged source of pleasure, "grown-ups" act like children, and parental strictures no longer apply. Many of the show's most appealing segments deal with the disruption of domestic space, the undermining of adult authority, or the violation of basic cultural categories: the "crazy fridge" scenes, where fruits and vegetables dance and perform acrobatics while making a shambles of Pee-Wee's icebox; the dinosaur family whose patriarch is constantly being humiliated by the pranks and misconduct of his offspring; the robot who keeps bumping into furniture; Penny, whose satirical comments often ridicule adult values; and the enormous foil ball that threatens to overwhelm everything in its path. Pee-Wee invites us to enter an anarchic realm where desire and disorder are indistinguishable and where infantile urges are given free rein.

The children seem fascinated with the playhouse and its oddly shaped doors, off-kilter roof, impenetrable clutter, and anthropomorphized furnishings: "Pee-Wee's playhouse is a funhouse. You never know what's going to happen" (Jackie). The playhouse figures prominently in children's drawings of the program (fig. 1), sometimes even displacing the show's star altogether: "He's inside the house where you can't see him" (Jackie).

The playhouse represents for these children an unruly, disorderly, and cluttered domestic space, where normal categories do not seem to apply, where nothing is in its proper place either literally or figuratively. One girl drew a picture of the playhouse with an anthropomorphized television that looked remarkably like a young girl (fig. 2): "Pee-Wee's house is a funny place. He has a TV with long hair and eyes and a nose and a mouth and . . . hahaha freckles." Later, seeing a friend's portrait of Pee-Wee as a punk rocker, which appears to have been modeled after a Strawberry Shortcake doll (fig. 3), she decides her own picture really depicted the show's star too, suggesting just how malleable the program materials (and children's drawings) can be. Another girl included a talking door, an image consistent with program content though no such character exists on the show (see fig. 1). Some children speculated, with great amusement, about what such a door might say:

Q: What do you think a talking door would say?
Bill: (deep voice) Hello, Mister. I'm a talking door.
(All laugh.)
Bill: Knock, knock.

Figure 1.

Q: Who's there?
Bill: Ding dong!
Jackie: Ding dong who?
Bill: Awk! Awk! It's a Silverhawk! Awk!
Kate: You're pretty crazy.
(All laugh.)[13]

Henry drew a picture of Pee-Wee's "crazy closet" full of an assortment of "crazy toys" that did "crazy things all the time."

Young children, whose own comprehension of the world around them is far from perfect, and who feel highly dependent upon adult authorities for guidance, sometimes take great pleasure in phenomena that call into question the more rigid cultural categories by which "grown-ups" order their social environment and that openly acknowledge the inconsistencies of adult content. Martha Wolfenstein attributes the persistent images of disorderly worlds, of the destruction of property and the breakdown of social order, found in children's jokes to their confusion and anxiety over the apparently contradictory behavior of their parents.[14] These ambigui-

Figure 2.

ties are vividly expressed in Kate's attempt to recount the plot of a particular episode:

Q. Can you tell me what happened during the episode today? What do you remember about it?

Kate: I remember that Pee-Wee said stop all that racket and stuff because the people, they were doing all this stuff that was wrong to do.

Q: What kind of stuff?

A: Jumping on the couch, spinning the round head too fast, and that's all I remember. You see, sometimes, people do all that racket. And see, when it does that, some people next door says something to them, and they can't do it anymore. And then sometimes I have a neighbor at my house and sometimes my mom and dad fight and Lucy hears it and gripes at them about it.

Kate's description suggests a compelling need to comprehend the paradoxes of the adult world: how could her parents maintain authority over her if, at the same time, they face rebuke from other adults because of their own childish conduct? How can they be both parent and child? To resolve these contradictions, she must overlook Pee-Wee's own infantile behavior, casting the program's star as an idealized father who, through analogy, may discipline her own parents when they act in childish ways. For Wolfenstein, children's jokes, through their representation of worlds where the Law of the Father no longer applies, are the playful manifestation of Oedipal tensions and allow for a harmless outlet for the youngsters' fundamental need to create some distance from parental authority in order to come to terms with its inconsistencies. Not atypically, Kate's account suggests that she finds the prospect of a world that makes as little sense to adults as it does to children, where the certainties of the adult order break down, a source of real fascination, capable of producing both great pleasure and great anxiety.

Similarly, the children were drawn toward the grotesque figures of some of the program characters: the oversized head and minuscule body of the door-to-door salesman; the disembodied head of the genie; the mismatched heads and bodies of Pee-Wee's toy collection; the talking fist

Figure 3.

Figure 4.

with the lipstick mouth and eyes; and Pee-Wee's mask-like face, which must be shrunk in one episode so that he may extract it from a mouse hole. For children who are just gaining mastery over their bodily functions, who are still a bit confused about how the various parts work together, and who are intrigued by the range of different physiques they encounter as they increasingly move outside the relatively homogenous space of the home, these mutant, misshapen bodies are an object of intense interest and perhaps even a little anxiety. Such figures appear frequently in their drawings, while the more normal-looking characters (Dixie, Captain Karl, etc.) rarely do. Pee-Wee's all-too-obvious lack of bodily control and equally apparent joy in manipulating his face strikes a familiar chord for these youngsters.

References to the body run through their conversations, both in direct reference to the program content ("She looks like a pig!" "How did he get such a big head?!!") and more generally. A girl drawing a portrait of herself and a friend watching television (fig. 4) obsessively enumerates the various body parts as she draws them: "Here's my head and nose, ears, eyes, arm, okay, and here's another arm. Then leg, leg, then Jackie's head, heh heh, fat head! Heh heh. And here's your arms and here's your legs and your other arm and an eye and a nose. There. All done." Another remarks seemingly at random and to no one in particular, "Have you ever seen a boy with orange hair?"

Although such questions do not originate from watching the show, Pee-Wee provides children with one way in which they can explore their feelings toward their own bodies and their fascination with physical difference, topics that frequently make adults feel uncomfortable. Befitting their roles as socializing agents, parents discuss the body with children in a prohibitory fashion ("Don't pick your nose!"). Pee-Wee, subversive spokesman for spontaneity and childishness, addresses such concerns in an open and exploratory fashion ("See what I can do with my nose!"), justifying the pleasures kids find in playing with their bodies. Here, again, we find that *Pee-Wee's Playhouse* becomes a perfect program for children to explore their feelings about themselves and their world precisely because it transgresses adult standards of taste and decorum and upholds children's meanings over those of their parents.

The Importance of Being Bonkers: Pee-Wee and the Preschool Experience

> Q. Do you think, er, do you think most kids think Pee-Wee is a grown-up or a kid?
> A: A kid.
> Q: A kid. How can you tell?
> A. Because they see that he goes bonkers all of the time and no grown-up acts like Pee-Wee. Pee-Wee acts like a one-year-old.
> Q: He does, doesn't he?
> A: Yeah. Except he doesn't cry and whine and stuff.
>
> —Henry

For these preschoolers, the fascination of *Pee-Wee's Playhouse* predominantly rests on the ambiguity surrounding its central character—Pee-Wee's "otherness," which one boy described as "the greatest mystery of them all," and his uncontrollable and frequently disruptive conduct. Children often represent Pee-Wee as a blur of scribbled activity; Henry reproduced the character's face as a great spiral, which he drew with such intensity that his pencil shredded the page (fig. 5). While adults often attribute the uneasiness that Pee-Wee provokes to a sense of sexual ambiguity, androgyny, or perhaps homosexuality, these children perceive it as a question of immaturity. For some, Pee-Wee represents an adult who lacks the social skills necessary to function in the "grown-up" world: "No grown-up acts like Pee-Wee" (Henry). For others, Pee-Wee repre-

Figure 5.

sents an oversize child who has somehow stumbled into a world of his own, outside of adult control, where he is free to indulge in his most infantile pleasures.

The question of social maturity is a central concern in these preschoolers' lives. Their entry into kindergarten marks the end of an era of relative freedom. (Only one of the children had daycare experience prior to kindergarten; the others had remained at home under their parents' care and supervision). Now, they must respond to institutional demands for conformity and decorum. Impulsiveness must give way to regimentation as they learn new rules of conduct and new ways of organizing their lives.

Children absorb these institutional norms to a surprising degree, often criticizing each other for their failure to behave appropriately. The threat of discovering that they are "still too little," not really mature enough yet to move on to first grade, is never far from the surface, and as a result, the children feel compelled to distance themselves from any signs of infantile behavior. Those with younger siblings obnoxiously remind people that they are old enough to go to school while the others are not. The worst insult is to be accused of "acting like a baby." Henry explicitly rejected several classmates from his guest list because he felt uncomfortable with their classroom conduct. One boy was characterized as a "clown" who "always acts crazy." Another was described as "always going bonkers," and "knocking things over." Such inappropriate conduct is ill-received by children struggling to suppress all signs of their own childishness. But at the same time, these children experience feelings of nostalgia for their earlier years when they did not face such pressures, frequently dragging out family albums with a disbelief that they could ever have been "that little," reverting to earlier types of conduct when they are tired or hungry. The pleasures of infantilism compete with their pride over their newly discovered maturity.

The duality of man/child, Pee-Wee, makes him a useful vehicle for exploring children's conflicting desires. Frequently, these children employ the same words to denigrate their own misconduct and to praise Pee-Wee's antics that they find particularly amusing. One girl drew a picture of Pee-Wee with very long hair and characterized him as a "punk rocker" (see fig. 3). Her discussion of that drawing suggests that she has created a vague mental category that includes a range of social figures that violate institutional norms or cause disruptions through inappropriate behavior:

Cassandra: Here's Pee-Wee acting crazy as ever. Wee wee wee.
Jackie: Pee-Wee's got long hair as ever. Aw gawd! Now he's a punk rocker!!! And now mine has hair sticking out on top of him!
Cassandra: Now my Pee-Wee is a punk rocker too!
Jackie: . . . Pee-Wee has as long as hair as ever so don't laugh at Pee-Wee no matter what anybody calls him!
Bill: You're as funny as a bug!
(All laugh.)
Jackie: It would be worser if he went to school, don't you think?
Q: What's a crazy punk rocker do?
Jackie: He acts crazy, just like Pee-Wee does.

Her references to Pee-Wee going to school and to the names other children might call him suggest just how close a link exists in her mind between Pee-Wee and her own impulsive behavior. Similarly, Henry's anxiety about conforming to institutional norms and confronting adult authorities finds direct expression in his story about Pee-Wee's late library book. The absurd overstatement—the library's demand for "all the money in two galaxies" as a penalty for a book that is only "one hundred days late," the disruption caused by his refusal to pay that price, and the

Figure 6.

librarian's grotesque response—gives comic release to the very real tensions about his own powerlessness before the kinds of seemingly unreasonable demands that adult authorities place upon him. For Henry, as for Jackie, Pee-Wee becomes a focal point for his confusion about the gap between the need to act maturely and his own infantile desires and impulses. The very personification of the return of the repressed, Pee-Wee embodies their unfulfilled desires and sublimated urges, allowing them to experience the triumph of the pleasure principle over rational control. But he can act in this role only by becoming an other, both adult and infant, belonging fully to neither camp.

Pee-Wee's grey suit and red bow tie, which persistently appear in children's representations of him (fig. 6), allow children to deny the obvious parallels between this eccentric figure and their own social position and thereby to contain some of the tensions that he might otherwise produce. No matter how childlike he may act, he dresses and looks like a "grown-up." Martha Wolfenstein and Erik Erikson consider it essential for comic figures, like circus clowns and moron jokes, to mask their essentially infantile nature in order to allow children a way to break from too intense an identification with them.[15]

In fact, Pee-Wee may be doubly displaced from the realm of their lived experience since children also describe him as "acting like he was just born" or "acting like a two-year-old," phrases that mean something fundamentally different to a five-year-old than they do to an adult. Pee-Wee is perceived as a younger sibling, not yet mature enough to handle the responsibilities of kindergarten, allowing the children to feel a strong sense of superiority over him. He does things that they would never do.

Several of the children felt a compelling need to place Pee-Wee in a world well beyond their reach. Hodge and Tripp employ the term "modality" to describe the relationship that young viewers ascribe to the difference between a given media representation and social reality, a choice that helps them determine their emotional response to the depicted events. Through their manipulation of modality, viewers may pull a represented event toward them so that it can be experienced more immediately and more intensely, or shove it away to create necessary emotional and psychological distance from it.

Bill constructs a land of make-believe to contain his brief Pee-Wee story:

> Once upon a time there was a little boy, er, man named Pee-Wee. He lived far far away in Pee-Wee Land where all people (who) looked like Pee-Wee came to play with Pee-Wee and live with him happily ever after. The end.

Bill's ambiguity about Pee-Wee's age, his dependence on traditional fairy tale structures, and his need to create a world ("Pee-Wee Land") where the star's usually anomalous appearance and behavior are normal and rational ("all the people looked like Pee-Wee") suggest the degree to which he is relying upon modality to deny any obvious connection between himself and the show's comic hero and to contain the disturbing questions that his otherness provokes.

Kate makes a subtler, though no less significant, attempt to define the program events as occupying a space quite distinct from the world of her own experience. Asked to write a story about Pee-Wee, she instead imagines what it might be like to own her own construction company. Attempting to direct discussion back to the program, my wife asked her how she might respond if Pee-Wee came to her with a commission:

Q: What would you do if you got an order from Pee-Wee to build a new playhouse?

A: Um. No! I don't watch TV because I work all day.

Q: Ah. Well, what if he hired you to build his house for his new TV show?

A: I would, er. One day, I would go home and I would watch TV and then, I would be done and I would go back to work . . . and then, you know, I would tell them that I saw that show that they wanted, but I have a lot of work to do and I can't do it. . . . And I don't like, when I go home, you see, my boss, he likes me to work and not go home to watch TV all the time.

While Kate's story concerns a real world of adult concerns, Pee-Wee can exist in such a world only on television; no direct interaction with him is possible.

Not all children create such sharp distinctions between *Pee-Wee's Playhouse* and their own lives. In my son's stories, Pee-Wee awakens early on Saturday mornings to watch some of Henry's favorite television shows and even comes to visit his apartment and play with some of his toys: "He likes the same things I do." Although we must be cautious about making psychological claims about individual children, such differences in the assignment of modality may be indicative of very real differences in the ways that these kids resolve the kinds of tensions that the figure of Pee-Wee provokes. Those who feel the greatest anxiety about the socialization process or about disorderly conditions within their surroundings may find it relatively difficult to allow Pee-Wee to remain in close proximity to the realm of their lived experience because his spontaneity might call into question the kinds of painful compromises they are forced to make in their adjustments to the demands of school life. Yet, even these children, frightened though they may be of the things he represents, feel a need to play with the potent meanings that the Pee-Wee man/child suggests to them. The dilemmas that he poses are too central to the socialization process to be long ignored.

The Uses of Immaturity: Television Play and Socialization

For children of the television age, the most readily available play materials are those that the media bring into their homes. Children draw upon the prefabricated characters and situations of popular culture to make sense of their own social experience, reworking them to satisfy their own needs and desires. The children's manipulation of these televisual materials rarely stops when the broadcast does. Rather, program content is fragmented and dissected and the most meaningful bits, the "good parts," are integrated into the child's other play activities, into dreams and into waking thoughts. The parents in my study reported that their children often drew upon their favorite shows to give content to their drawings and pretend games. All of the children owned dolls or other toys directly tied to television programs. In such play, children feel little compulsion to remain faithful to the original series concepts, to "stay within the lines." In fact, children seem almost compulsively intertextual, blurring the normal boundaries between texts, mixing and matching the contents of multiple shows at their whim, creating stories where, say, Batman and Dr. Who join forces to combat Count Dracula and the Stay-Puft Marshmallow Man, or parodying, albeit crudely, the codes and conventions of favored programs. Henry wrote a story "making fun" of Mr. Rogers by showing how differently Pee-Wee would act in the same situations. Just as the children at the party treated a He-Man stuffed toy as, interchangeably, a seat belt and a naughty boy, a child may take a "pro-social" program and endow it with countercultural meanings, or with equal dexterity, may find rational logic behind the most nonsensical elements of their favorite shows.

These skills are not totally lost as the child is molded into a young adult. Indeed, many of the activities enjoyed by adult media fans reflect these same kinds of play with program content.[16] Rather, newer interpretive skills are layered over them as he or she learns to read television in more socially sanctioned ways. Fragmentation and association may come to coexist with integration and interpretation as alternative (and perhaps complimentary) ways of responding to popular texts. Yet, the reality principle dictates that pleasure will be more frequently subordinated to some "higher purpose" as our impulsiveness is constrained by our inclusion within a larger cultural community. Maturation should be perceived as a process whereby basic emotional needs are embedded within new mental structures necessary for future survival and yet potentially antagonistic to human impulsiveness. As Hodge and Tripp write, "Earlier stages survive because they are functional. They are the site of pleasure and the play of emotional energy. If later stages are essential for power, earlier stages are essential for desire."[17] Nobody wants a world in which children never reach maturity, a kind of "never-never land" where one can act infantile forever. The socialization process is essential for human accomplishment and fulfillment. But we must be cautious that in furthering the development of our children, we do not push too hard toward the rationalization of all experience, destroying within them those qualities that make them most human: their capacity to play, to find pleasure, to be creative. If, as adults, we feel compelled to find something educational and pro-social in all of children's television, perhaps this is the lesson we can learn from a visit to Pee-Wee's Playhouse: the importance of "going bonkers."

8

"Complete Freedom of Movement"

Video Games as Gendered Play Spaces

A Tale of Two Childhoods

Sometimes I feel nostalgic for my boyhood spaces in suburban Atlanta in the 1960s. My big grassy front yard sloped sharply downward into a ditch where we could float boats on rainy days. Beyond, there was a pine forest where my brother and I could toss pine cones like grenades or smack sticks together like swords. In the backyard, there was a patch of grass where we could wrestle or play kickball, and also a treehouse that sometimes bore a pirate flag and, at other times, the Stars and Bars of the Confederacy. Beyond our yard, there was a bamboo forest where we could play Tarzan, and vacant lots, construction sites, sloping streets, and a neighboring farm (the last vestige of a rural area turned suburban).

Between my house and the school, there was another forest, which, for the duration of my youth, remained undeveloped. A friend and I would survey this land, claiming it for our imaginary kingdoms of Jungleloca and Freedonia. We felt a proprietorship over that space, even though others used it for schoolyard fisticuffs, smoking cigarettes, or playing kissing games. When we were there, we rarely encountered adults, though when we did, it usually spelt trouble. We would come home from these secret places, covered with Georgia red mud.

Of course, we spent many afternoons at home, watching old horror movies or action-adventure series reruns, and our mothers would fuss at us to go outside. Often, something we had seen on television would inspire our play, as we stalked through the woods like Lon Chaney Jr.'s Wolfman or "sock"-ed "pow"-ed each other under the influence of Batman. Today, each time I visit my parents, I am shocked to see that most of those "sacred" places are now occupied by concrete, bricks, or asphalt. They managed to get a whole subdivision out of Jungleloca and Freedonia!

My son Henry, now sixteen, has never had a backyard. He has grown up in various apartment complexes, surrounded by asphalt parking lots with, perhaps, a small grass buffer from the street. Children were prohibited by apartment policy from playing on the grass, or racing their tricycles in the basements, or doing much of anything else that might annoy the non-childbearing population, cause damage to the facilities, or put themselves at risk. There was, usually, a city park some blocks away to which we could go on outings a few times a week and where we could watch him play. Henry could claim no physical space as his own, except his toy-strewn room, and he rarely got outside earshot of his parents. Once or twice, when I became exasperated by my son's constant presence around the house, I would forget all this and tell him he should go outside and play. He would look at me with confusion and ask, "Where?"

But he did have video games, which took him across lakes of fire, through cities in the clouds, along dark and gloomy back streets, and into dazzling neon-lit Asian marketplaces. Video games constitute virtual playing spaces that allow homebound children like my son to extend their reach, to explore, manipulate, and interact with a more diverse range of imaginary places than constitute the often drab, predictable, and overly familiar spaces of their everyday lives. Keith Feinstein, president of the Video Game Conservatory, argues that video games preserve many aspects of traditional play spaces and culture, maintaining aspects that motivate children to "learn about the environment that they find themselves living in."

> Video games present the opportunity to explore and discover, as well as to combat others of comparable skill (whether they be human or electronic) and to struggle with them in a form that is similar to children wrestling, or scrambling for the same ball—they are nearly matched, they aren't going to really do much damage, yet it feels like an all-important fight for that child at that given moment. Space Invaders gives us visceral thrill and poses mental/physical challenges similar to a schoolyard game of dodge-ball (or any of the hundred of related kids games). Video games play with us, a never tiring playmate.[1]

Feinstein's comment embraces some classical conceptions of play (such as spatial exploration and identity formation), suggesting that video game play isn't fundamentally different from backyard play. To facilitate such immersive play, video game spaces require concreteness and vividness. The push in the video games industry for more than a decade has been toward the development of more graphically complex, more visually engaging, more three-dimensionally rendered spaces, and toward quicker, more sophisticated, more flexible interactions with those spaces.

Video games advertise themselves as taking us places very different from where we live:

> Say hello to life in the fast lane. Sonic R for Sega Saturn is a full-on, pedal-to-the-metal hi-speed dash through five 3D courses, each rendered in full 360 degree panoramas. . . .You'll be flossing bug guts out of your teeth for weeks.
>
> —*Sonic R* advertisement, *Next Generation*, January 1998

> Take a dip in these sub-infested waters for a spot of nuclear fishin'. . . . Don't worry. You'll know you're in too deep when the water pressure caves your head in.
>
> —*Critical Depth* advertisement, *Next Generation*, January 1998

> Hack your way through a savage world or head straight for the arena. . . . Complete freedom of movement.
>
> —*Die By the Sword* advertisement, *Next Generation*, January 1998

> Strap in and throttle up as you whip through the most realistic and immersive powerboat racing game ever made. Jump over roadways, and through passing convoys, or speed between oil tankers, before they close off the track and turn your boat to splinters. Find a shortcut and take the lead, or better yet, secure your victory and force your opponent into a river barge at 200 miles per hour.
>
> —*VR Sports* advertisement, *Next Generation*, January 1998

Who wouldn't want to trade in the confinement of your room for the immersion promised by today's video games? Watch children playing these games, their bodies bobbing and swaying to the on-screen action, and it's clear they are there—in the fantasy world, battling it out with the orcs and goblins, pushing their airplanes past the sound barrier, or splashing their way through the waves in their speed boats. Perhaps my son finds in his video games what I found in the woods behind the school, on my bike whizzing down the hills of the suburban back streets, or settled into my treehouse during a thunderstorm with a good adventure novel—intensity of experience, escape from adult regulation; in short, "complete freedom of movement."

This essay will offer a cultural geography of video game spaces, one that uses traditional children's play and children's literature as points of comparison to the digital worlds contemporary children inhabit. Specifically, I examine the "fit" between video games and traditional boy culture and review several different models for creating virtual play spaces for girls. As we attempt to offer video games for girls, we need to better understand what draws boys to video games and whether our daughters should feel that same attraction.

Video games are often blamed for the listlessness or hyperactivity of our children, yet sociologists find these same behavioral problems occurring among all children raised in highly restrictive and confined physical environments.[2] Social reformers sometimes speak of children choosing to play video games rather than playing outside, when, in many cases, no such choice is available. More and more Americans live in urban or semi-urban neighborhoods. Fewer of us own our homes, and more of us live in apartment complexes. Fewer adults have chosen to have children, and our society has become increasingly hostile to their presence. In many places, "no children" policies severely restrict where parents can live. For a variety of reasons, parents are frightened to have their children on the streets, and place them under "protective custody." "Latch-key" children return from school and lock themselves in their apartments.[3]

In the nineteenth century, children living along the frontier or on America's farms enjoyed free range over ten square miles or more of space. Elliott West describes boys of nine or ten going camping alone for days on end, returning when they were needed to do chores around the house.[4] The early twentieth century saw the development of urban playgrounds in response to a growing sense of children's diminishing access to space and an increased awareness of child welfare,[5] but autobiographies of the period stress the availability of vacant lots and back allies that children could claim as their own play environments. Sociologists writing about the suburban America of my boyhood found that children enjoyed a play terrain of one to five blocks of spacious backyards and relatively safe subdivision streets.[6] At the end of the twentieth century, many children have access only to the one to five rooms inside their apartments. Video game technologies expand the space of their imagination.

Let me be clear—I am not arguing that video games are as good for kids as the physical spaces of backyard play culture. As a father, I wish that my son could come home covered in mud or with scraped knees rather than carpet burns. However, we sometimes blame video games for problems they do not cause—perhaps because of our own discomfort with these technologies that were not part of our childhood. Video games did not make backyard play spaces disappear; rather, they offer children some way to respond to domestic confinement.

Moving Beyond "Home Base": Why Physical Spaces Matter

The psychological and social functions of playing outside are as significant as the impact of "sunshine and good exercise" upon our physical well-being. In his book *Children's Experience of Place*, for example, Roger Hart stresses the importance of children's manipulations and explorations of their physical environment to their development of self-confidence and autonomy. Our physical surroundings are "relatively simple and relatively stable" compared to the "overwhelmingly complex and ever shifting" relations between people, and thus, they form core resources for identity formation.[7] The unstructured spaces, the play forts and treehouses, children create for themselves in the cracks, gullies, back allies, and vacant lots of the adult world constitute what Robin C. Moore calls "childhood's domain" or Willem Van Vliet has labeled as a "fourth environment" outside the adult-structured spaces of home, school, and playground.[8] These informal, often temporary play spaces are where free and unstructured play occurs. Such spaces surface most often on the lists children make of "special" or "important" places in their lives. M. H. Matthews stresses the "topophilia," the heightened sense of belonging and ownership, children develop as they map their fantasies of empowerment and escape onto their neighborhoods.[9] Frederick Donaldson proposed two different classifications of these spaces—home base, the world which is secure and familiar, and home region, an area undergoing active exploration, a space under the process of being colonized by the child.[10] Moore writes:

> One of the clearest expressions of the benefits of continuity in the urban landscape was the way in which children used it as an outdoor gymnasium. As I walked along a Mill Hill street with Paul, he continually went

darting ahead, leapfrogging over concrete bollards, hopping between paving slabs, balancing along the curbside. In each study area, certain kids seemed to dance through their surroundings on the look out for micro-features with which to test their bodies. . . . Not only did he [David, another boy in the study], like Paul, jump over gaps between things, go "tightrope walking" along the tops of walls, leapfrogging objects on sight, but at one point he went "mountain climbing" up a roughly built, nine-foot wall that had many serendipitously placed toe and handholds.[11]

These discoveries arise from children's active exploration and spontaneous engagement with their physical surroundings. Children in the same neighborhoods may have fundamentally different relations to the spaces they share, cutting their own paths, giving their own names to features of their environment. The "wild spaces" are far more important, many researchers conclude, than playgrounds, which can only be used in sanctioned ways, since they allow many more opportunities for children to modify their physical environment.

Children's access to spaces is structured around gender differences. Observing the use of space within 1970s suburban America, Hart found that boys enjoyed far greater mobility and range than girls of the same age and class background. In the course of an afternoon's play, a typical ten- to twelve-year old boy might travel a distance of 1,200 yards, while the average girl of the same age might travel only 760 yards. For the most part, girls expanded their geographic range only to take on responsibilities and perform chores for the family, while parents often turned a blind eye to a boy's movements into prohibited spaces. The boys Hart observed were more likely to move beyond their homes in search of "rivers, forts and treehouses, woods, ballfields, hills, lawns, sliding places, and climbing trees," while girls were more likely to seek commercially developed spaces, such as stores or shopping malls. Girls were less likely than boys to physically alter their play environment, to dam creeks or build forts. Such gender differences in mobility, access, and control over physical space increased as children grew older.[12]

One study found that parents were more likely to describe boys as being "outdoor" children and girls as "indoor" children.[13] Another study, which inventoried the contents of children's bedrooms, found boys more likely to possess a range of vehicles and sports equipment designed to encourage outside play, while the girls rooms were stocked with dolls, doll clothes, and other domestic objects.[14] Parents of girls were more likely to express worries about the dangers their children face on the streets and to structure girls' time for productive household activities or educational play.[15]

Historically, girl culture was formed under closer maternal supervision, and girls' toys were designed to foster female-specific skills and competencies to prepare them for their future domestic responsibilities as wives and mothers. The doll's central place in girlhood reflected maternal desires to encourage daughters to sew; the doll's china heads and hands fostered delicate gestures and movements.[16] However, these skills were not acquired without some resistance. Nineteenth-century girls were apparently as willing as today's girls to mistreat their dolls by, for example, cutting their hair or driving nails into their bodies.

Putting Boy Culture Back in the Home

> Clods were handy and the air was full of them in a twinkling. They raged around Sid like a hail storm; and before Aunt Polly could collect her surprised faculties and sally to the rescue, six or seven clods had taken personal effect, and Tom was over the fence and gone. . . . He presently got safely beyond the reach of capture and punishment, and hasted toward the public square of the village, where two "military" companies of boys had met for conflict, according to previous appointment. Tom was the general of one of these armies; Joe Harper (a bosom friend) general of the other. . . . Tom's army won a great victory, after a long and hard-fought battle. Then the dead were counted, prisoners exchanged, the terms of the next disagreement agreed upon, and the day for the necessary battle appointed; after which the armies fell into line and marched away, and Tom turned homeward alone.
>
> —Mark Twain, *Adventures of Tom Sawyer*

What E. Anthony Rotundo calls "boy culture"[17] emerged in the context of the growing separation of the male public sphere and the female private sphere in the wake of the industrial revolution. Boys were cut off from the work life of their fathers and left under the care of their mothers. According to Rotundo, boys escaped from the home into outdoor play spaces, freeing them to participate in a semi-autonomous "boy culture" that cast itself in opposition to maternal culture:

> Where women's sphere offered kindness, morality, nurture and a gentle spirit, the boys' world countered with energy, self-assertion, noise, and a frequent resort to violence. The physical explosiveness and the willingness to inflect pain contrasted so sharply with the values of the home that they suggest a dialogue in actions between the values of the two spheres—as if a boy's aggressive impulses, so relentlessly opposed at home, sought extreme forms of release outside it; then, with stricken consciences, the boys came home for further lessons in self-restraint.[18]

The boys took transgressing maternal prohibitions as proof they weren't "mama's boys." Rotundo argues that this break with the mother was a necessary step toward autonomous manhood. One of the many tragedies of our gendered division of labor may be the ways that it links misogyny—an aggressive fighting back against the mother—with the process of developing self-reliance. Fathers, on the other hand, offered little guidance to their sons, who, Rotundo argues, acquired masculine skills and values from other boys. By contrast, girls' play culture was often "interdependent" with the realm of the mother's domestic activities, insuring a smoother transition into anticipated adult roles, but allowing less autonomy.

What happens when the physical spaces of nineteenth-century boy culture are displaced by the virtual spaces of contemporary video games? Cultural geographers have long argued that television is a poor substitute for backyard play, despite its potential to present children with a greater diversity of spaces than can be found in their immediate surroundings, precisely because it is a spectatorial rather than a participatory medium. Moore, however, leaves open the prospect that a more interactive digital medium might serve some of the same developmental functions as backyard play.[19] A child playing a video game, searching for the path around obstacles, or looking for an advantage over imaginary opponents, engages in many of the same "mapping" activities as children searching for affordances in their real-world environments. Rotundo's core claims about nineteenth-century boy culture hold true for the "videogame-culture" of contemporary boyhood. This congruence may help us to account for the enormous popularity of these games with young boys. This "fit" should not be surprising when we consider that the current game genres reflect intuitive choices by men who grew up in the 1960s and 1970s, when suburban boy culture still reigned.

CULTURAL INDEPENDENCE. Nineteenth-century "boy culture" was characterized by its independence from the realm of both mothers and fathers. It was a space where boys could develop autonomy and self-confidence. Contemporary video-game culture also carves out a realm for modern-day children separate from the space of their parents. They often play the games in their rooms and guard their space against parental intrusion. Parents often express distaste for the games' pulpy plots and lurid images. Here, however, the loss of spatial mobility is acutely felt—the "bookworm," the boy who spent all of his time in his room reading, had a "mama's boy" reputation in the old "boy culture." Modern-day boys have had to accommodate their domestic confinement with their definitions of masculinity, perhaps accounting, in part, for the hyper-masculine and hyper-violent content of the games themselves.

RISK-TAKING. In nineteenth-century "boy culture," youngsters gained recognition from their peers for their daring, often proven through stunts (such as swinging on vines, climbing trees, or leaping from rock to rock as they cross streams) or through pranks (such as stealing apples or doing mischief on adults). In video-game culture, children gain recognition for their daring as demonstrated in the virtual worlds of the game, overcoming obstacles, beating bosses, and mastering levels. Nineteenth-century boys' trespasses on neighbor's property or confrontations with hostile shopkeepers are mirrored by the visual vocabulary of the video games, which often pit smaller protagonists against the might and menace of much larger rivals. Much as cultural geographers describe the boys' physical movements beyond their home bases as developing "home territories," the video games allow boys to gradually develop their mastery over the entire digital terrain, securing their future access to spaces by passing goal posts or finding warp zones.

MASTERY AND SELF-CONTROL. The central virtues of nineteenth-century "boy culture" were mastery and self-control. Boys set tasks and goals for themselves that required discipline in order to complete. Through this process of setting and meeting challenges, they acquired the virtues of manhood. The central virtues of video game culture are also mastery (over the technical skills required by the games) and self-control (manual dexterity). Putting in the long hours of repetition and failure necessary to master a game also requires discipline and the ability to meet and surpass self-imposed goals. Most contemporary video games are ruthlessly goal-driven. Boys will often play the games, struggling to master a challenging level, well past the point of physical and emotional exhaustion. Children are not so much "addicted" to video games as they are unwilling to quit before they have met their goals, and the games seem always to set new goalposts, inviting us to best "just one more level." One of the limitations of the contemporary video game, however, is that it provides only pre-structured forms of interactivity; in that sense, video games are more like playgrounds and city parks than wild spaces.

COMPETITION. Nineteenth-century "boy culture" was hierarchical, with a member's status dependent upon competitive activity, direct confrontation, and physical challenges. The boy fought for a place in the gang's inner circle, hoping to win admiration and respect. Video-game culture can also be hierarchical, with a member gaining status by being able to complete a game or log a big score. Video-game masters move from house to house to demonstrate their technical competency and to teach others how to "beat" particularly challenging levels. The video arcade becomes a proving ground for contemporary masculinity, and many games are designed for the arcade, demanding a constant turnover of coins for play and intensifying the action into roughly two-minute increments.

AGGRESSION. Nineteenth-century "boy culture" was sometimes brutally violent and physically aggressive; children hurt each other or got hurt trying to prove their mastery and daring. Video-game culture displaces this physical violence into a symbolic realm. Rather than beating each other up behind the school, boys combat imaginary characters, finding a potentially safer outlet for their aggressive feelings. We forget how violent previous boy culture was. Rotundo writes:

> The prevailing ethos of the boys' world not only supported the expression of impulses such as dominance and aggression (which had evident social uses), but also allowed the release of hostile, violent feelings (whose social uses were less evident). By allowing free passage to so many angry or destructive emotions, boy culture sanctioned a good deal

of intentional cruelty, like the physical torture of animals and the emotional violence of bullying. . . . If at times boys acted like a hostile pack of wolves that preyed on its own kind as well as on other species, they behaved at other times like a litter of playful pups who enjoy romping, wrestling and testing new skills.[20]

Even feelings of fondness and friendship were expressed through physical means, including greeting each other with showers of brickbats and offal. Such a culture is as violent as the world depicted in contemporary video games, which have the virtue of allowing growing boys to express their aggression and rambunctiousness through indirect means.

SCATOLOGY. Nineteenth-century "boy culture" expressed itself through scatological humor. Such bodily images (of sweat, spit, snot, shit, and blood) reflected boys' growing awareness of their bodies and signified their rejection of maternal constraints. Video-game culture has often been criticized for its dependence upon similar kinds of scatological images, with the blood and gore of games like *Mortal Kombat* (with its "end moves" of dismemberment and decapitation) providing some of the most oft-cited evidence in campaigns to reform video-game content.[21] Arguably, these images serve the same functions for modern boys as for their nineteenth-century counterparts—allowing an exploration of what it's like to live in our bodies and an expression of distance from maternal regulations. As in the earlier "boy culture," this scatological imagery sometimes assumes overtly misogynistic form, directed against women as a civilizing or controlling force, staged toward women's bodies as a site of physical difference and as the objects of desire/distaste.

ROLE-PLAYING. Nineteenth-century "boy culture" depended on various forms of role-playing, often imitating the activities of adult males. Rotundo notes the popularity of games of settlers and Indians during an age when the frontier had only recently been closed, casting boys sometimes as their settler ancestors and other times as "savages." Such play mapped the competitive and combative boy culture ethos onto the adult realm, thus exaggerating the place of warfare in adult male lives. Through such play, children tested alternative social roles, examined adult ideologies, and developed a firmer sense of their own abilities and identities:

Boy culture emphasized exuberant spontaneity; it allowed free rein to aggressive impulses and revealed in physical prowess and assertion. Boy culture was a world of play, a social space where one evaded the duties and restrictions of adult society. . . . Men were quiet and sober, for theirs was a life of serious business. They had families to support, reputations to earn, responsibilities to meet. Their world was based on work, not play, and their survival in it depended on patient planning, not spontaneous impulse. To prosper, then, a man had to delay gratification and restrain desire. Of course, he also needed to be aggressive and competitive, and he needed an instinct for self-advancement. But he had to channel those assertive impulses in ways that were suitable to the abstract battles and complex issues of middle-class men's work.[22]

Today, the boys are using the same technologies as their fathers, even if they are using them to pursue different fantasies.

SOCIALIZATION. In nineteenth-century "boy culture," play activities were seen as opportunities for social interactions and bonding. Boys formed strong ties that in turn formed the basis for adult affiliations, such as participation in men's civic clubs and fraternities, and for business partnerships. The track record of contemporary video-game culture at providing a basis for a similar social networking is more mixed. In some cases, the games constitute both play space and playmates, reflecting the physical isolation of contemporary children from each other. In other cases, the games provide the basis for social interactions at home, at school, and at the video arcades. Children talk about the games together, over the telephone or the Internet, as well as in person, on the playground, or at the school cafeteria. Boys compare notes, map strategies, share tips, and show off their skills, and this exchange of video-game lore provides the basis for more complex social relations.

Far from a "corruption" of the culture of childhood, video games show strong continuities to the boyhood play fondly remembered by previous generations. There is a significant difference, however. Nineteenth-century "boy culture" enjoyed such freedom and autonomy precisely because boys' activities were staged within a larger expanse of space, and because they could occupy that environment largely unsupervised by adults. Nineteenth-century boys sought indirect means of breaking with their mothers, escaping to spaces that were outside their control, engaging in secret activities they knew would have met parental disapproval. The mothers, on the other hand, rarely had to confront the nature of this "boy culture" and often didn't even know that it existed. The video-game culture, on the other hand, occurs in plain sight, in the middle of the family living room or, at best, in the children's rooms. Mothers come face to face with the messy process by which Western culture turns boys into men, and it becomes the focus of open antagonisms and the subject of tremendous guilt and anxiety. Current attempts to police video-game content reflect a long history of attempts to shape and regulate children's play culture, starting with the playground movements of progressive America and the organization of social groups for boys such as the Boy Scouts or Little League, which tempered the more rough-and-tumble qualities of "boy culture" and channeled them into games, sports, and other adult-approved pastimes.

Many of us might wish to foster a boy culture that allowed the expression of affection or the display of empowerment through nonviolent channels, that disentangled the development of personal autonomy from the fostering of misogyny, and that encouraged boys to develop a more nurturing, less domineering attitude toward their social and natural environments. These goals are worth pursuing. We can't simply adopt a "boys will be boys" attitude. However, one wonders about the consequences of such policing in a world that no longer offers "wild" outdoor spaces as a safety valve for boys to escape parental control. Perhaps, our sons—and daughters—need an unpoliced space for social experimentation, a space where they can vent their frustrations and imagine alternative adult roles without inhibiting parental pressure. The problem, of course, is that unlike nineteenth-century "boy culture," the video-game culture is not a world children construct for themselves but rather one made by adult companies and sold to children. There is no way that we can escape adult intervention in shaping children's play environments as long as those environments are built and sold rather than discovered and appropriated. As parents, we are thus implicated in our children's choice of play environments, whether we wish to be or not, and we need to be conducting a dialogue with our children about the qualities and values exhibited by these game worlds. One model would be for adults and children to collaborate in the design and development of video-game spaces, thereby developing a conversation about the nature and meanings of the worlds being produced. Another approach would be to create tools to allow children to construct their own play-spaces and then give them the space to do what they want.[23] Right now, parents are rightly apprehensive about a play-space that is outside their own control and is shaped according to adult specifications but without their direct input.

One of the most disturbing aspects of "boy culture" is its gender segregation. Nineteenth-century "boy culture" played an essential role in preparing boys for entry into their future professional roles and responsibilities; some of that same training has also become essential for girls at a time when more and more women are working outside the home. The motivating force behind the "girls' game" movement is the idea that girls, no less than boys, need computers at an early age if they are going to be adequately prepared to get "good jobs for good wages."[24] Characteristically, the girls' game movement has involved the transposition of traditional feminine play cultures into the digital realm. However, in doing so, we run the risk of preserving, rather than transforming, those aspects of traditional "girl culture" that kept women restricted to the domestic sphere, while denying them the spatial exploration and mastery associated with "boy culture." Girls, no less than boys, need to develop an exploratory mindset, a habit of seeking unknown spaces as opposed to settling placidly into the domestic sphere.

Gendered Games/Gendered Books: Toward a Cultural Geography of Imaginary Spaces

These debates about gendered play and commercial entertainment are not new, repeating (and in a curious way, reversing) the emergence of a gender-specific set of literary genres for children in the nineteenth century. As Elizabeth Segel notes, the earliest children's book writers were mostly women, who saw the genre as "the exercise of feminine moral 'influence'" upon children's developing minds, and who created a literature that was undifferentiated according to gender but "domestic in setting, heavily didactic and morally or spiritually uplifting."[25] In other words, the earliest children's books were "girls' books" in everything but name, which isn't surprising at a time when novel-reading was still heavily associated with women. The "boys' book" emerged in the mid-nineteenth century, as "men of action," industrialists and adventurers, wrote fictions intended to counter boys' restlessness and apathy toward traditional children's literature. The introduction of boys' books reflected a desire to get boys to read. Boys' book fantasies of action and adventure

reflected the qualities of their pre-existing play culture, fantasies centering on "the escape from domesticity and from the female domination of
the domestic world."[26] If the "girls' game" movement has involved the rethinking of video game genres (which initially emerged in a male-dominated space) in order to make digital media more attractive to girls (and
thus to encourage the development of computational skills), the "boys'
book" movement sought to remake reading (which initially emerged in a
female-dominated space) to respond to male needs (and thus to encourage literacy). In both cases, the goal seems to have been to construct fantasies that reflect the gender-specific nature of children's play and thus to
motivate those left out of the desirable cultural practices to get more involved. In this next section, I will consider the continuity that exists between gender/genre configurations in children's literature and in the digital games marketplace.

Adventure Islands: Boy Space

> Alex looked around him. There was no place to seek cover. He was too
> weak to run, even if there was. His gaze returned to the stallion, fasci-
> nated by a creature so wild and so near. Here was the wildest of all wild
> animals—he had fought for everything he had ever needed, for food, for
> leadership, for life itself; it was his nature to kill or be killed. The horse
> reared again; then he snorted and plunged straight for the boy.[27]
>
> —Walter Farley, *The Black Stallion* (1941)

The space of the boy book is the space of adventure, risk-taking, and
danger, of a wild and untamed nature that must be mastered if one is to
survive. The space of the boys' book offers "no place to seek cover," and
thus encourages fight-or-flight responses. In some cases, most notably in
the works of Mark Twain, the boys' book represented a nostalgic docu-
mentation of nineteenth-century "boy culture," its spaces, its activities,
and its values. In other cases, as in the succession of pulp adventure stories that form the background of the boys' game genres, the narratives
offered us a larger-than-life enactment of those values, staged in exotic
rather than backyard locales, involving broader movements through
space and amplifying horseplay and risk-taking into scenarios of actual

combat and conquest. Boys' book writers found an easy fit between the ideologies of American "manifest destiny" or British colonialism and the adventure stories boys preferred to read, which often took the form of quests, journeys, or adventures into untamed and uncharted regions of the world—into the frontier of the American west (or, in the twentieth century, the "final frontier" of Mars and beyond), into the exotic realms of Africa, Asia, and South America. The protagonists were boys or boy-like adult males, who had none of the professional responsibilities and domestic commitments associated with adults. These heroes sought adventure by running away from home to join the circus (*Toby Tyler*), to sign up as cabin boy on a ship (*Treasure Island*), or to seek freedom by rafting down the river (*Huckleberry Finn*). They confronted a hostile and untamed environment (as when *The Jungle Book*'s Mowgli must battle "tooth and claw" with the tiger, Sheer Khan, or when Jack London's protagonists faced the frozen wind of the Yukon.) They were shipwrecked on islands, explored caves, searched for buried treasure, plunged harpoons into slick-skinned whales, or set out alone across the desert, the bush, or the jungle. They survived through their wits, their physical mastery, and their ability to use violent force. Each chapter offered a sensational set piece—an ambush by wild Indians, an encounter with a coiled cobra, a landslide, a stampede, or a sea battle—that placed the protagonist at risk and tested his skills and courage. The persistent images of blood-and-guts combat and cliff-hanging risks compelled boys to keep reading, making their blood race with promises of thrills and more thrills. This rapid pace allowed little room for moral and emotional introspection. In turn, such stories provided fantasies boys could enact within their own environments. Rotundo describes nineteenth-century boys playing pirates, settlers and Indians, or Roman warriors, roles drawn from boys' books.

The conventions of the nineteenth- and early twentieth-century boys' adventure story provided the basis for the current video game genres. The most successful console game series, such as Capcom's *Mega Man* or Nintendo's *Super Mario Brothers* games, combine the iconography of multiple boys' book genres. Their protagonists struggle across an astonishingly eclectic range of landscapes—deserts, frozen wastelands, tropical rain forests, urban undergrounds—and encounter resistance from strange hybrids (who manage to be animal, machine, and savage all rolled into one). The scroll games have built into them the constant construction of frontiers—home regions—that the boy player must struggle to master and push beyond, moving deeper and deeper into uncharted space. Action is relentless. The protagonist shoots fireballs, ducks and charges, slugs it out, rolls, jumps and dashes across the treacherous terrain, never certain what lurks around the next corner. If you stand still, you die. Everything you encounter is potentially hostile so shoot to kill. Errors in judgment result in the character's death and require starting all over again. Each screen overflows with dangers; each landscape is riddled with pitfalls and booby traps. One screen may require you to leap from precipice to precipice, barely missing falling into the deep chasms below. Another may require you to swing by vines across the treetops, or spelunk through an underground passageway, all the while fighting it out with the alien hordes. The game's levels and worlds reflect the set-piece structure of the earlier boys' books. Boys get to make lots of noise on "adventure island," with the soundtrack full of pulsing music, shouts, groans, zaps, and bomb blasts. Everything is streamlined: the plots and characters are reduced to genre archetypes, immediately familiar to the boy gamers, and defined more through their capacity for action than anything else. The "adventure island" itself is the archetypal space of both boys' books and boys' games—an isolated world far removed from domestic spaces or adult supervision, an untamed world for people who refuse to bow before the pressures of the civilizing process, a never-never-land in which you seek your fortune. The "adventure island," in short, is a world that fully embodies the "boy culture" and its ethos.

Secret Gardens: Girl Space

If it was the key to the closed garden, and she could find out where the door was, she could perhaps open it, and see what was inside the walls and what had happened to the old rose-trees. It was because it had been shut up so long that she wanted to see it. It seemed as if it must be different from other places and that something strange must have happened to it during ten years. Besides that, if she liked it she could go into it every day and shut the door behind her, and she could make up some play of her own and play it quite alone, because nobody would ever know where she was, but would think the door was still locked and the key buried in the earth.[28]

—Frances Hodgson Burnett, *The Secret Garden* (1911)

Girl space is a space of secrets and romance, a space of one's own in a world that offers you far too little room to explore. Ironically, "girls' books" often open with fantasies of being alone and then require the protagonist to sacrifice her private space in order to make room for others' needs. The "girls' book" as an entertainment genre emerged through imitation of the gothics and romances preferred by adult women readers. As Segel writes:

> The liberation of nineteenth century boys into the book world of sailors and pirates, forest and battles, left their sisters behind in the world of childhood—that is, the world of home and family. When publishers and writers saw the commercial possibilities of books for girls, it is interesting that they did not provide comparable escape reading for them (that came later, with the pulp series books) but instead developed books designed to persuade the young reader to accept the confinement and self-sacrifice inherent in the doctrine of feminine influence. This was accomplished by depicting the rewards of submission and the sacred joys of serving as "the angel of the house."[29]

If the boys' book protagonist escaped all domestic responsibilities, the girls' book heroine learned to temper her impulsiveness and to accept family and domestic obligations (*Little Women, Anne of Green Gables*) or sought to be a healing influence on a family suffering from tragedy and loss (*Rebecca of Sunnybrook Farm*). Segel finds the most striking difference between the two genre traditions in the books' settings: "the domestic confinement of one book as against the extended voyage to exotic lands in the other."[30] Avoiding the boys' books' purple prose, the girls' books describe naturalistic environments, similar to the realm of readers' daily experience. The female protagonists take emotional risks, but rarely physical ones. The tone is more apt to be confessional than confrontational.

Traditional girls' books, such as *The Secret Garden*, do encourage some forms of spatial exploration, an exploration of the hidden passages of unfamiliar houses or the rediscovery and cultivation of a deserted rose garden. Norman N. Holland and Leona F. Sherman emphasize the role of spatial exploration in the gothic tradition, a "maiden-plus-habitation" formula whose influence is strongly felt on *The Secret Garden*.[31] In such stories, the exploration of space leads to the uncovering of secrets, clues, and symptoms that shed light on character's motivations. Hidden rooms often contain repressed memories and sometimes entombed relatives. The castle, Holland and Sherman note, "can threaten, resist, love or confine, but in all these actions, it stands as a total environment" that the female protagonist can never fully escape.[32] Holland and Sherman claim that gothic romances fulfill a fantasy of unearthing secrets about the adult world, casting readers in a position of powerlessness, and daring them to overcome their fears and confront the truth. Such a fantasy space is, of course, consistent with what we have already learned about girls' domestic confinement and greater responsibilities to their families.

Purple Moon's *Secret Paths in the Forest* fully embodies the juvenile gothic tradition while significantly enlarging the space open for girls to explore. Purple Moon removes the walls around the garden, turning it into woodlands. Producer Brenda Laurel has emphasized girls' fascination with secrets, a fascination that readily translates into a puzzle game structure, though *Secret Paths* pushes further than existing games to give these "secrets" social and psychological resonance. Based on her focus group interviews, Laurel initially sought to design a "magic garden," a series of "romanticized natural environments" responsive to "girls' highly touted nurturing desires, their fondness for animals." She wanted to create a place "where girls could explore, meet and take care of creatures, design and grow magical or fantastical plants" (personal correspondence, 1997). What she found was that the girls did not feel magical animals would need their nurturing and in fact, many of the girls wanted the animals to mother them. The girls in Laurel's study, however, were drawn to the idea of the secret garden or hidden forest as a "girls' only" place for solitude and introspection. Laurel explains:

> Girls' first response to the place was that they would want to go there alone, to be peaceful and perhaps read or daydream. They might take a best friend, but they would never take an adult or a boy. They thought that the garden/forest would be a place where they could find out things that would be important to them, and a place where they might meet a wise or magical person. Altogether their fantasies were about respite and looking within as opposed to frolicsome play. (Personal correspondence, 1997)

The spaces in Purple Moon's game are quiet, contemplative places, rendered in naturalistic detail but with the soft focus and warm glow of an impressionistic watercolor.

The world of *Secret Paths* explodes with subtle and inviting colors—the colors of a forest on a summer afternoon, of spring flowers and autumn leaves and shifting patterns of light, of rippling water and moonlit skies, of sand and earth. The soundtrack is equally dense and engaging, as the natural world whispers to us in the rustle of the undergrowth or sings to us in the sounds of the wind and the calls of birds. The spaces of *Secret Paths* are full of life, as lizards slither from rock to rock or field mice dart for cover, yet even animals that might be frightening in other contexts (coyotes, foxes, owls) seem eager to reveal their secrets to our explorers. Jesse, one of the game's protagonists, expresses a fear of the "creepy" nighttime woods, but the game makes the animals seem tame and the forest safe, even in the dead of night. The game's puzzles reward careful exploration and observation. At one point, we must cautiously approach a timid fawn if we wish to be granted the magic jewels that are the tokens of our quest. The guidebook urges us to be "unhurried and gentle" with the "easily startled" deer.

Our goal is less to master nature than to understand how we might live in harmony with it. We learn to mimic its patterns, to observe the notes (produced by singing cactus) that make a lizard's head bob with approval and then to copy them ourselves, to position spiders on a web so that they may harmonize rather than create discord. And, in some cases, we are rewarded for feeding and caring for the animals. In the novel *The Secret Garden*, Mary Lennox is led by a robin to the branches that mask the entrance to the forgotten rose garden:

> Mary had stepped close to the robin, and suddenly the gusts of wind swung aside some loose ivy trails, and more suddenly still she jumped toward it and caught it in her hand. This she did because she had seen something under it—a round knob which had been covered by the leaves hanging over it. . . . The robin kept singing and twittering away and tilting his head on one side, as if he were as excited as she was. (p. 80)

Such animal guides abound in *Secret Paths*: the cursor is shaped like a ladybug during our explorations and like a butterfly when we want to venture beyond the current screen. Animals show us the way, if we only take the time to look and listen.

Unlike twitch-and-shoot boys' games, *Secret Paths* encourages us to stroke and caress the screen with our cursor, clicking only when we know where secret treasures might be hidden. A magic book tells us: "As I patiently traveled along [through the paths], I found that everything was enchanted! The trees, flowers and animals, the sun, sky and stars—all had magical properties! The more closely I listened and the more carefully I explored, the more was revealed to me." Nature's rhythms are gradual and recurring, a continual process of birth, growth, and transformation. Laurel explains:

> We made the "game" intentionally slow—a girl can move down the paths at whatever pace, stop and play with puzzles or stones, or hang out in the tree house with or without the other characters. I think that this slowness is really a kind of refuge for the girls. The game is much slower than television, for example. One of the issues that girls have raised with us in our most recent survey of their concerns is the problem of feeling too busy. I think that "Secret Paths" provides an antidote to that feeling from the surprising source of the computer. (Personal correspondence, 1997)

Frances Hodgson Burnett's "Secret Garden" is a place of healing, and the book links Mary's restoration of the forgotten rose garden with her repairing a family torn apart by tragedy, restoring a sickly boy to health, and coming to grips with her mother's death:

> So long as Mistress Mary's mind was full of disagreeable thoughts about her dislikes and sour opinions of people and determined not to be pleased by or interested in anything, she was a yellow-faced, sickly, bored and wretched child. . . . When her mind gradually filled itself with robins, and moorland cottages crowded with children . . . with springtime and with secret gardens coming alive day by day. . . there was no room for the disagreeable thoughts which affected her liver and her digestion and made her yellow and tired. (p. 294)

Purple Moon's *Secret Paths* has also been designed as a healing place, where girls are encouraged to "explore with your heart" and answer their emotional dilemmas. As the magical book explains, "You will never be alone here, for this is a place where girls come to share and to seek help from one another." At the game's opening, we draw together a group of female friends in the treehouse, where each confesses her secrets and tells of her worries and sufferings. Miko speaks of the pressure to always be the best and the alienation she feels from the other children; Dana recounts her rage over losing a soccer companionship; Minn describes her humiliation because her immigrant grandmother has refused to assimilate to New World customs. Some of them have lost parents; others face scary situations or emotional slights that cripple their confidence. Their answers lie along the secret paths through the forest, where the adventurers can find hidden magical stones that embody social, psychological, or emotional strengths. Along the way, the girls' secrets are literally embedded within the landscape, so that clicking on our environment may call forth memories or confessions. If we are successful in finding all of the hidden stones, they magically form a necklace, and, when given to the right girl, they allow us to hear a comforting or clarifying story. Such narratives teach girls how to find emotional resources within themselves and how to observe and respond to others' often unarticulated needs. Solving puzzles in the physical environment helps us to address problems in our social environment. *Secret Paths* is what Brenda Laurel calls a "friendship adventure," allowing young girls to rehearse their coping skills and try alternative social strategies.

The Play Town: Another Space for Girls?

> Harriet was trying to explain to Sport how to play Town, "See, first you make up the name of the town. Then you write down the names of all the people who live in it. . . . Then when you know who lives there, you make up what they do. For instance, Mr. Charles Hanley runs the filling station on the corner. . . . Harriet got very businesslike. She stood up, then got on her knees in the soft September mud so she could lean over the little valley made between the two big roots of the tree. She referred to her notebook every now and then, but for the most part she stared intently at the mossy lowlands which made her town.[33]
> —Louise Fitzhugh, *Harriet the Spy* (1964)

Harriet the Spy opens with a description of another form of spatial play for girls—Harriet's "town," a "micro-world" she maps onto the familiar contours of her own backyard and uses to think through the complex social relations she observes in her community. Harriet controls the inhabitants of this town, shaping their actions to her desires: "In this town, everybody goes to bed at nine-thirty" (p. 4). Not unlike soap operas, her stories depend on juxtapositions of radically different forms of human experience: "Now, this night, as Mr. Hanley is just about to close up, a long, big old black car drives up and in it there are all these men with guns. . . . At this same minute Mrs. Harrison's baby is born" (p. 6). Her fascination with mapping and controlling the physical space of the town makes her game a pre-digital prototype for *Sim City* and other simulation games. However, compared to Harriet's vivid interest in the distinct personalities and particular experiences of her townspeople, *Sim City* seems alienated and abstract. *Sim City*'s classifications of land use into residential, commercial, and industrial push us well beyond the scale of everyday life and, in so doing, strip the landscape of its potential as a stage for children's fantasies. *Sim City* offers us another form of power— the power to "play God," to design our physical environment, to sculpt the landscape or call down natural disasters, but not the power to imaginatively transform our social environment.[34] *Sim City* embraces stock themes from boys' play, such as building forts, shaping earth with toy trucks, or damming creeks, playing them out on a much larger scale. For Harriet, the mapping of the space was only the first step in preparing the ground for a rich saga of life and death, joy and sorrow—the very elements that are totally lacking in most simulation games.

As Fitzhugh's novel continues, Harriet's interests shift from the imaginary events of her simulated town and into real-world spaces. She "spies" on people's private social interactions, staging more and more "daring" investigations, trying to understand what motivates adult actions, and writing her evaluations and interpretations of their lives in her notebook. Harriet's adventures take her well beyond the constricted space of her own home. She breaks into houses and takes rides on dumbwaiters, sneaks through back alleys and peeps into windows. She barely avoids getting caught. Harriet's adventures occur in public space (not the private space of the secret garden), a populated environment (not the natural worlds visited in *Secret Paths*). Yet, her adventures are not so much direct struggles with opposing forces (as might be found in a boys' book adventure) as covert operations to ferret out knowledge of social relations.

The games of Theresa Duncan (*Chop Suey, Smarty, Zero Zero*) offer a digital version of Harriet's "Town." Players can explore suburban and urban spaces and pry into bedroom closets in search of the extraordinary dimensions of ordinary life. Duncan specifically cites *Harriet the Spy* as an influence, hoping that her games will grant young girls "a sense of inquisitiveness and wonder."[35] *Chop Suey* and *Smarty* take place in small Midwestern towns, a working-class world of diners, hardware stores, and beauty parlors. *Zero Zero* draws us further from home—into fin de siècle Paris, a world of bakeries, wax museums, and catacombs. These spaces are rendered in a distinctive style somewhere between the primitiveness of Grandma Moses and the colorful postmodernism of *Pee-Wee's Playhouse*. Far removed from the romantic imagery of *Secret Paths*, these worlds overflow with city sounds—the clopping of horse hooves on cobblestones, barking dogs, clanging church bells in *Zero Zero*—and the narrator seems fascinated with the smokestacks and signs that clutter this manmade environment. As the narrator in *Zero Zero* rhapsodizes, "Smoke curled black and feathery like a horse's tale from a thousand chimney pots" in this world "before popsicles and paperbacks." While the social order has been tamed, posing few dangers, Duncan has not rid these worlds of their more disreputable elements. The guy in the candy shop in *Chop Suey* has covered his body with tattoos. The Frenchmen in *Zero Zero* are suitably bored, ill-tempered, and insulting; even flowers hurl abuse at us. The man in the antlered hat sings rowdy songs about "bones" and "guts" when we visit the catacombs, and the women puff on cigarettes, wear too much make-up, flash their cleavage, and hint about illicit rendezvous. Duncan suggests: "There's a sense of bittersweet experience in *Chop Suey*, where not everyone has had a perfect life but they're all happy people. Vera has three ex-husbands all named Bob. . . . Vera has problems, but she's also filled with love. And she's just a very vibrant, alive person, and that's why she fascinates the little girls." Duncan rejects our tendency to "project this fantasy of purity and innocence onto children," suggesting that all this "niceness" deprives children of "the richness of their lives" and does not help them come to grips with their "complicated feelings" toward the people around them.[36]

Duncan's protagonists, June Bug (*Chop Suey*), Pinkee LeBrun (*Zero Zero*), are smart, curious girls who want to know more than they have been told. Daring Pinkee scampers along the roofs of Paris and pops down chimneys or steps boldly through the doors of shops, questioning adults about their visions for the new century. Yet, she is also interested in smaller, more intimate questions, such as the identity of the secret admirer who writes love poems to Bon Bon, the singer at the Follies. Clues unearthed in one location may shed light on mysteries posed elsewhere, allowing Duncan to suggest something of the "interconnectedness" of life within a close community. Often, as in *Harriet the Spy*, the goal is less to evaluate these people than to understand what makes them tick. In that sense, the game fosters the character-centered reading practices that Segel associates with the "girls' book" genres, reading practices that thrive on gossip and speculation.

Zero Zero and Duncan's other games take particular pleasure in anarchistic imagery, in ways we can disrupt and destabilize the environment, showering the baker's angry face with white clouds of flour, ripping off the table cloths, or shaking up soda bottles so they will pop their corks. Often, there is something vaguely naughty about the game activities, as when a visit to Poire, the fashion designer, has us matching different pairs of underwear. In that sense, Duncan's stories preserve the mischievous and sometimes antisocial character of Harriet's antics and the transformative humor of Lewis Carroll, encouraging the young gamers to take more risks and to try things that might not ordinarily meet their parents' approval. Pinkee's first actions as a baby are to rip the pink ribbons from her hair! Duncan likes her characters free and "unladylike."

Harriet the Spy is ambivalent about its protagonist's escapades: her misadventures are clearly exciting to the book's female readers, but the character herself is socially ostracized and disciplined, forced to more appropriately channel her creativity and curiosity. Pinkee suffers no such punishment: at the end of the game we find her watching the fireworks that mark the change of the centuries, taking pleasure in the knowledge that she will be a central part of the changes that are coming: "tonight belongs to Bon Bon but the future belongs to Pinkee."

Conclusion: Toward a Gender-Neutral Play Space?

Brenda Laurel and Theresa Duncan offer two very different conceptions of a digital play space for girls—one pastoral, the other urban; one based on the ideal of living in harmony with nature, the other based on an anarchistic pleasure in disrupting the stable order of everyday life and making the familiar "strange." Yet, in many ways, the two games embrace remarkable similar ideals—play spaces for girls adopt a slower pace, are less filled with dangers, invite gradual investigation and discovery, foster an awareness of social relations and a search for secrets, and center around the emotional lives of their characters. Both allow the exploration of physical environments but are really about the interior worlds of feelings and fears. Laurel and Duncan make important contributions when they propose new and different models for how digital media may be used. The current capabilities of our video and computer game technologies reflect the priorities of an earlier generation of game makers and their conception of the boys' market. Their assumptions about what kinds of digital play spaces were desirable defined how the bytes would be allocated, valuing rapid response time over the memory necessary to construct more complex and compelling characters. Laurel and Duncan shift the focus, prioritizing character relations and "friendship adventures." In doing so, they are expanding what computers can do and what roles they can play in our lives.

On the other hand, in our desire to open digital technologies as an alternative play space for girls, we must guard against simply duplicating in the new medium the gender-specific genres of children's literature. The segregation of children's reading into boys' and girls' book genres, Segel argues, encouraged the development of gender-specific reading strategies—with boys reading for plot and girls for character relationship. Such differences, Segel suggests, taught children to replicate the separation between a male public sphere of risk-taking and a female domestic sphere of care-taking. The classification of children's literature into boys' books and girls' books "extracted a heavy cost in feminine self-esteem," restricting girls' imaginative experience to what adults perceived as its "proper place."[37] Boys developed a sense of autonomy and mastery both from their reading and from their play. Girls learned to fetter their imaginations, just as they restricted their movements into real-world spaces. At the same time, this genre division limited boys' psychological and emotional development, insuring a focus on goal-oriented, utilitarian, and violent plots. Too much interest in social and emotional life was a vulnerability in a world where competition left little room to be "led by your heart." We need to design digital play spaces that allow girls to do something more than stitch doll clothes, mother nature, or heal their friend's sufferings, and for boys to do something more than battle it out with the barbarian hordes.

Segel's analysis of "gender and childhood reading" suggests two ways of moving beyond the gender segregation of our virtual landscape. First, as she suggests, the designation of books for boys and girls did not preclude (though it certainly discouraged) reading across gender lines: Reading boys' books gave girls (admittedly limited) access to the boy culture and its values. Segel finds evidence of such gender-crossing in the nineteenth century, though girls were actively discouraged from reading boys' books because their contents were thought too lurid and unwholesome. At other times, educational authorities encouraged the assignment of boys' books in public schools since girls could read and enjoy them, while there was much greater stigma attached to boys reading girls' books. The growing visibility of the "quake girls," female gamers who compete in traditional male fighting and action/adventure games, suggests that there has always been a healthy degree of "crossover" interest in the games market and that many girls enjoy "playing with power."[38] Girls may compete more directly and aggressively with boys in the video game arena than would ever have been possible in the real world of backyard play, since differences in actual size, strength, and agility have no effect on the outcome of the game. They can return from combat without the ripped clothes or black eyes that told parents they had done something "unladylike." Unfortunately, much as girls who read boys books were likely to encounter the misogynistic themes that mark boys' fantasies of separation from their mothers, girls who play boys' games find that the games' constructions of female sexuality and power are designed to gratify preadolescent males, not to empower girls.

We need to open up more space for girls to join—or play alongside—the traditional boy culture down by the river, in the old vacant lot, within the bamboo forest. Girls need to learn how to explore "unsafe" and "unfriendly" spaces. Girls need to experience the "complete freedom of movement" promised by the boys' games—if not all the time, then at least some of the time—if they are going to develop the self-confidence and competitiveness demanded of contemporary professional women. Girls need to be able to play games where Barbie gets to kick some butt. However, this focus on creating action games for girls still represents only part of the answer, for as Segel notes, the gender segregation of children's literature was almost as damaging for boys as it was for girls. Boys may need to play in secret gardens or toy towns just as much as girls need to explore adventure islands. In the literary realm, Segel points to books such as *Little House on the Prairie* or *Wrinkle in Time*, which fuse the boys and girl genres, rewarding both a traditionally masculine interest in plot action and a traditionally feminine interest in character relations.

Sega Saturn's *Nights into Dreams* represents a similar fusion of the boys' and girls' game genres. Much as in *Secret Paths*, our movement through the game space is framed as an attempt to resolve the characters' emotional problems. In the frame stories that open the game, we enter the mindscape of the two protagonists as they toss and turn in their sleep.

Claris, the female protagonist, hopes to gain recognition on the stage as a singer, but has nightmares of being rejected and ridiculed. Elliot, the male character, has fantasies of scoring big on the basketball court yet fears being bullied by bigger and more aggressive players. They run away from their problems, only to find themselves in Nightopia, where they must save the dream world from the evil schemes of Wileman the Wicked and his monstrous minions. In the dream world, both Claris and Elliot may assume the identity of Nights, an androgynous harlequin figure, who can fly through the air, transcending all the problems below. Nights' complex mythology has players gathering glowing orbs that represent different forms of energy needed to confront Claris's and Elliot's problems—purity (white), wisdom (green), hope (yellow), intelligence (blue), and bravery (red)—a structure that recalls the magic stones in *Secret Paths through the Forest*.

Spring Valley is a sparkling world of rainbows and waterfalls and Emerald Green forests. Other levels allow us to splash through cascading fountains, or sail past icy mountains and frozen wonderlands, or bounce on pillows and off the walls of the surreal Soft Museum, or swim through aquatic tunnels. The game's 3-D design allows an exhilarating freedom of movement. *Nights into Dreams* also retains some of the dangerous and risky elements associated with the boys' games. There are spooky places in this game, including nightmare worlds full of Day-Glo serpents and winged beasties, and there are enemies we must battle, yet there is also a sense of unconstrained adventure, of floating through the clouds. When we lose Nights' magical, gender-bending garb, we turn back into boys and girls and must hoof it as pedestrians across the rugged terrain below, a situation that makes it far less likely we will achieve our goals. To be gendered is to be constrained; to escape gender is to escape gravity and to fly above it all.

Sociologist Barrie Thorne has discussed the forms of "borderwork" that occurs when boys and girls occupy the same play spaces: "The spatial separation of boys and girls [on the same playground] constitutes a kind of boundary, perhaps felt most strongly by individuals who want to join an activity controlled by the other gender."[39] Boys and girls are brought together in the same space, but they repeatedly enact the separation and opposition between the two play cultures. In real-world play, this "borderwork" takes the form of chases and contests on the one hand, and "cooties" or other pollution taboos on the other. When "borderwork" occurs, gender distinctions become extremely rigid and nothing passes between the two spheres. Something similar occurs in many of the books Segel identifies as gender-neutral—male and female reading interests co-exist, side by side, like children sharing a playground, and yet they remain resolutely separate and the writers, if anything, exaggerate gender differences in order to proclaim their dual address. In *Peter Pan*, Wendy and the "lost boys" travel to Neverland but Wendy plays house and the "lost boys" play Indians or pirates. The "little house" and the "prairie" exist side by side in Laura Wilder's novels, but the mother remains trapped inside the house, while Pa ventures into the prairie. The moments when the line between the little house and the prairie are crossed, such as a scene where a Native American penetrates into Ma Wilder's parlor, become moments of intense anxiety.

As we develop digital play spaces for boys and girls, we need to make sure this same pattern isn't repeated, that we do not create blue and pink ghettos inside it. On the one hand, the opening sequences of *Nights into Dreams*, which frame Elliot and Claris as possessing fundamentally different dreams (sports for boys and musical performance for girls, graffiti-laden inner city basketball courts for boys and pastoral gardens for girls), perform this kind of borderwork, defining the proper place for each gender. On the other hand, the androgynous Nights embody a fantasy of transcending gender and thus achieving the freedom and mobility to fly above it all. To win the game, the player must become both the male and the female protagonist, and the two must join forces for the final level. The penalty for failure in this world is to be trapped on the ground and to be fixed into a single gender.

Thorne finds that aggressive "borderwork" is more likely to occur in prestructured institutional settings such as schoolyards, where children are forced together by adults, than when they find themselves interacting more spontaneously in the informal settings of the subdivisions and apartment complexes. All of this suggests that our fantasy of designing games that will provide common play spaces for girls and boys may be an illusive one, as full of complications and challenges on its own terms as creating a "girls' only" space or encouraging girls to venture into traditional male turf. We are not yet sure what such a gender-neutral space will look like. Creating such a space would mean redesigning not only the nature of computer games but also the nature of society. The danger may be that in such a space, gender differences are going to be more acutely felt, as boys and girls will be repelled from each other rather than drawn together. There are reasons why this is a place where neither the feminist entrepreneurs nor the boys' game companies are ready to go, yet as the girls' market is secured, the challenge must be to find a way to move beyond our existing categories and to once again invent new kinds of virtual play spaces.

9

"Her Suffering Aristocratic Majesty"
The Sentimental Value of Lassie

> Nostalgia is a sadness without an object, a sadness which creates a longing that of necessity is inauthentic because it does not take part in lived experience. Rather, it remains behind and before that experience. Nostalgia, like any form of narrative, is always ideological: the past it seeks has never existed except as narrative, and hence, always absent, that past continually threatens to reproduce itself as a felt lack.
>
> —Susan Stewart, *On Longing* (1993)

> His mother had asked him to forget about Lassie but he could not. He could pretend to and he could stop talking about her. But in his mind Lassie would always go on living. . . . He would sit at his desk at school and dream of her. He would think that perhaps some day—some day—like a dream come true, he would come out of school and there she would be, sitting at the gate.
>
> —Eric Knight, *Lassie Come-Home* (1940)

The year is 1954. A television legend debuts. Jeff Miller, a simple farm boy, squirms in his suit and tie as he listens to the reading of a neighbor's will. The bored boy is overjoyed when he learns that he is to receive "the best thing," a collie named Lassie. However, Lassie refuses to leave the house where she has lived since she was a puppy. When Jeff takes her away by force, she escapes and runs back "home." As "Gramps" explains, "The Lord made animals free just like human beings and you can't force them to love you."

Actually, Lassie is protecting the old man's savings from the untrust-worthy handyman. She fights fiercely when he tries to steal the money; Jeff brings help, capturing the crook. Then, at last, Lassie consents to live with Jeff and obey his commands. "She's my dog now, isn't she, Gramps?" Jeff enthuses, and "Gramps" confirms his rightful ownership, "Yes— she's all yours now. She's done her deciding." Thus begins *Lassie*, the longest-running children's series in American television history.

In "Inheritance," the series pilot, the issue of Lassie's legal and eco-nomic ownership is settled quickly. No one contests the old man's will. However, the issue of the animal's moral allegiance lingers. "Inheritance" must assess both the worth of the dog (which another boy discounts, "Who wants an old she-dog? All they do is have pups!") and the worth of its potential owner (which is proven through patience, love, and courage). *Lassie* ascribes a moral intelligence to the collie—she can divine human motives and character. Both the handyman's criminality and Jeff's virtues are instantly legible to Lassie. She faithfully repays her old master before doing her "deciding."

The episode's core images—the dog who remains loyal beyond her owner's death, who comes home even when she is given away, and who rewards the virtuous and punishes the corrupt—reflect a larger history, the sentimentalization of dogs in the previous century.[1] In the late nine-teenth century, the bourgeois imagination created a mythic image of ca-nine fidelity, compatible with prevailing romanticist tendencies. Many ex-perienced the onset of modernity with a sense of nostalgic loss. Old social commitments were breaking down and the organic ties of traditional communities were giving way to alienated and individualistic urban life. However, no matter what else changed, you could count on "man's best friend." Dogs' loyalty to their masters stood in stark contrast to the per-ceived breakdown of social ties between their human owners. As social historian Kathleen Kete notes, many of these idealistic images of canine fidelity had entered children's stories by the twentieth century. Yet, Kete does not address what these images might mean in the context of chil-dren's fiction, where the fidelity of the dog spills over into and gives new life to widely circulating myths about childhood innocence. Addressing that question in turn opens up the whole issue of children's fiction, its re-lation to adult needs, its mythic construction of the child, and its ties to nostalgic longing.

Lassie stands at the nexus of two central ideological reconceptualiza-tions, both of which occurred during the late nineteenth century: the first centered around the transformation of dogs from domesticated animals (whose value resided in their productive labor or exchange price) into "pets" (whose value was primarily sentimental); the second centered around the "sacralization" of the child, that is, the displacement of children as sources of economic revenue and productive labor and the need to create a compensatory affective value. Probably the most popular in a series of dog books written in the twentieth century and aimed primarily at children, *Lassie Come-Home* represented a systematic exploration of human affective investments in and sentimental attachments to dogs. These issues cling to Lassie as she travels across different media and is re-groomed to fit changing tastes.

This essay will investigate the sentimental and symbolic value of Lassie as a "popular hero" of literature, film, and television.[2] As she roams, Lassie gets entangled within contemporary discourses about class, gender, nationalism, modernity, and childhood. First, I will identify the issues of ownership and emotional bonds that structure Eric Knight's book, and then I will look more closely at some key turning points within the television series involving the exchange of Lassie (starting with the 1954 pilot episode and moving through the 1964 shift from Timmy to Ranger Stuart). Since undying fidelity defines the ideal pet, these negotiations of ownership constitute potential crisis points where viewer loyalties must also be transferred between series protagonists. In each case, melodramatic devices insure a smooth transition, yet potential ideological problems surface that threaten the long-term stability of Lassie's "family values." This essay is, first and foremost, an investigation of the process of nostalgic longing and sentimental investment, of the ways children and dogs become vehicles for the hopes and fears of human adults.

Like most children's works, *Lassie* seems to exist outside of any historical context (history being a grown-up concern) and "innocent" of all but the most blatant ideological content (the morals at the end of the stories speak all the truths). *Lassie* appears in our minds in broadly drawn images, like the pages of a coloring book: the mother in the kitchen and the father in the tool shed; Timmy and Lassie romping across the open countryside; the dog rescuing an injured camper or mothering a lost fawn; the collie winning a blue ribbon at the country fair; a tearful boy clutching Lassie's white mane.[3] We preserve childhood as a utopian space free from adult concerns and controversies, a period of naive idealism and trust betrayed by the adult world. We are too cynical to embrace those feelings once again, yet our need to hold onto them is too urgent, and so we treat children's fictions as banal and meaningless.[4] This essay represents an attempt to cut through our foggy cultural myth of "childhood innocence" in order to reconstruct the historical contexts shaping the popular circulation and consumption of *Lassie*, a series I take to be central both to our cultural understanding of the dog and to the post–World War II construction of American boyhood.

Perhaps not surprisingly, the most significant meanings to be found in children's fictions are adult anxieties about our children's world and adult fantasies about how children (and dogs) may become vehicles for social transformation and personal redemption. What James Kincaid has said of the child holds for the dog as well: "The child carries for us things we somehow cannot carry for ourselves, sometimes anxieties we want to be divorced from and sometimes pleasures so great we would not, without the child, know how to contain them."[5] In the adult symbolic order, dogs and children are primarily beasts of burden, who are assumed powerless to speak for themselves. The muteness of dogs and the inarticulateness of children are mysteries the adult imagination seeks to penetrate—part of their charm, part of their fascination. To serve adult purposes, the innocence of children and the intelligence and fidelity of dogs have been fetishized, endowed with a broad range of connotative associations and meanings. Dogs and children are assumed to be supra- or non-human: the child's innocence pulls it away from the adult realm while the dog's intelligence pulls it toward that realm, yet both remain outside. They exist in a state of nature, or so the mythology goes, so that the meanings that seem to originate from within them are pre-social and pre-ideological. The communication between children and dogs is immediate, concrete, and closed to grown-ups. Ideology gets naturalized through its association with children and dogs, and thus they remain our most powerful symbols for speaking about what is most "precious," "pure," and "valuable" in the face of modernity and change.

Home and Hardship: Lassie Come-Home

The opening of Eric Knight's 1940 children's novel *Lassie Come-Home* is preoccupied with Lassie's value. In a dog-centered Yorkshire culture where, Knight tells us, "the dogs [are] rich-coated and as sturdy as the people who live there," Lassie is universally admired: "Every man in the village agreed that she was the finest collie he had ever laid eyes on."[6] Her value lies in her physical beauty, her intelligence and good habits ("You can set your clock by her"), and, most importantly, her symbolic function. In a period of economic hardship, Lassie's owners have refused to sell her, even when offered lordly sums, and so Lassie "represented some sort of pride that money had not been able to take away from them" (p. 4). Her economic value (as an "expensive" animal) has been translated into sentimental and symbolic worth (as a "priceless" animal).

This tension between dog's economic and sentimental value can be traced back to what Kete describes as "the embourgeoise-ment of the beast" in the nineteenth century.[7] By mid-century, dogs were understood as falling into two broad categories—the work dogs owned by the lower class and the show dogs or lap dogs owned by the wealthy. French tax policy sought to draw a distinction between "useful" and "useless" dogs, and, by so doing, to restrict dog ownership to those who either depended upon work dogs for their economic livelihood or could afford a pet's expenses. Owners of work animals suffered little taxation, while pets were taxed as luxuries. Dogs were viewed as pets if they roamed freely in the home, accompanied the master on walks, or played with children. However, as pet ownership expanded from an upper-class phenomenon to an activity of ordinary citizens, the ideologies surrounding human attachments to animals spread across the culture.[8] Bourgeois pet-keepers claimed that a dog's emotional support and physical protection were essential aspects of modern life. In this context, myths circulated about dog's fidelity to man—which exceeded all reason or human understanding.

Especially popular were stories about dogs that traveled tremendous distances to be rejoined with their human owners. Victor Hugo, for example, wrote of a beloved dog which, in a moment of bad judgment, he gave to a Russian count; astonishingly, the dog found his way from Moscow to Paris. Such stories formed the foundation for *Lassie Come-Home*, which similarly deals with a dog's incredible journey. These tales privilege the emotional relations between humans and their pets over economic exchanges that threaten to sever those bonds. The dog becomes a moral arbiter of all exchanges, instinctively negating deals that unjustly break its moral allegiances. Against both economic arrangements and natural barriers, the dog returns home to redeem its master.

Knight's decision to make Lassie a collie seems ideally suited for exploring competing bids on a dog's worth. Collies were almost totally unknown in the United States when Knight wrote the book, which was dedicated to Dr. Harry Jarrett, the American veterinarian who sought to introduce the breed. For Knight, the choice of the collie evoked nostalgia for the Yorkshire country of his youth, where these gentle-natured dogs are more common.[9] The collie enjoyed a dual status in British culture: on the one hand, the breed was a favorite of Queen Victoria, closely associated with the aristocracy and highly valued as a show dog among breeders; on the other hand, the collie was an excellent work dog, especially good at herding.[10] Knight plays with this contradiction between the collie's aristocratic and common associations: "You can go into any one of the hundreds of small mining villages in this largest of England's counties, and see, walking at the heels of humbly clad workmen, dogs of such a fine breed and aristocratic bearing as to arouse the envy of the wealthier dog fanciers from other parts of the world" (p. 1). Knight speaks of the "suffering aristocratic majesty" (p.34) of Lassie in captivity; characters affectionately refer to her as "Her Majesty" (p. 157) and "Herself" (p.146). At the same time, her ties to working-class culture are never in doubt. As she moves across the British countryside, she forms bonds and affections almost exclusively with the poor—with an elderly farm couple still mourning the wartime loss of their son; with a traveling busker eking out a meager living; and, most powerfully, with the Carracloughs, a poor mining family momentarily on the dole.

Yet, interestingly, Knight tells us nothing of collies' economic functions. Sam Carraclough is a miner, not a herdsman, and so the collie contributes nothing to his livelihood. Rather, the dog is experienced as an expense, increasingly difficult to justify in hard times. As Knight writes, "The poor man sits and thinks about how much coal he will need that winter, and how many pairs of shoes will be necessary, and how much food his children ought to have to keep them sturdy" (p. 3). There is no difference, he claims, between the love rich men and poor men bestow on their dogs. Yet, he seems to suggest something quite different: that for the rich, dogs are often things that can be bought and bargained over, while for the poor they are creatures who must be loved and sacrificed for.

By the second chapter, despite Sam's reluctance, the dog has been sold to the Duke of Rudling to become a prize show dog. The sale sets off a contest between the intense emotional and moral bonds that link Lassie to the Carracloughs and the Duke's legal right to possess the dog as the object of an economic exchange. Sam possesses a rock-hard morality and sees the economic transaction as irreversible: "No matter how many words tha says, tha can't alter that she's sold, and we've taken the Duke's brass and spent it, and now she belongs to him" (p.52). Yet, in Knight's world, the ownership of a dog is a moral contract, which, once violated, must be set right no matter what the cost. And so the book tells us the story of Lassie's many attempts to escape from the Duke and return home, including a torturous thousand-mile journey from the lord's Scottish estate back to her family in Yorkshire.

The book plays with the double meanings attached to the phrase "come-home dogs." Early in the book, Hymes, the Duke's unpleasant and shiftless kennel-keeper, accuses the Carracloughs of training their dog to escape and "come home" so that she can be sold more than once. By the book's conclusion, Joe, the boy, praises Lassie as a "come-home dog," because she has suffered and endured endless hardship to "come home" to the people she loves and who love her. The contradiction resolves itself when the Duke concedes her to her original owners, hires Carraclough to run his kennels, and invites them to come live on his estate. As the Duke explains to his granddaughter, "For five years I've sworn I'd have that dog. And now I've got her. But I had to buy the man to get her" (p. 192).

Lassie's incredible journey has temporarily resolved the book's core class conflict, reconciling the competing claims made for her possession. Joe reads this social transformation in the most utopian of terms: "When she [Lassie] had been home, things had been right. When she was sold and gone, nothing had gone right any more. And now that she was back, everything was fine again, and they were all very happy" (p. 197). Many readers, and some critics, take Joe's thoughts at face value—as the moral of the tale, as a celebration of a child's simple faith and the redemptive power of dogs.[11]

Certainly, the book's sentimental ending is all of this, yet such a reading is profoundly reductive. At the time he wrote *Lassie Come-Home*, first as a short story for *Saturday Evening Post* and, later, expanded into a novel, Knight was known primarily as a journalist and a writer of adult novels.[12] Like his close friend, documentary filmmaker Paul Rotha, Knight was interested in documenting the economic conditions and personal hardship faced by the British working class. In his "local color" novels, *Invitation to Life, Song on Your Bugles, The Happy Land,* and *This Above All,* Knight wrote with nostalgia and remorse about the decline of the world of his boyhood and about the problems confronting small English village life in the modern era; he described British workers as having "lost their pride . . . their dignity of being through the industrial paralysis, the narcotic of the dole, the meaningless slavery of the labor camps, the dunderheaded stubbornness of the middle class, the inertia of the leaders."[13] Contemporary critics compared his novels to Richard Llewellyn's *How Green Was My Valley* and J. M. Barrie's *The Little Minister*. Like Llewellyn and Barrie, Knight hoped that his sentimental realism would awaken public consciousness about the decline of traditional British culture. In creating *Lassie Come-Home*, Knight was aware that he was writing a children's book, yet he hoped that Lassie might also further social reform. Lassie was, he wrote to Rotha, less about a dog than about the "tremendous economic problem" that forces the family to sell her.[14] Here, Knight translates the consequences of this social and economic crisis into the image of a child's trust betrayed and a dog's loyalty violated.

His linkage of those two sentimental icons—the boy and the dog—was no accident. As Kete's discussion of the French tax codes suggests, the interactions between dogs and children helped to define the legal status of canines as domestic "pets." Moreover, the period between the 1870s and the 1930s had witnessed what historian Viviana A. Zelizer describes as the "sacralization" of childhood.[15] Zelizer investigates the changing economic and emotional "value" of children through close examination of debates about child labor, issues surrounding insurance and funeral expenses for children, and a variety of other everyday economic transactions that shaped family life during this key transitional period. The birth of a child in nineteenth-century America was greeted as an expansion of the family's earning power. Reflecting middle-class security from immediate want, a new conception of the child, based on sentimental rather than economic value, gained popular circulation by century's end. The "priceless" bourgeois child was to be protected from the harsh realities of the adult work world. Middle-class reformers sought to impose this new conception of the child as "innocent," "pure" and "dependent" upon the larger society, passing laws restricting child labor or regulating child abuse. This economic and legal transformation coincided with medical breakthroughs that insured that a higher proportion of children would live into adulthood; the primary focus of concern shifted from disease and other health risks to concerns for children's mental and emotional well-being. The result was a greater affective investment in the individual child. The expenses of raising a child needed to be rationalized in terms of the affective rewards of parenting, not in terms of the child's potential economic contribution to the family's welfare.

The figure of the innocent child quickly became a vehicle for social criticism against the corrupting influences of the modern world. Mary Lynn Stevens Heininger's examination of representations of children in literature, art, and material culture confirms Zelizer's arguments, seeing fictional children as speaking both to popular pessimism about the present and to utopian hopes for the future. The desire to separate children from the adult sphere highlighted the "vicious, materialistic and immoral qualities of American society."[16] On the one hand, popular representations posed children as "soft and smiling foils to a more grim and grownup reality." They were pure victims of contemporary social ills. On the other hand, as Heininger notes, the notion of the "pristine" child embodied a utopian fantasy of renewal and rebirth. The child came to represent the modern era's hopes for the future.

The dual mythic functions of "childhood innocence" can be linked to the two different children in *Lassie Come-Home*: Joe, the poor boy who is so beloved by Lassie, and Priscilla, the Duke's much-prized granddaughter. Joe is almost suprahumanly innocent, naive about the harsh economic realities his family confronts, unable to understand the sacrifices his parents have already made, and eternally optimistic that the dog will find its way home. The violation of his blind trust seems almost too painful to bear. Knight allows the child-reader to recognize the signs of poverty (the father reaching for a pipe he can no longer fill with tobacco, the mother cutting back on sugar or bursting into tears when Joe asks about meat), and thus to confront the painful truths Joe is never forced to face. Priscilla, on the other hand, seems suprahumanly precocious, the only upper-class character who fully grasps the Carracloughs' love for Lassie. Her understanding comes from recognition of common emotional experience, while Hymes maintains a profound distrust of the working class and her grandfather simply relishes the shrewd bargain. Priscilla prods and probes the adults, ultimately forcing them to recognize human costs and consequences. Priscilla aids Lassie in escaping from her grandfather's estate, rejoices when she is returned to her rightful owner, and coaxes her grandfather into hiring Sam. Priscilla embodies the innocent child as the hope for the future.

In a children's book more in keeping with the American ideology of a "classless" society, we might picture a romance between the poor boy and the rich girl. However, Knight is too much a realist (and too British) to tolerate such imagery, merely suggesting their friendship at the end. Both Joe and Priscilla beam with pride as Lassie nurses a litter of pups, the competing interests of the working and ruling classes reconciled through this classic rebirth image. Strikingly, the birth of Lassie's pups seems to result from an immaculate conception, as if they were brought about through the combined faith and goodness of the two children. No father is ever mentioned, despite the book's ongoing preoccupation with issues of breeding. Lassie is a pure maternal force, outside of brute barnyard reproduction. Part of the construction of childhood innocence, after all, involves denying children both sexuality and sexual knowledge.

However, sexual anxieties surface earlier in the book, when Lassie must fight against a pack of mongrel farm dogs. The purity and superiority of Lassie's "blood" gives her an intelligence and authority the mutts must ultimately respect: "Lassie had something that the others had not. She had blood. She was a pure-bred dog, and behind her were long generations of the proudest and the best of her kind. . . . Where the mongrel dog will whine and slink away, the pure-bred will still stand with uncomplaining fearlessness" (p.104). As Harriet Ritvo has noted, the elaborate set of breed classifications, which emerged in the Victorian dog show culture, became a way of managing and making sense of other problems of race and class distinctions.[17] Middle-class dog owners could claim status through their ownership of pedigreed animals, even if they were locked out of the bloodlines of human aristocracy, while hybrids, half-breeds, and mongrels were seen as debased and potentially dangerous, often standing in for the lower classes in popular discourse about dogs.[18]

Knight consistently makes claims about the traits (sometimes physical, sometimes intellectual or moral) that separate Lassie as a purebred collie from other breeds:

> For collies do not rush and hold. Their way of fighting is not like that of the bulldog; nor like that of the terrier which dodges and worries and shakes. (p.103)

> Lassie had lain still, like a captive queen among lesser prisoners. . . . She did not drop this air of dignity even when the grilled backdrop of the van was opened. The other dogs of mixed breeds yelped anew and darted about. (p.116)

Such distinctions closely parallel the language he uses to speak of class and regional differences among the human characters:

Joe had in him the blood of men who might think slowly and stick to old ideas and bear trouble patiently—but who do not run away. (p.182)

In such passages, stereotypical differences between unreliable cockneys, "hard-headed Scots," and "slow-thinking" but honest Yorkshire men assume the same status as "natural facts" as the breed distinctions among collies, bulldogs, and terriers. The two sets of classifications work side by side to create a legible moral universe. At the same time, they rigidify class and national boundaries. A working-class man can no more become an aristocrat than a bulldog can become a collie, or indeed, than a mongrel can hold its own against a purebred.

When Lassie confronts the mongrel pack, she stands threatened by animals that are not of her kind, who come from the lower orders and thus possess impure "blood" (all the worse since these animals were of collie descent). With all of this emphasis upon the purity of blood, these animals bring with them a threat of rape and miscegenation, a besmirching of Lassie's bloodlines. No wonder Knight describes the scene with such melodramatic excess, the virginal Lassie standing her ground, learning how to fight, and finally forcing the curs to submit. Within this discourse of bloodlines, the stakes are extraordinarily high, having to do with what British sources called telegony, "the contamination of future generations by the first male to mount the bitch."[19] So, if these mongrel animals were to "dominate" (or mount) our heroine, their debased blood would taint all of her future offspring, including the pups so admired by Joe and Priscilla. Knight does not directly articulate this threat to her sexual purity, any more than he explains who actually does sire her pups; it becomes a matter of adult knowingness, seemingly unfit for childhood innocence, yet this question of "blood" lingers over the entire book.

The persistence of this adult knowingness argues against a purely utopian or simplistic reading of the book. Knight knows much more than he can tell—at least, more than he can tell the children. Knight, the documentarist, the realist novelist, seems compelled by the conventions of the children's story to give *Lassie Come-Home* a happy ending. He gives in to the nostalgia that shadows the book, a nostalgia for the simple truths and pure relations of his Yorkshire childhood, one that would appeal to a Britain being torn apart by the forces of modernization.

Yet, as literary critic Susan Stewart suggests, nostalgia sparks "a sadness without an object," a longing for a past that never existed except through the narratives of our own memories and imaginations. However much the book's "local color" reflects Knight's personal memories, the close-knit Carraclough family has no relationship to his own childhood experiences. Knight's father, a Quaker jeweler, deserted the family two years after Eric was born. His mother departed the following year, moving to Russia to serve as governess for the Princess Xenia's children and leaving him with an elderly aunt and uncle. By thirteen—just one year older than Joe is in the book—Eric was forced to work to support the family. His mother moved to the United States and began to send for his siblings one by one; he was the last one to be brought over, some two years after the rest. The separation anxiety that runs through the book, displaced onto the loss of a beloved dog, seems to be the one element that grows most directly from Knight's childhood, while the images of the happy family, of domestic solidarity, are the stuff of nostalgic imaginings. A sense of loss, mourning, death, and separation are integral to the myth of the faithful dog. For Knight, as for the characters in the Lassie saga, this beloved tricolor collie becomes an angelic figure of redemption and healing who can make a damaged and damaging world whole again, who can reverse—at least for one family—the economic crisis destroying traditional British culture.

Domestic Angels and Pastoral Ideals: The Timmy Years

The year is 1957. One night, Lassie stumbles upon the body of a sleeping boy, huddled in the Millers' barn. Hearing the noise, Jeff comes outside. Using Lassie's intelligence and tricks as a vehicle, he tries to communicate with the confused and frightened youngster: "She's smart. If you tell her your name, she can remember it." The boy refuses to speak, and throughout much of the episode, he is believed to be mute. Though tough and strong-willed, the boy, Timmy, radiates innocence and trust, "a little angel with a dirty face." We soon learn that he is an orphan left in the care of elderly and largely indifferent relatives. As his uncle explains, "It ain't any kinda life for a boy on our place. It's lonely with just us." Timmy has run away from home because the boy feared "he wasn't earning his keep," because he was not able to contribute directly to the family's economic well-being. Without the affective bonds of family life, the "priceless" child experiences himself as "worthless." The Millers invite Timmy to stay with them on the farm for the summer, while Jeff and Lassie offer him their friendship and protection.

"The Runaway" begins the process by which the homeless Timmy gets situated within Lassie's construction of the ideal domestic life. Timmy's emotional wounds are nursed and healed by the loving collie. At the same time, "The Runaway" begins the transfer of Lassie's ownership from Jeff to Timmy. Actor Tommy Rettig was perceived as too old to play the boy, and so the producers replaced him with Jon Provost. As one producer explained, "Boys grow up, dogs don't."[20] However, the ideological construction of the faithful dog made it difficult to execute this transfer without considerable care and preparation. Neither the boy nor the dog could be seen to be breaking the intense bond between them without powerful motivation. Jeff could acquire Lassie through the death of her owner and through the power of his love. Timmy, on the other hand, came to own Lassie because of his intense needs for protection and affection.

To facilitate this transference of affection, the producer introduced Timmy half a season before Jeff's departure.[21] Timmy was shown as consistently needing Jeff's help. Playing the older brother role, Jeff moves from child to adult. In "The Spartan," for example, Jeff's lessons on manhood—telling Timmy that boys don't complain—backfires when Timmy catches pneumonia and almost dies. In "The Graduation," Jeff takes on his first job as a vet's assistant, but courts disaster when he leaves Timmy in charge of the clinic and the younger boy frees a rabid dog. The stories hinge upon Jeff's maturity (not yet fully secured) and Timmy's boyish curiosity and emotional vulnerability.

Despite such preparations, "Transition" involved a series of traumatic shifts in the previously secure and stable family life depicted on the program, shifts intensified by the death of George Cleveland, the actor who played the beloved "Gramps." As the episode opens, the characters are mourning "Gramps," whose death forces Jeff to become "the man of the family" and assume responsibility for the farm. Jeff wants to adopt Timmy, but the child welfare office and his mother both insist "Timmy belongs in a home with a mother and a father." In financial trouble, Jeff sells the family farm to the Martins and moves to the city. The Martins become attached to Timmy and provide him a home Recognizing both that Lassie will be unhappy in an urban environment and that Timmy needs her love more than he does, Jeff bestows the beloved beast upon his replacement: "Take good care of him. You always took good care of me." Amid tearful reaction shots, Lassie signals her consent by slowly moving from Jeff to Timmy, and the Miller's car pulls off leaving us with the image of a secure, happy, nuclear family.

To break the bonds between Jeff and Lassie, the producers were forced to disrupt the entire series framework, questioning the stability of the traditional family, the economic security of middle-class farm life, and the "timelessness" of childhood. The producers reintroduced into *Lassie* the problems its "family values" sought to exclude. As writers like Richard Dyer and Fredric Jameson remind us, the utopian fantasies offered by popular entertainment often require the admission of real-world pains, traumas, and anxieties, so that they may be symbolically resolved through commercial fantasy.[22] Much as the original novel reworked class inequalities and economic injustice through the shared love of a dog, television's *Lassie* seeks to cure the uncertainties of postwar American family life. The fatherless Jeff and the orphan Timmy represented the image of a broken family on television at a time when most of the other images of American childhood centered on nuclear families. In reality, of course, in the wake of World War II there were many fatherless children and, despite a postwar decline in divorce, many children of divorce. Childrearing experts such as Benjamin Spock treated such children as "special cases," addressed in the back of the book but excluded from their image of normalcy. *Lassie*, on the other hand, depended upon the creation of such broken families precisely so that they could be healed through Lassie's commitment and affection. So successful was this process of adoption and redemption that the series and its viewers seemed to quickly forget that Timmy was not the natural offspring of the Martins and that this cohesive family was brought together under such abrupt and arbitrary circumstances.

A core paradox within our culture's conception of children's fiction centers on its persistent dependence upon traumatic shifts in fortune, upon melodramatic loss and suffering, given the dominant ideology of "childhood innocence" and the strong imperative to protect children from harsh adult realities. Why does a genre based on "family values" depend so heavily on the threat of the disintegration of the family? Children's fiction often seems to secure our faith in the family by posing a threat—the prospect of a harsher life that tests children's innocence and rewards their commitment to core values, their ability to maintain their virtues even in the face of the worst aspects of the modern world. In this way, children's fictions both shelter children from adult knowingness about the contemporary life and draw narrative power from the threat that the modern world poses for traditional family life.

While few American children's books of the period dealt as frankly as Knight did with the issue of class inequality, *Lassie Come-Home*'s balance between pessimism (the focus on economic problems) and optimism (the prospect of moral healing) was consistent with a growing emphasis upon realism and common experience in the children's books of the 1930s and early 1940s. Lassie's contemporaries, such as *Homer Price* (1943), *Johnny Tremain* (1943), *The Yearling* (1938) or *My Friend Flicka* (1941), sought something akin to the naturalism we associate with adult writers like John Steinbeck, depicting "ordinary people, living under recognizable pressures."[23] These writers temper the pessimism of naturalism, however, with an optimism facilitated by the "innocent child." Reviewing the dominant tendencies in postwar children's fiction, Sally Allen McNall writes:

> Despite the greater realism of their settings, these books showed problems being solved with ease by boys and girls of common sense and good will. The material and social constraints so carefully detailed are then transcended. . . . It was taken for granted that children and young people would be more idealistic and hopeful than their elders, and those who tampered with these qualities were antagonists.[24]

The child's simple faith and determination restores adult hope. In animal stories, the beloved pet often functions as a similar kind of domestic angel, who rewards those worthy of owning her.

Scenes of redemption, reconciliation, and regeneration run through the seven Lassie films made by MGM in the 1940s and early 1950s. In *Son of Lassie* (1945), the dog becomes a symbol of British wartime pluck and courage when she accompanies Peter Lawford safely through occupied Norway. In *Courage of Lassie* (1946), a shell-shocked collie must undergo rehabilitation in postwar England and, in the process, restore meaning to the lives of her disillusioned owners. In *Hills of Home* (1948) she brings about a reconciliation between father and son, and in *The Sun Comes Up* (1949), between a young orphan and an embittered widow.[25]

These films share three aspects of the original novel that did not carry over to the television series: first, Lassie is owned by adults and families, not by children. Despite her obvious ties to Joe, she is consistently described as "Sam Carraclough's Lassie," that is, as the possession of the father. The shift of Lassie's ownership from adults to children would come with the television series. Second, Lassie remains a British subject. Lassie loses her English accent when she moves to American television.[26] While the wartime years fostered a shared national commitment between England and the United States, cold-war America demanded firm nationalistic allegiances; Lassie could not be tainted with foreignness. As Lassie's "biographer," Ace Collins, explained: "It was decided that the father would have been lost during military service, like Eric Knight himself, thus putting more of a focus on the mother's and grandfather's roles and creating a patriotic stance for the show. Because the family was poor and lacked an active young adult male member, the farm would be a bit run-down, presenting a nostalgic look much like a Norman Rockwell painting. . . . Even with America becoming more urban, folks still yearned for the ideals of a simpler time."[27] Through this process, television's Lassie became a distinctly American myth. Third, the initial crisis originates within the owner's family and must be resolved through Lassie. On television, major problems arise elsewhere—with visiting characters—while the "togetherness" of the Millers and the Martins is never called into question.

This last shift is consistent with a tendency that Nina C. Leibman identifies across a broad range of 1950s and 1960s series about the American family, such as *Leave It to Beaver*, *Father Knows Best*, and *My Three Sons*: while most of the series draw on conventions of Hollywood family melodramas, they offer a more "optimistic" retelling of those stock narratives based on "idealized versions of family life, often pitted against outsider, dysfunctional units."[28] Such a transformation of the domestic melodrama reflects the needs of episodic television for repetition and stability.

Throughout most of its seventeen-season run on American network television, *Lassie* served as the anchor point on CBS's early Sunday evening line-up, helping to establish this time slot's close association with "family television." *Lassie* provided a solid lead-in for other CBS programs, such as *Dennis the Menace*, *My Favorite Martian*, *It's About Time*, and *Gentle Ben*, while other networks counter-programmed with series such as *Shirley Temple's Storybook*, *National Velvet*, *Bullwinkle*, *Walt Disney's Wonderful World of Color*, *New Adventures of Huck Finn*, and *Wild Kingdom*. What all of these series shared was a need to construct and maintain an audience consisting of both children and adults. Saturday morning had become the semi-official "children's hour," where broadcasters could focus their full attention on the young, but Sunday night prime-time still needed to appeal to a broader demographic that included wage-earning and consuming adults. The "wholesomeness" of *Lassie* (a quality which its long-time sponsor, Campbell's, hoped to attach to its soups) made Sunday night television safe for even the most conservative viewer (and this perhaps accounts for *Lassie*'s later adoption by the Family Channel, a cable network owned by the Christian Broadcasting System.)[29]

Life magazine's television critic, Cyclops, protested "the sentimentalization and inflating, the scouring away of the story's social context, the Disneyization of *Lassie*." Lassie had become "Super-Collie . . . the Hound of Heaven" whose extraordinary intelligence, loyalty, and communicativeness "make you look at your own mutt and wonder if somebody put stupidity pills into the Gaines-burger."[30] Many of Cyclops's criticisms seem valid: the core "realism" of the 1940s children's book, its focus on economic hardship and injustice, was stripped away. The Millers and the Martins are hardworking farmers, common to the core and often contrasted with snobby rich folks, but the series rarely gives us any sense of the difficult economic status of the "family farm" in the 1950s and 1960s. Similarly, the relocation of Lassie from Yorkshire to the United States involved something more than her Americanization. Television's *Lassie* lacks geographic specificity; its idyllic pastoral space could exist in any part of the country, and Lassie's various encounters with woodland creatures cut across all known biomes. CBS clearly wanted the Millers' farm to seem like "home" to all Americans, and, as a result, they abandoned Knight's careful attempts to document a particular way of life.

Most of the episodes centered on everyday mishaps: Jeff and Porky babysit for a six-year-old brat who causes them endless trouble; Lassie brings home a litter of kittens but the Millers can't get them to eat; Timmy accidentally breaks Uncle Petrie's guitar and has to raise money to fix it. Many of these stories could have been told just as well on any of the other domestic situation comedies. Here, Lassie, not the father, knows best. Where more serious incidents occurred, offering opportunities for Lassie's curative powers, they tended to come from outside the core family—escaped convicts, bankrupt traveling circuses, blinded Korean War returnees, eccentric old ladies who live on the outskirts of town, Japanese-American families hoping to settle in the community, crop dusters down on their luck, or deer poachers, to cite only examples from *Lassie*'s first two seasons. In these cases, Lassie is given the chance to reform the wicked and restore the weary.

Having made the virtues of rural living and the American family its ideological bedrock, *Lassie* confronts the threats posed to this traditional culture by the city (which, throughout the American sentimental tradition, has been cast as the source of evil and corruption) and by technology (which is often seen as threatening to break down organic communal bonds). City folk are either so green that they get into trouble (falling into wells, sliding off cliffs, getting lost in the woods) or they bring crime and violence (kidnapping Lassie, hitting her with a car, organizing pit-bull fights). In both cases, these urban visitors provide ideal foils for the family's closeness to the natural world and their fundamental honesty. Most often, technological changes are initiated by members of the family and must be negotiated against Lassie's commitments to more traditional lifestyles.

In "The New Refrigerator," for example, trouble starts when the Martins purchase an electric refrigerator, a long coveted luxury: "let others have their mink coats." The episode, however, has established a solid friendship between Lassie and the ice man, who is resigned to his displacement by modern technology; even his wife has bought a fridge. Lassie loudly resists the displacement of traditional social networks in favor of the convenience of consumer culture, barking fiercely at the "white monster." As June protests, "Lassie, you're a reactionary." The conflict is presented as a struggle between "two stubborn females," each insistent on protecting their desired way of life. The equation of the mother and the dog is most powerfully asserted when June pleads, "Lassie, can't you try to get along with my new refrigerator? I wouldn't bark at something you've always wanted." Despite repeated efforts to train her, Lassie refuses to eat food from the new machine. Ultimately, a crisis secures Lassie's acceptance—Timmy pulls a barrel down on his head and Lassie races to the refrigerator to bring him ice. For Lassie, the technology must be seen as central to the family's survival before she can give her blessing.

Given the series' emphasis upon the fundamentally conservative nature of rural life and the stability of the nuclear family, the disruptions and anxieties unleashed in "Transition" are startling. Suddenly, in a single episode, the Millers must confront death, bankruptcy, the selling of the family farm, a move to the city, Jeff's manhood, and, perhaps most traumatically, the loss of Lassie. "Transition" attests to the power of the sentimental attachments between a boy and his dog. Nothing short of total cataclysm could break them apart.

Escaping Domesticity: The Ranger Stuart Years

The year is 1964. During the last week of summer, the Martins load up the family station wagon and take Timmy and Lassie camping. While Alice prepares food, the others go out in a boat to fish. An unexpected storm capsizes their boat. Timmy and Paul make it to shore, but Lassie has disappeared. The parents tell Timmy that "all we can do now is wait and hope," but privately, they are worried. The Martins have little success getting the local authorities interested in the case: "They have to deal with a lot of human problems right now and a missing collie report just doesn't seem that important to them." As the episode closes we catch a glimpse of Lassie swimming toward a boat, but it will take four episodes to unite Lassie and Timmy again. Timmy spends the time pining for the lost dog, while his parents urge him to come to terms with harsh facts: "We can cry for her but we've got to live with reality. . . . We've had more than our share of happiness having a dog like Lassie. Now all we can do is accept the sadness and go on from there." Learning to deal with such traumatic loss is "part of life, part of growing up," as nature suddenly seems far less benign than in previous episodes.

Meanwhile, viewers watch Lassie get rescued by a park ranger, Corey Stuart, and form an intense partnership with him as they travel together rescuing other victims of the storm, stopping a poacher from killing game on federal land, and surviving both a forest fire and an avalanche. In the end, Corey returns the dog to Timmy, disappointed that they will have to go their separate ways. Understanding their bond, Timmy laments, "I wish there could be two Lassies." For once, the uniqueness of this "priceless" dog seems a liability rather than an asset.

This four-part story arc began the season-long process of transferring Lassie from Timmy to Ranger Stuart. Here, the melodrama arises from two equally intense bonds and only one Lassie. One or the other must relinquish their claims. If Stuart makes the first sacrifice, just moments after declaring "it would take a department directive and a herd of wild horses to get her away from me," he will ultimately possess her. As the episodes' succession of cliff-hanging spectacles suggests, Lassie will be removed from the safety of pastoral America (with its ties to domestic melodrama). Stuart will teach Lassie to experience the call of the wild: "Listen to the birds, girl. The wind in the trees. The sound of the river. That's the song of the forest." Having heard its cry, Lassie can no longer be fully domesticated, and the logic of the series will push her further and further from well-worn paths. By the series' final season on network television, Lassie has become a lone wanderer, cut off from all permanent ties, yet always stopping along her journey to aid and assist humans in trouble. Lassie, the "come-home dog," no longer has a home. As the ranger explains, "I never know from day to day where I'll be." The result is a rethinking of the series' generic placement.

Throughout the nineteenth century, the growing emphasis on the sentimental value of the individual child was linked to the development of more specialized categories of children's fictions, books aimed at the particular needs of growing girls or boys. Whereas earlier children's books had been undifferentiated in their address, the new children's books prepared boys for participation in a public sphere of individualistic action and girls for participation in a domestic sphere of familial relations.[31] *Lassie* as a book and as a television series struggles to bridge the rigid separation of boys' and girls' books, making the sentimental values associated with the girls' book acceptable to male readers and domesticating the action elements associated with the boys' book.[32]

Lassie Come-Home contrasts sharply with a classic boys' book like Jack London's *Call of the Wild*. The books open in similar ways, with Buck, the purebred German shepherd, kidnapped from his loving bourgeois owners and sold into servitude in the wilds of Alaska, while Lassie is sold to the Duke and transported to Scotland. Both dogs go on a lengthy journey and confront a series of life-risking adventures before they arrive at their desired destinations. Buck, however, responds to the call of the wild, finding his place as the powerful leader of a wolf pack; his adventure breaks down his ties to the human realm and establishes his dominance within a brutal natural hierarchy ("the law of club and fang"). Lassie responds to the call of the hearth; she remains in the grips of powerful domestic urges. Something inside her demands that she wait for Joe outside the school gate and she braves everything to get there. Buck is strengthened by his encounters with natural elements, erupting in uncontainable phallic power:

> His muscles were surcharged with vitality, and snapped into play sharply, like steel springs. Life streamed through him in splendid flood, glad and rampant; until it seemed that it would burst him asunder in sheer ecstasy and pour forth generously over the world.[33]

Lassie is worn down by her exile from the domestic sphere, arriving home a pained martyr with bleeding paws and limping limbs:

> This was a dog that lay, weakly trying to lift a head that would no longer lift; trying to move a tail that was torn and matted with thorns and burrs, and managing to do nothing very much except to whine in a weak, happy, crying way. (pp. 175–76)

That Buck is the "dominant primordial beast" and Lassie is "her suffering aristocratic majesty" has much more to do with human assumptions about gender than breed distinctions between German shepherds and collies.

Lassie's femininity allows her to slide comfortably into the melodramatic traditions associated with the girls' sentimental novel. Her saga is a variant on the maternal melodrama where a mother struggles to reclaim possession or access to her children, or of the slave story where she is sold "up river" to a bad owner, kept in chains, but escapes and makes her way to freedom.[34] Lassie's status as a dog, however, allows her to escape the constraints placed on human females and translate melodrama's passive suffering into decisive action; she fights back, tooth and claw, against anything that stands between her and the people she loves.

This emphasis upon Lassie's maternalism becomes more central to the television series. Throughout the Jeff and Timmy years, Lassie remains fairly close to home, having adventures on or around the family farm. All things are relative. Compared to the fenced-in suburban backyards experienced by her viewers, Lassie and Timmy enjoyed extraordinary freedom to roam across a vast range of open spaces. Roger Hart, who studied suburban children's use of play space in the early 1970s, found that children in the fourth and fifth grades enjoy mobility only within 300 yards of their houses, while ten- and eleven-year-olds could count on doubling that distance once they owned bikes.[35] Such mobility was greater than that enjoyed by city children of those same periods. Timmy's play space was much larger still and offered more opportunities to get into trouble or encounter strangers. However, compared to the thousand-mile journey across Scotland and Northern England in the Knight novel, television's Lassie was cribbed and confined. (Interestingly, given the series' focus on the great outdoors, most of the Lassie merchandise seemed designed for indoor play, such as board games, view-master slides, stuffed dolls, figurines, breakfast dishes, and paint-with-water sets).[36]

As the story became more homebound, the boys, Jeff and Timmy, became more and more central to the program's appeal. Like "Beaver" or Dennis the Menace, Jeff and Timmy were the inheritors of the "bad boy" tradition that literary critics and historians associate with *Tom Sawyer* and *Huckleberry Finn*.[37] In keeping with the permissive era faith in childhood innocence, the more mean-spirited and anti-authoritarian aspects of this earlier literary tradition have been discarded; Jeff and Timmy are not active rebels against the maternal sphere. They are simply innocent explorers of adult spaces, naturally boisterous inhabitants of a world where "boys will be boys." If the nineteenth-century "bad boy" escaped the constraints of maternal authority, the ever-watchful Lassie goes out into the woods with Timmy and makes sure he doesn't get into trouble. As Cully explains to Timmy in one episode, "Lassie's always looked after you like her own puppy." Under Lassie's maternal supervision, the wildest corner of the woods remains as safe as a suburban backyard.

Ranger Stuart's relationship to Lassie is profoundly different. As an adult unmarried male, he has no family, no mother, no domestic entanglements of any kind, and so, under his ownership, Lassie is freed to roam the entire North American continent. Stuart and Lassie part and come together multiple times, having adventures separately and as part of a team. Lassie's worth gets redefined in terms of her professional accomplishments—the rescues she performs, the messages she delivers. She battles fires, saves stranded campers from avalanches, survives being swept away by rapids, and helps a man caught under a fallen power-line. Stuart consistently refers to her as his "partner" or, more suggestively, his "girlfriend." The ideal of pastoral America, the world of civilized communities, gives way almost entirely to images of a wild frontier space, where men and dogs are tested and tempered through their encounters with the natural realm. With the introduction of the ranger, *Lassie* fully embraces the boys' book tradition, becoming a series more about the call of the wild than the yearning for the hearth.

This generic and geographic relocation reflects larger shifts in the way popular entertainment represented the natural order. In the 1950s, when Lassie debuted, the collie existed alongside a succession of popular representations of dogs, horses, cats, and other domesticated animals. Walt Disney alone was responsible for bringing to the screen *Lady and the Tramp* (1955), *Old Yeller* (1957), *The Shaggy Dog* (1959), *101 Dalma-*

tians (1961), *Nikki, Wild Dog of the North* (1961), *Greyfriars Bobby* (1961), *Big Red* (1962), *Savage Sam* (1963), and *The Incredible Journey* (1963), all classic dog stories, many of which became staples of *Walt Disney's Wonderful World of Color.* Television viewers could watch *The Adventures of Rin Tin Tin* (1954–59), *My Friend Flicka* (1956–58), and *National Velvet* (1960–62). By the mid-1960s, popular representations of animals tended to favor wild and untamed creatures rather than domesticated animals. On television, *Flipper* (1964–68) dealt with a boy and his dolphin, and *Gentle Ben* (1967–69) a boy and his black bear. Films like *Born Free* (1966), *The Jungle Book* (1967), and *Maya* (1966) and television series such as *Daktari* (1966–69) and *Cowboy in Africa* (1967–68) departed from the "civilized" realms of England and America to deal with the "untamed" wildlife of Africa and Asia. By 1969, *Lassie* was going head-to-head on Sunday nights with *Wild Kingdom,* a series full of lurid images of predators and prey and deadly poisonous snakes. *Lassie's* shift toward outdoor adventure during the Ranger Stuart years both anticipates and participates in this renewed focus on undomesticated fauna.

This shift in focus from domesticated to wild animals finds its parallels in child-rearing literature of the period. Most of the 1950s and early 1960s films and television series we have discussed can be traced to pre–World War II literary sources. The focus on finely trained and domesticated animals was consistent with the then-dominant behaviorist paradigm, with its focus on regimentation, discipline, control, and domestication. In the postwar period, on the other hand, child-rearing literature was characterized by a shift toward permissiveness, popularized by Benjamin Spock. Permissiveness stressed freedom rather than discipline and the "natural" development of children outside tight parental control; it spawned a cult of primitivism, drawing close analogies from the anthropological literature of Margaret Mead. Permissive children were wild and untamed, demanding a world that respected their natural impulses. Although encyclopedic on other aspects of children's lives, permissive writers say almost nothing about dogs and other pets. They do see a value in children engaging with the natural world, but they emphasize camping trips, walks in the woods, or visits to the zoo. This idealization of the untamed natural world required Lassie, no less than *Born Free's* Elsa, to leave the constraints of domestic space for the freedom of the wild kingdom.

In liberating Lassie from the domestic space, the producers, however, broke apart the complex set of generic compromises between the sentimental girls' book tradition and the blood-and-guts boys' book tradition that gave the series immunity from popular criticism. Popular discourse about children's television circled around distinctions between classic children's literature and comic books, education and entertainment, realism and sensationalism. Reformers such as Newton Minow consistently urged producers to seek their inspiration from respected literary works rather than comic books and pulp magazines.[38] Children's programs were viewed positively by teachers and reformers if they encouraged children to read. Often, there was an implicit (or even explicit) preference for the sentimental values associated with girls' books and a vilification of the suspense and adventure elements associated with boys' books. *Lassie's* ties to a recognized literary classic and its status as in-between boys' and girls' genres helped the series to overcome some of these most basic objections, paving the way for its widespread acceptance as "wholesome" entertainment. *A Parent's Guide to Children's Reading* (1958), for example, specifically praises *Lassie,* along with Mary Martin's *Peter Pan* and Walt Disney's *Davy Crockett* as programs that encourage youngsters to return to the library shelves.[39] Moreover, at a time when post-Sputnik parents were eager for children to embrace science and natural history, everything from *Lassie* to *Mr. Wizard* was cited for their potential educational benefits.

On the other hand, the sensational boys' book elements, however subdued in the Jeff and Timmy years, were still potentially problematic and became more so in the Ranger Stuart period. One television producer, for example, cited *Lassie* in 1967 as an example of how the vividness and immediacy of television added luridness: "*Lassie* is one of the scariest shows for kids. They see a real kid and a real dog in real danger."[40] The animal-centered adventure series were consistently panned by the National Association for Better Radio and Television and other such groups. In 1956, for example, the group condemned *Rin Tin Tin* as one of the "most objectionable" programs on television: "Tense situations exist throughout the program and unbelievable problems are solved by this incredible dog. . . . Whole-some episodes are the exception."[41] Such critics feared that suspenseful storylines, especially those involving children in jeopardy, overstimulated children's active imaginations.[42] *Flipper,* for example, was condemned for "story themes [which] abound in crime and involve youngsters in extremely dangerous situations."[43] *PTA* magazine wrote with outrage about the debut of *Gentle Ben:* "For years there have been warnings to children and adults against feeding and playing with bears. . . . How CBS could permit a program with a black bear for a pet—not a cub either—but a gigantic adult bear—is beyond our comprehension."[44] Though *Lassie*'s mid-1960s episodes are not noticeably different from those of *Flipper* or *Gentle Ben*, it continued to get the approval of the PTA and other reform-oriented groups while the competing animal series were condemned.

Once again, the transfer of ownership (from Timmy to Ranger Stuart) and the breaking of the intense bonds between master and pet occurs only by throwing family togetherness and pastoralism into crisis. This time, images of boyhood, family, and farm will be banished altogether to pave the way for greater mobility, more suspense, and a wilder conception of the natural world. As the episode opens, both Timmy and his adopted father are eagerly awaiting the mail. Timmy wants the delivery of a dog tag for Lassie, while the father awaits more dramatic news about a "wonderful opportunity for all of us." He plans to move the all-American Martin family to Australia, where he insists there is lots of land and not enough people. However, bad news follows. Lassie will have to be placed on a six-month quarantine before she will be admitted into the country. For a dog used to the freedom Lassie has enjoyed, such confinement would be unendurable. Timmy refuses to speak to his father, begs to stay behind with Ranger Stuart, and finally threatens to run away from home. "It's tearing us to pieces. I've never seen him act this way before," Ruth exclaims, startled by her normally goody-goody son's willfulness. Paul understands, however, the boy's powerless rage: "He's just a little boy in a grown-up world and that ain't an easy thing to be. Things get decided for you and there isn't nothing you can do about it."

In Knight's *Lassie Come-Home*, Joe never questions his father's "right" to sell his dog, even though the boy continues to hope for its return. When his father speaks, Joe obeys. The boy is silenced on several occasions by a firmly expressed "no." However, the issue of parental authority had undergone a dramatic transformation in the postwar period, with more child-centered parenting styles seen as fundamentally democratic and most appropriate for raising children into American citizenship. Rudolf Dreikurs's *Children: The Challenge* (1964) charts the different political models behind prewar and postwar child-rearing practices:[45]

Autocratic society	Democratic society
Authority figure	Knowledgeable leader
Power	Influence
Pressure	Stimulation
Demanding	Winning cooperation
Punishment	Logical consequences
Reward	Encouragement
Imposition	Permit self-determination
Domination	Guidance
Children are seen and not heard.	Listen! Respect the child.
YOU do because I said to.	WE do because it is necessary.

A conscious effort was made following World War II to reconstruct both the American family and children's culture according to these "democratic" principles.

Many of the key architects of postwar children's culture had served together as part of Frank Capra's propaganda unit during the Second World War.[46] Capra assembled a remarkable group that included Ted Geissel ("Doctor Seuss"), Chuck Jones (Looney Toons), P. D. Eastman (*Are You My Mother?*), Stanley Kramer (*Boy with the Green Hair, 5000 Fingers of Dr. T*), and Eric Knight. Knight was killed during the war, so he did not directly participate in the postwar shifts in popular discourse about parents and children or in the attempt to create a more playful, pleasure-centered culture. However, television's *Lassie* embraced at least some permissive doctrines. The sudden introduction of the issue of parental authority represented a significant shift in the program ideology.

Lassie cannot be taken from Timmy by force of parental autocracy or legal fiat. The episode must reconcile father and son. First, Lassie distances herself from Timmy. Timmy explains to his elderly friend, Cully, "Lassie's acting strange. She's usually right by my side but now she's gone." Cully links the shift to Timmy's coming of age, suggesting that as a boy turns into a man, he no longer needs the maternal presence of the dog: "You're growing up and Lassie's sensing it. . . . Lassie knows you've got to be on your own. You've got to stand on your own two feet." Second, Paul apologizes to Timmy for being too domineering: "Maybe I was wrong when I made such a big decision without all of us talking it over." Timmy, however, has accepted the move and the "sacrifice" he must make. By episode's end, he turns the dog over to Cully. After a series of further misadventures, Cully, in turn, grants custody to Ranger Stuart, explaining that he thinks this is what Timmy would have wanted: "Lassie's a special dog. She needs to be right in the middle of things." It is this need for immediacy and excitement that propels *Lassie* from domestic melodrama into outdoor adventure.

Postscript: 1996

Nostalgia, Susan Stewart tells us, is "sadness without an object," a longing for a more perfect past that never quite existed.[47] Children and dogs are central figures for nostalgia, evoking images of innocence that adults cannot reclaim and loyalty that defies human understanding. These are culturally powerful myths, serving to reconcile and resolve, at least temporarily, any number of ideological contradictions. They seem to offer us a way out of our adult human problems into a world of simpler moral choices and undying commitments. Yet, as we have seen, the need to tell that story, to communicate our ideals about children and dogs through narrative rather than static images, requires the constant enactment of a threat to their world: things cannot remain simple and pure for long. In the *Lassie* series, such threats surface most dramatically in those episodes that center on a change in Lassie's ownership, since these storylines require a dissolution of one set of social ties between children and dogs and the forging of an alternative set of affections. Such a transformation unleashes all of the threats that traditional children's literature tries to protect children from confronting. In the process the series' generic formulas often also undergo a shift, which also requires some alteration in the symbolic and sentimental values attached to the beloved collie. *Lassie*'s status as a "timeless" myth of core human values is contradicted by the way that the series has been subjected to historic change. However, our emotional attachment to the program may still be governed by things that do not change in our memory, the kinds of stock images that supplant any specific plot-lines when we try to remember what it was like watching *Lassie* as boys and girls.

This is an essay about the way our culture lives with nostalgia, the ways that certain myths about children and dogs spring forth to help us deal with our anxieties about change. Yet, this essay is also a personal exercise in nostalgia, a way back to my own boyhood and to my own dog, Brownie, a half-breed female collie. Brownie was my companion from kindergarten through most of high school; she had three litters of puppies and mothered a succession of pet rabbits, ducks, chicks, turtles, and neighborhood children. Brownie loved to take boat rides and would lap at the wake. However, she lived most of her life in a fenced-in suburban backyard. As a preadolescent, I was obsessed with the idea that when this dog died, my childhood would be over. Unlike Lassie, Brownie did not go on to bigger adventures with forest rangers when she passed from my possession. She simply died, and she was put in an old cardboard box and left out at the street for the garbage man to take her away. That's how we were legally required to dispose of dead pets in the early 1970s.

Once, I loved a dog. Now, I hate dogs. Living, breathing canines fill me not with longing but rather with an intense loathing. I plot sinister revenge on my neighbor's yapping dog that somehow senses and amplifies my hostility. When I think of dogs, I think of the smell of dog breath in the tight confines of the backseat of the family station wagon and the scent of fresh urine in the plush carpet; I think of the slippery feeling of saliva on my hands after a dog licks it; I think of the unsettling sensation of slipping and sliding barefoot on dog poop hidden in the freshly cut grass; I think of ear-wrenching yelps and barks, of toenails scratching on linoleum; I think of that grayish jelly junk that forms on the top of cans of dog food. I have trouble seeing past the body of the farting, panting, drooling, barking, shitting beast and into the spirit, the romantic ideal, of the domesticated pet. I find the myth of the dog fascinating, the reality disgusting. Across twenty years of American television, nobody ever stepped in Lassie's poop.

Perhaps this all seems too embarrassingly personal, yet what I want to suggest has to do with our shared cultural construction of the dog—what it contains, what it excludes. Our mythic reconstruction of the dog involves an isolation of the animal from the reality of its body, just as our myth of childhood innocence involves the isolation of the child from its sexuality and a denial of its agency. Dogs and children are stripped of all their messy bits so they can fetch and carry things for us. When I remember Brownie, I sometimes remember her with the mythic aura that surrounds Lassie, as a larger-than-life embodiment of maternal love and childhood freedom. Yet, those other more tactile and pungent memories are part of my lived experience of dog ownership, the part we don't talk about, and the part that the longing of nostalgia tends to suppress.

When I write about Lassie, I am writing about a dog I never had, indeed, a dog I never could have had. Through writing about her, I reclaim access to a pastoral, conservative, American ideal whose values I do not fully share but which, on occasion, I long for nevertheless. I mourn the death of Brownie, the loss of Lassie, and the end of a world where I found it hard to separate the two. The myth of the faithful dog, Kete tells us, stood as a compensation for the reality of faithless people, a bulwark against modern fears of death and loneliness, and the myth always carries with it a sense of mourning and loss.

The essential point about nostalgia is that things are not the same.

In "Heavy Petting," Marjorie Garber tells us that 1994 was "the Year of the Dog."[48] She cites the popular success of books like *The Hidden Life of Dogs*, *The Intelligence of Dogs*, and *Animal Happiness*, which rediscover the power of personification, insisting that we can understand how dogs think through the power of empathetic identification. She points to popular films like *Homeward Bound* and *Look Who's Talking Now* as well as of the chic photograph books of William Wegman and Thierry Poncelet. She even points to the release of a new *Lassie* movie and a series of tie-in books. Yet, throughout it all, I remain unconvinced. Things are not the same. There is something annoyingly artificial, self-conscious, even posing about these postmodern representations of the dog, as if we weren't supposed to take them all so seriously and, above all, as if we weren't supposed to feel the sentimental tug of dog-love. If the nineteenth-century French bourgeoisie invested their sense of loss into a compensatory myth of canine loyalty, we tend to discard such feelings behind a facade of carefree parody.

As I sit down to write, I find an article in the *New York Times* that sums it all up too perfectly.[49] Dog and cat owners, we are told, are employing a "high-tech method to identify their pets in case they are lost or stolen." A small microchip with an information number is implanted just under its skin, allowing for a precise identification should the animal be separated from its owner. One particular California-based Humane Society has "chipped" between 10,000 and 11,000 pets. "It's not so easy with a 125-pound Rottweiler to find a tattoo," one vet explains.[50]

As I ponder the image of Lassie as a cyborg collie, I recall the centrality of the issue of her unique identity to the whole saga. In the concluding passage of *Lassie Come-Home*, the Carracloughs give their come-home dog a makeover not so that they can fool the Duke into thinking she is another dog but rather so they can convince him to relinquish his claims on her ownership. Under the hands of a skilled dog's man, Lassie is transformed:

For where Lassie's skull was aristocratic and slim, this dog's head was clumsy and rough. Where Lassie's ears stood in the grace of twin-lapped symmetry, this dog had one screw ear and the other standing up Alsatian fashion, in a way that would give any collie breeder the cold shivers. More than that. Where Lassie's coat faded to delicate sable, this curious dog had ugly splashes of black; and where Lassie's apron was a billow-ing expanse of white, this dog had muddy puddles of off-white, blue-merle mixture. (p. 188)

The Duke recognizes Lassie on first glance, even though it flies in the face of human comprehension that she could have made her thousand-mile journey. And, if there is any doubt, he looks at her paws, "crossed and recrossed with half-healed scars where thorns had torn and stones had lacerated" (p. 189). The Duke knows, in his soul, that this dog is Lassie, just as Joe does not have any difficulty identifying the exhausted and emaciated animal he finds waiting for him after school. Still, miracle of miracles, the Duke releases Lassie back to her morally rightful owners: "This is no dog of mine. 'Pon my soul and honor, she never belonged to me. No! Not for a single second did she ever belong to me!" (p. 189). And with those words, with this moment of sublime recognition, Sam is re-leased from his unfortunate deal.

Neither the Duke nor Joe, neither Jeff nor Timmy, nor any of the oth-ers who were blessed to own Lassie through the years, needed a mi-crochip to identify her. I recognize that the microchip is an act of love, a response to a changed society, a harsh reality we have to live with. But re-ality falls far short of our cherished myths. Lassie was unique, priceless, without possible imitation or counterfeit. Her spiritual qualities, her moral authority, her "suffering aristocratic majesty" was possessed by no other dog, and only those who understand that distinction were allowed to possess a dog like Lassie. And, even if her human owners were con-fused, Lassie would have known and would have made her wishes known. Something has broken down in the relations between dogs and their masters. The myth of the faithful dog no longer offers us condo-lences in the face of a feckless world. If the myths of canine fidelity and childhood innocence were central tropes through which our culture dealt with the threats of modernity, such myths of authenticity and of natural social relations have no place in a postmodern world.

It is perhaps symptomatic of such a realm that people have read the above postscript and not known whether I was telling the truth about my dog, my nausea, my tears, or my nostalgia. That ambiguity is an essential aspect of nostalgia—we want to believe, and yet, at the same time, we can't; we know that the past we create through our myths, our memories, our popular fictions, is only partially true. My relation to dogs is reducible neither to my very real mourning of a lost object of desire nor to my equally real distaste for shit and spit. Our cultural relations to dogs are reducible neither to postmodern chic nor authentic celebration. Dogs conjure up complex feelings, contradictory emotions, irreconcilable myths. All of it is true, but none of it is all true. And, so, in the end, nostalgia always frustrates the desires that fuel its search for a more perfect past. We can't trust our feelings, memories or myths.

Things are not the same.

They never were.

Notes

NOTES TO THE INTRODUCTION

1. Steven Johnson, *Everything Bad Is Good for You: How Today's Popular Culture Is Actually Making Us Smarter* (New York: Riverhead Books, 2005).

2. Walter De Leon, "The Wow Finish," *Saturday Evening Post*, February 14, 1925; reprinted in Charles W. Stein, ed., *American Vaudeville as Seen by Its Contemporaries* (New York: Alfred A. Knopf, 1984), p. 194.

3. Ibid., pp. 198–99.

4. My use of the sexually charged phrase "The Wow Climax" as the book's title is also intended as a tribute to the film critic Pauline Kael, whose collections of essays consistently dealt with the emotional dimensions of popular cinema, which she often signaled through the use of double entendres in her titles, such as *I Lost It at the Movies*, *Kiss Kiss Bang Bang*, *Going Steady*, and *When the Lights Go Down*.

5. Henry Jenkins, *What Made Pistachio Nuts? Early Sound Comedy and the Vaudeville Aesthetic* (New York: Columbia University Press, 1992).

6. Sergei Eisenstein, "Montage of Attractions," in Richard Taylor, ed., *The Eisenstein Reader* (London: British Film Institute, 1998), p. 30.

7. Ibid.

8. See David Bordwell, *The Cinema of Eisenstein* (Cambridge, MA: Harvard University Press, 1993), p. 119.

9. Daniel Gerould, "Russian Formalist Theories of Melodrama," *Journal of American Culture* 1, no. 1 (Spring 1978): 154–55.

10. David Bordwell, *Planet Hong Kong: Popular Cinema and the Art of Entertainment* (Cambridge, MA: Harvard University Press, 2000), p. 8.

11. Tom Gunning, "The Cinema of Attractions: Early Film, Its Spectator, and the Avant-Garde," *Wide Angle* 3 (1986): 56–62.

12. David Freeman, *Creating Emotion in Games* (New York: New Riders, 2003), p. 16.

13. C. S. Lewis, "On Stories," in *On Stories and Other Essays on Literature* (New York: Harvest, 1966), pp. 7–8.

14. Bordwell, *Planet Hong Kong*, p. 13.

NOTES TO PART I INTRODUCTION

1. Gilbert Seldes, *The Seven Lively Arts* (New York: Sagmore Press, 1957).

2. Pierre Bourdieu, *Distinction: A Social Critique of Taste* (Cambridge, MA: Harvard University Press, 1984), p. 33.

3. Ibid., p. 34.

4. Ibid.

5. Ibid.

6. Lawrence Levine, *Highbrow/Lowbrow: The Emergence of Cultural Hierarchy in America* (Cambridge, MA: Harvard University Press, 1990), p. 26.

7. John F. Kasson, *Rudeness and Civility: Manners in Nineteenth-Century Urban America* (New York: Hill and Wang, 1990).

8. Alan McKee, ed., *Beautiful Objects in Popular Culture*, full citation coming.

9. J. Hoberman, "Vulgar Modernism," in *Vulgar Modernism: Writing on Movies and Other Media* (Philadelphia: Temple University Press, 1991), pp. 32–39.

NOTES TO CHAPTER I

1. Shigeru Miyamoto, as quoted in Marc Saltzman, ed., *Game Design Secrets of the Sages*, 2d ed. (Indianapolis: Macmillan, 2000), p. 10.

2. Jack Kroll, "Emotional Engines? I Don't Think So," *Newsweek*, February 27 2000, p. 4.

3. Hal Barwood, "The Envelope Please?" *Game Developer*, February 2002.

4. The core argument in this essay initially took shape as remarks presented in 2000 at the conference *Video and Computer Games Come of Age*, jointly sponsored by the MIT Comparative Media Studies Program and the Interactive Digital Software Association, Cambridge, Massachusetts. It was presented as a talk at various venues, including the Game Developers Conference in San Jose, California; the Electronic Entertainment Exposition in Los Angeles; the Queensland Institute of Technology; and the University of Western England–Bristol. It was expanded and published as "Artform for the Digital Age," *Technology Review*, September–October 2000, and subsequently reprinted in abbreviated form as Henry Jenkins, "Think Tank: Zap! Rat-a-Tat-Tat! Ping! Ah, 'Tis Art Aborning," *New York Times*, October 14, 2000, p. B11. I am grateful for the feedback it has received in these various venues. On the current revision I am especially thankful to Kurt Squire, Alex Chisholm, Philip Tan Boon, Eric Zimmerman, and Kevin Johnson, as well as the insights of the larger Games to Teach team and the great variety of people in the games industry who have volunteered their time to help us with our efforts.

5. Kurt Squire, "Educating Game Designers: An Interview with Warren Spector," *Joystick 101*, May 23, 2001.

6. For more on Matthew Barney and his relationship to the aesthetics of popular culture, see Chapter 2 of this volume.

7. For examples of the new scholarship emerging around games, see Noah Wardrip-Fruin and Pat Harrigan, eds., *First Person: New Media as Story, Performance, and Game* (Cambridge, MA: MIT Press, 2006); Lucian King and Conrad Bain, eds., *Game On* (London: Barbican, 2002); the online journal *Game Studies*, http://www.gamestudies.org/; or the current volume.

8. For a useful overview of Seldes's contributions to American arts and letters, see Michael G. Kammen, *The Lively Arts: Gilbert Seldes and the Transformation of Cultural Criticism in the United States* (Oxford: Oxford University Press, 1996). Although Seldes borrowed the concept of the "Seven Arts" from the classical tradition, his book *The Seven Lively Arts* remains ambiguous about how to break down the topics he discusses into distinct traditions. What one takes from Seldes is less a taxonomy of popular arts than a way of understanding the relationships between popular, middlebrow, and high art.

9. Gilbert Seldes, *The Seven Lively Arts* (New York: Sagmore Press, 1957), p. 193.

10. Barwood, "The Envelope Please?"

11. Seldes, *The Seven Lively Arts*, p. 272.

12. Ibid., p. 228.

13. Ibid., p. 293. Seldes's arguments about sensory restoration need to be understood in the context of larger discourses about sensation and expression at the turn of the century. For an overview of those discussions, see Ben Singer, *Melodrama and Modernity: Early Sensational Cinema and Its Contexts* (New York: Columbia University Press, 2001); and Henry Jenkins, *What Made Pistachio Nuts? Early Sound Comedy and the Vaudeville Aesthetic* (New York: Columbia University Press, 1992).

14. Seldes, *The Seven Lively Arts*, p. 223.

15. Ibid., p. 300.

16. Ibid., p. 299.

17. These historical transitions have attracted considerable scholarly attention within film studies circles. For a useful overview, see Thomas Elsaesser and Adam Barker, eds., *Early Cinema: Space-Frame-Narrative* (London: British Film Institute, 1990).

18. Seldes, *The Seven Lively Arts*, p. 288.

19. Ibid., p. 16.

20. Ibid., p. 18.

21. Ibid., p. 288.

22. Kroll, "Emotional Engines? I Don't Think So," p. 64.

23. Steven Poole, *Trigger Happy: Videogames and the Entertainment Revolution* (New York: Arcade Publishing, 2000), pp. 218–20.

24. Frank Lantz and Eric Zimmerman, "Checkmate: Rules, Play and Culture," *Merge* (1999), http://www.ericzimmerman.com/texts/RulesPlayCulture .htm. See also Eric Zimmerman, "Do Independent Games Exist?" in Lucian King and Conrad Bain, eds., *Game On* (London: Barbican, 2002): "Games suffer from cinema envy. What passes for 'realism' in games is an awkward and unimaginative use of 3D computer graphics. It's time for game developers to stop trying to replicate the pleasures of film. Games need to find their own forms of expression, capitalizing on their unique properties as dynamic, participatory systems" (p. 125).

25. Seldes, *The Seven Lively Arts*, p. 286.

26. Poole, *Trigger Happy*, p. 226.

27. Seldes, *The Seven Lively Arts*, p. 19.

28. Ibid., p. 186.

29. Squire, "Educating Game Designers."

30. Sergei Eisenstein, "Montage of Attractions," *Drama Review* (March 1974): 77–85.

31. Vadim Uraneff, "Commedia Dell'Arte and American Vaudeville," *Theatre Arts* (October 1923): 326.

32. For a useful discussion of the aesthetics of early video games, see Van Burnham and Ralph H. Baer, *Supercade* (Cambridge, MA: MIT Press, 2001).

33. I am indebted to the participants of the Comparative Media Studies–Electronic Arts Creative Leaders workshop series for these insights into the game design process.

34. Seldes, *The Seven Lively Arts*, p. 175.

35. Robert Lytell, "Vaudeville Old and Young," *New Republic*, July 1 1925, p. 156.

36. David Perry, as quoted in Saltzman, *Game Design Secrets of the Sages*, p. 18.

37. James Newman, "On Being a Tetraminoe: Mapping the Contours of the Videogame Character," paper delivered at the International Game Cultures Conference, Bristol, England, June–July 2001.

38. Dikarika, "Tales from a DDR Addict," *Joystick 101*, January 12, 2002.

39. Alex Rigopulos, e-mail correspondence with the author, March 1, 2002.

40. "Gamers Set for Sensory Overload," *BBC News*, March 1, 2002, http://news.bbc.co.uk/1/hi/sci/tech/1846561.stm.

41. David Bordwell, *Planet Hong Kong: Popular Cinema and the Art of Entertainment* (Cambridge, MA: Harvard University Press, 2000), p. 244.

42. Ibid., p. 232.

43. Seldes, *The Seven Lively Arts*, p. 37.

44. Henry Jenkins, "Game Design as Narrative Architecture," in Wardrip-Fruin and Harrigan, eds., *First Person*, pp.118–30.

45. See Chapter 8 of this volume.

46. Kurt Squire and Henry Jenkins, "The Art of Contested Spaces," in King and Bain, eds., *Game On* (London: Barbican, 2002), pp. 64–76.

47. Squire, "Educating Game Designers."

48. Seldes, *The Seven Lively Arts*, p. 289.

49. Gilbert Seldes, *The Great Audience* (New York: Viking, 1950).

NOTES TO CHAPTER 2

1. Matthew Barney, as quoted in Richard Flood, "The Land of Everlasting Hills," in *Cremaster 2* (Minneapolis: Walker Art Center, 1999), p. 2.

2. David Cronenberg, as quoted in Ian Conrich, "An Aesthetic Sense: Cronenberg and Neo-Horror Film Culture," in Michael Grant, ed., *The Modern Fantastic: The Films of David Cronenberg* (Westport, CT: Praeger, 2000), p. 37.

3. Matthew Barney, personal correspondence with author.

4. Jerry Saltz, "The Next Sex," *Art in America*, October 1999, pp. 82–91.

5. Michael Kimmelman, "The Importance of Matthew Barney," *New York Times Magazine*, October, 10 1999, pp. 62–69.

6. Dan Cameron, "Matthew Barney, Escape Artist," in Matthew Barney, *Cremaster 1, Cremaster 4* (Barcelona: Fundació la Caixa, 1998), p. 33.

7. Flood, "The Land of Everlasting Hills."

8. All quotations by Clive Barker are from Stephen Jones, ed., *Shadow in Eden: The Books, Films and Art of Clive Barker* (Lancaster, UK: Underwood-Miller, 1991), and are cited by page number in the text.

9. Robin Wood, *Hollywood from Vietnam to Reagan* (New York: Columbia University Press, 1986).

10. On the production of *Cabinet of Dr. Caligari*, see Mike Budd, *The Cabinet of Dr. Caligari: Texts, Contexts, Histories* (New Brunswick, NJ: Rutgers University Press, 1990).

11. Unless otherwise noted, quotations by David Cronenberg are from Chris Rodley, ed., *Cronenberg on Cronenberg* (London: Faber and Faber, 1992), and are cited by page number in the text.

12. Joan Hawkins, *Cutting Edge: Art-Horror and the Horrific Avant-Garde* (Minneapolis: University of Minnesota Press, 2000).

13. David Sanjek, "Fans' Notes: The Horror Film Fanzine," in Ken Gelder, ed., *The Horror Reader* (New York: Routledge, 2000), pp. 314–23.

14. Mark Kermode, "I Was a Teenage Horror Fan, Or, How I Learned to Stop Worrying and Love Linda Blair," in Martin Barker and Julian Petley, eds., *Ill Effects: The Media/Violence Debate* (London: Routledge, 1997), pp. 126–34.

15. Judith Halberstam, *Skin Shows: Gothic Horror and the Technology of Monsters* (Durham, NC: Duke University Press, 1995), p. 8.

16. Ibid.

17. See, for example, Philip Brophy, "Horrality—the Textuality of Contemporary Horror Films," in Gelder, ed., *The Horror Reader*, pp. 276–84.

18. Linda Ruth Williams, "The Inside-Out of Masculinity: David Cronenberg's Visceral Pleasures," in Michael Aaron, ed., *The Body's Perilous Pleasures: Dangerous Desires and Contemporary Culture* (Edinburgh: Edinburgh University Press, 1999), p. 34.

19. Cronenberg, as quoted in Conrich, "An Aesthetic Sense," p. 37.

20. Charles Burns, *Black Hole* (New York: Random House), n.p.

21. Ibid., n.p.

22. Fuchs, quoted in H. R. Giger, *Retrospective, 1964–1984* (Zurich: ABC Verlag, 1985).

23. The quotes come, respectively, from Thryza Nichols Goodeve, "Travels in Hypertophia," *Art Forum*, May 1995; ibid; Neville Wakefield, "Matthew Barney's Fornication with the Fabric of Space," *Parkett*, no. 39 (1994); ibid.

24. Linda Williams, "Body Genres: Gender, Genre, and Excess," in Sue Thornham, ed., *Feminist Film Theory: A Reader* (New York: New York University Press, 1999), pp. 267–81.

25. Saltz, "The Next Sex."

26. See, for example, Hy Bender and Neil Gaiman, *The Sandman Companion* (New York: Vertigo Books, 1999).

27. For a useful introduction to Cordwainer Smith's work, see *The Rediscovery of Man: The Complete Short Stories of Cordwainer Smith*, ed. James A. Mann (Boston: New England Science Fiction Association, 1993).

NOTES TO PART II INTRODUCTION

1. Robert Warshow, *The Immediate Experience: Movies, Comics, Theatre and Other Aspects of Popular Culture* (Cambridge, MA: Harvard University Press, 2001), p. xxxvii.

2. Ibid., p. xxxviii.

3. Ibid., p. xl.

4. Ibid.

5. Ibid.

6. Ibid., p. xli.

7. For a fuller discussion of the concept of immediacy, see Henry Jenkins, Tara McPherson, and Jane Shattuc, "The Culture That Sticks to Your Skin: A Manifesto for a New Cultural Studies," in Jenkins, McPherson, and Shattuc,

eds., *Hop on Pop: The Politics and Pleasures of Popular Culture* (Durham, NC: Duke University Press, 2003, pp. 3–25.

8. Rhona J. Berenstein, *Attack of the Leading Ladies: Gender, Sexuality and Spectatorship in Classic Horror Cinema* (New York: Columbia University Press, 1995); Kevin Heffernan, *Ghouls, Gimmicks, and Gold: Horror Films and the American Movie Business, 1953–1968* (Durham, NC: Duke University Press, 2004); Eric Schaefer, *"Bold! Daring! Shocking! True!": A History of Exploitation Films, 1919–1959* (Durham, NC: Duke University Press, 1999).

9. Lawrence Grossberg, *Dancing in Spite of Myself: Essays on Popular Culture* (Durham, NC: Duke University Press, 1997); Jackie Stacey, *Star Gazing: Hollywood Cinema and Female Spectatorship* (London: Routledge, 1994); Richard Dyer, *Only Entertainment* (London: Routledge, 1992).

10. Robert Warshow, "Paul, the Horror Comics, and Dr. Wertham," *in The Immediate Experience*, p. 72.

11. For more of my writing on contemporary debates about media violence, see Henry Jenkins, *Fans, Bloggers, and Gamers: Essays on Participatory Culture* (New York: New York University Press, 2006).

12. Robert Warshow, "The Gangster as Tragic Hero," in *The Immediate Experience*, p. 99.

13. Robert Warshow, "Movie Chronicle: The Westerner," in *The Immediate Experience*, p. 122.

14. Pierre Bourdieu, *Distinction: A Social Critique of Taste* (Cambridge, MA: Harvard University Press, 1984), p. 56.

15. Norbert Elias and Eric Dunning, *The Quest for Excitement: Sport and Leisure in the Civilizing Process* (New York: Basil Blackwell, 1986).

16. Henry Jenkins, "Wrestling with Theory, Grappling with Politics," in Nick Sammond, ed., *Steel Chair to the Head: The Pleasure and Pain of Professional Wrestling* (Durham, NC: Duke University Press, 2005), p. 299.

17. Linda Williams, "Film Bodies: Gender, Genre, and Excess," in Sue Thornham, ed., *Feminist Film Theory: A Reader* (New York: New York University Press, 1999), p. 269.

18. Ibid.

19. Ibid., p. 270.

20. Henry Jenkins, "So You Want to Teach Pornography," in Pamela Church Gibson, ed., *More Dirty Looks: Gender, Pornography and Power* (Berkeley: University of California Press, 2004), pp. 1–8; Henry Jenkins, "'He's in the Closet But He's Not Gay': Male-Male Desire in Penthouse Letters," in Peter Lehman, ed., *Pornography: Film and Culture* (New Brunswick, NJ: Rutgers University Press, forthcoming).

21. See Henry Jenkins, *What Made Pistachio Nuts? Early Sound Comedy and the Vaudeville Aesthetic* (New York: Columbia University Press, 1992).

22. José Esteban Muñoz, *Disidentifications: Queers of Color and the Performance of Politics* (Minneapolis: University of Minnesota Press, 1999), p. 6.

NOTES TO CHAPTER 4

1. "WWF Interview: A Talk with Jake 'the Snake' Roberts," *WWF Magazine*, February 1992, p. 17.

2. Roland Barthes, "The World of Wrestling," in *A Barthes Reader*, ed. Susan Sontag (New York: Hill and Wang, 1982), p. 23.

3. Ibid., p. 25.

4. Ibid., p. 29.

5. For useful background on the historical development of television wrestling, as well as an alternative reading of its narrative structures, see Michael R. Ball, *Professional Wrestling as a Ritual Drama in American Popular Culture* (Lewiston, ME: Edwin Mellen Press, 1990). For a performance-centered account of WWF Wrestling, see Sharon Mazer, "The Doggie Doggie World of Professional Wrestling," *The Drama Review*, Winter 1990, pp. 96–122.

6. John Fiske, *Television Culture* (London: Methuen, 1982); Tania Modleski, *Loving with a Vengeance: Mass Produced Fantasies for Women* (London: Methuen, 1982); Jane Feuer, "Melodrama, Serial Form and Television Today," *Screen* 25 (1984): 4–16.

7. Christine Gledhill, "The Melodramatic Field: An Investigation," in Christine Gledhill, ed., *Home Is Where the Heart Is: Studies in Melodrama and the Woman's Film* (London: British Film Institute, 1987), pp. 12–13. David Thorburn similarly finds melodramatic conventions underlying much of prime-time television programming. See Thorburn, "Television Melodrama," in Horace Newcomb, ed., *Television: The Critical Eye*, 4th ed. (New York: Oxford University Press, 1987), p. 7.

8. Norbert Elias and Eric Dunning, *The Quest for Excitement: Sport and Leisure in the Civilizing Process* (New York: Basil Blackwell, 1986), p. 41.

9. Ibid., pp. 64–65.

10. Ibid., p. 111.

11. Ibid., p. 49.

12. Ibid.

13. Ibid., p. 50.

14. Ibid., pp. 86–87.

15. Peter Brooks, *The Melodramatic Imagination: Balzac, Henry James, Melodrama, and the Mode of Excess* (New Haven: Yale University Press, 1976).

16. Gledhill, "The Melodramatic Field: An Investigation," p. 21.

17. Keith Elliot Greenberg, "One Step Too Far: Boss Man and Mountie Clash over Meaning of Justice," *WWF Magazine*, May 1991, p. 40.

18. Brutus was injured in a motorcycle accident and had his skull reconstructed; he is no longer able to fight but has come to represent the voice of aged wisdom within the WWF universe. Brutus constantly articulates the values of fairness and loyalty in the face of their abuse by the rule-breaking characters, pushing for reconciliations that might resolve old feuds, and watching these disputes erupt and destroy his barber shop.

19. "The Mark of Cain: Shawn Michaels Betrays His Tag Team Brother," *WWF Magazine*, March 1992, p. 18.

20. "WWF Superstars Talk about Wrestlemania," *WWF Magazine*, March 1992, p. 18.

21. Robert Bechtold Heilman, *The Iceman, the Arsonist, and the Troubled Agent: Tragedy and Melodrama on the Modern Stage* (Seattle: University of Washington Press, 1968), p. 76.

22. Brooks, *The Melodramatic Imagination*, p. 34.

23. "WWF Interview: A Talk with Jake 'the Snake' Roberts," p. 17.

24. Brooks, *The Melodramatic Imagination*, p. 4.

25. Ibid., p. 41.

26. Robert Bechtold Heilman, *Tragedy and Melodrama: Versions of Experience* (Seattle: University of Washington Press, 1968), p. 76.

27. "Elizabeth Balancing Family with Business," *WWF Wrestling Spotlight*, March 1992.

28. Eve Kosofsky Sedgwick, *Between Men: English Literature and Male Homosocial Desire* (New York: Columbia University Press, 1985).

29. "Meeting of the Minds: Jake and Andre—Psychological Interplay," *WWF Magazine*, August 1991, p. 52.

30. Ibid.

31. Keith Elliot Greenberg, "The Darkness Is in Me Forever . . . ," *WWF Magazine*, August 1991, p. 47.

32. This incident could also be read as a response to a series of rumors and tabloid stories centering on the sexuality of WWF athletes. The Ultimate Warrior was "outed" by one tabloid newspaper, while charges of sexual harassment surfaced on an episode of the Phil Donahue show. Complicating an easy reading of this incident is the strong popularity of wresting within the gay male community and the existence of gay fanzines publishing sexual fantasies involving wrestlers.

33. Bruce Palmer, *"Man over Money": The Southern Populist Critique of American Capitalism* (Chapel Hill: University of North Carolina Press, 1980), p. 3.

34. Ibid., p. 5.

35. "WWF Superstars Talk about Wrestlemania," p. 18.

36. "Personality Profile: Repo Man," *WWF Magazine*, February 1992, p. 11.

37. "Salt of the Earth: Sid Justice Comes from the Land," *WWF Magazine*, November 1991, pp. 47–48.

38. "Tatanka: Leader of the New Indian Nation," *WWF Magazine*, April 1992, p. 55.

39. "A Talk with Big Boss Man," *WWF Magazine*, November 1991, p. 18.

40. "American Pride: Sarge and Duggan Protect Old Glory from the Nastys," *WWF Magazine*, March 1992, p. 52.

NOTES TO CHAPTER 5

1. Daniel Kagen, "Corman's 'Slightly Corrupted' Fare," *Insight*, April 11, 1988, p. 61. For a useful discussion of the play between commerce and art in Corman's career, see William A. Routt, "Art, Popular Art," *Continuum: The Australian Journal of Media and Culture* 7, no.2 (1994): 2–3.

2. Recent feminist criticism has made much of Dorothy Arzner's "mannish lesbian" appearance in photographs as signaling her subcultural identifications and her exclusion from the dominant culture of Hollywood. See Judith Mayne, *Directed by Dorothy Arzner* (Bloomington: Indiana University Press, 1994). A similar reading could be made of Rothman's image—the fact that she looks so much like the women in her films, that she fits within a certain conception of feminine attractiveness and glamour, as suggesting a more comfortable fit with the conditions of exploitation film production, as signaling the heterosexual assumptions behind 1970s liberal feminism. Rothman is as femme as Arzner is butch, and that difference speaks to some of the differences in how feminist critics have taken up the two "cases" of female authorship.

3. Stephanie Rothman, "A New Beginning on Terminal Island," in Danny Peary, ed., *Omni's Screen Flights/Screen Fantasies: The Future According to Science Fiction Cinema* (Garden City: Doubleday, 1984), p. 142.

4. For a useful overview of Rothman's career, see Terry Curtis, "Fully Female," *Film Comment*, November–December 1976, pp. 46–52.

5. For background on Dimension, see Fred Olen Ray, *The New Poverty Row: Independent Filmmakers as Distributors* (Jefferson, NC: McFarland and Co., 1991), pp. 149–74; Ed Lowery, "Dimension Pictures: Portrait of a Seventies Independent," *The Velvet Light Trap*, no. 22 (1986): 65–74.

6. For useful discussions of Corman's role as a producer, see David Chute, "The New World of Roger Corman," *Film Comment*, March–April 1982, pp. 27–32; Dave Kehr, "B+: Four Auteurs in Search of an Audience," *Film Comment*, September–October 1977, pp. 6–15; Michael Goodwin, "Velvet Vampires and Hot Mamas: Why Exploitation Films Get to Us," *Village Voice*, July 7 1975; Jim Hillier and Aaron Lipstadt, *Roger Corman's New World*, BFI Dossier no. 7 (London: British Film Institute, 1981); Michael Pye and Lynda Myles, *The*

Movie Brats: How the Film Generation Took Over Hollywood (New York: Holt, Rinehart, and Winston, 1979); Kim Newman, "The Roger Corman Alumni Association," *Monthly Film Bulletin*, November–December 1985; Jim Hillier and Aaron Lipstadt, "The Economics of Independence: Roger Corman and New World Pictures, 1970–1980," *Movie*, Winter 1986, pp. 43–53.

7. Pam Cook, "Exploitation Films and Feminism," *Screen*, 1976, pp. 122–27.

8. Dave Chute, "The New World of Roger Corman," *Film Comment*, March–April 1982, pp. 27–32. Corman's comments are typically double-edged, since there were not many more women operating lathe drills in the early 1970s than directing movies; both images point to the battlegrounds where middle-class women were making claims for economic and professional equality.

9. J. Philip DiFranco, *The Movie World of Roger Corman* (New York: Chelsea House, 1979), p. 55.

10. Roger Corman and Jim Jerome, *How I Made a Hundred Movies in Hollywood and Never Lost a Dime* (New York: Delta Books, 1991), p. 184.

11. For key works in this tradition, see Claire Johnston, ed., *Notes on Women's Cinema* (London: Society for Education in Film and Television, 1973); Claire Johnston, ed., *Dorothy Arzner: Towards a Feminist Cinema* (London: British Film Institute, 1975). Cook has reintroduced debate about Rothman in these terms multiple times since the publication of her initial 1976 *Screen* essay (see n. 7 above). See, for example, Pam Cook, ed., *The Cinema Book* (London: British Film Institute, 1987), pp. 199–200; Pam Cook, "Exploitation Films" and "Stephanie Rothman," in Annette Kuhn with Susannah Radstone, eds., *The Women's Companion to International Film* (Berkeley: University of California Press, 1990), pp. 139–10, 347–48; Pam Cook, "The Art of Exploitation, or How to Get Into the Movies," *Monthly Film Bulletin* 52, no.623 (1985), pp. 367–69.

12. Laura Mulvey, "Visual Pleasure and Narrative Cinema," in Bill Nichols, ed., *Movies and Methods II* (Berkeley: University of California Press, 1985), pp. 303–15.

13. Claire Johnston, "Women's Cinema as Counter-Cinema," in Bill Nichols, ed., *Movies and Methods I* (Berkeley: University of California Press, 1976), p. 217.

14. Cook, "Exploitation Films and Feminism," p. 127.

15. Rothman, "A New Beginning on Terminal Island," p.141.

16. See, for example, Molly Haskell, *From Reverence to Rape: The Treatment of Women in the Movies* (New York: Penguin, 1974), for what was probably the earliest account of how women disappeared from 1970s films in response to the rise of feminism. Haskell, however, completely ignores the exploitation cinema.

17. Cook, "Exploitation Films and Feminism," p. 123.

18. "I think it is noteworthy that no one else at the time was making action pictures with female leads. In all the stories we tried to make the women

genuinely the protagonists in that they initiated the action." Roger Corman, as quoted in DiFranco, *The Movie World of Roger Corman*, p. 162. For similar claims, see Gary Morris, *Roger Corman* (Boston: Twayne, 1985), p. 147.

19. Quotes taken from the video box, *Bury Me an Angel*, New World Video, 1985.

20. Cook, "Exploitation Films and Feminism," p. 126.

21. The same double motives surface in James Cameron's *Aliens*, where Ripley both wants to protect society from the monsters and to assume maternal responsibility for Newt, the orphaned girl. The introduction of more traditionally feminine motives for her actions has been the subject of controversy given the allegedly asexual and degendered construction of Ridley Scott's *Alien*. Constance Penley argues, "What we get finally is a conservative moral lesson about maternity, futuristic or otherwise: mothers will be mothers, and they will always be women." Constance Penley, "Time Travel, Primal Scene, and the Critical Dystopia," in Constance Penley, Elisabeth Lyon, Lynn Spigel, and Janet Bergstrom, eds., *Close Encounters: Film, Feminism and Science Fiction* (Minneapolis: University of Minnesota Press, 1991), p. 73. I read the film somewhat differently. While it is true that the instabilities and contradictions of Ripley's character are consistent with the problems surrounding the exploitation film heroine, Cameron situates her within a world of androgynous possibility, where all of the characters mix and match traits associated with femininity and masculinity. The characters who survive are those who are comfortable with that mix, who have achieved some balance between the two (specifically Ripley, Newt, and Bishop) while those who die are most often the hypermasculine women (Vasquez) and hyperfeminine men (Hudson). Signs of traditional femininity mean something different, I would argue, in a world where gender is shown to be a construct that can be freely manipulated, and where sex itself is seen as socially constructed (since characters are identified as having naturally or artificially determined sexes).

22. Similar images of emotional and psychological instability surround the female protagonist in Cameron's *Terminator* films and have been the source of much debate by feminist critics.

23. Richard Dyer, "The Role of Stereotypes," in *The Making of Images: Essays on Representation* (London: Routledge, Chapman and Hall, 1993), pp. 11–18.

24. Cook, "Exploitation Films and Feminism," pp. 124–25. Cook's account of the exploitation film was influential in the development of arguments within the "progressive genre" debate. See Barbara Klinger, "Cinema/Ideology/Criticism Revisited: The Progressive Genre," in Barry Keith Grant, ed., *Film Genre Reader* (Austin: University of Texas Press, 1986), pp. 74–90.

25. A similar structure occurs in the other New World genres: The female outlaw films, such as *Bloody Mama*, *Boxcar Bertha*, or *Crazy Mama*, often

open with moments of victimization and trauma, though here, the proportions are different. The process of victimization dominates the women's prison film, while the process of rebellion and resistance dominates the female outlaw films.

26. Jonathan Demme's *Caged Heat* is a notable exception, a progressive intervention in the genre that is worth further consideration on multiple levels. Demme focuses specifically on abuses within the American prison system and on the plight of women within our society. He even refuses the characteristic demonization of the female prison warden, offering scenes that cast her in a more sympathetic light, and at one striking point, making her a mouthpiece for his feminist critique of the sexual exploitation of women.

27. Paul Willemen, "Roger Corman: The Millenic Vision," in Paul Willemen, David Pirie, David Will, and Lynda Myles, ed., *Roger Corman* (Edinburgh: Edinburgh Film Festival, 1970), pp. 8–33.

28. Peter Fitting, "So We All Became Mothers: New Roles for Men in Recent Utopian Fiction," *Science Fiction Studies* 12 (1985): 156–83.

29. Rothman, "Exploitation Films and Feminism," p. 142.

30. Ibid., p. 141.

31. One might usefully compare the remarkably similar representation of striptease in Rothman's *Working Women* and Dorothy Arzner's *Dance Girl Dance*, since both invite us to experience the burlesque audience from the performer's vantage point and to think about the economic and professional stakes in female erotic display.

32. While such devices are more common in Rothman's films than in most other exploitation movies, similar attempts to question the politics of female spectacle or to discomfort the male spectator occur in other New World productions. Demme's *Caged Heat*, for example, includes a number of uncomfortable jokes involving castration, impotency, and the mutilation of penises; a running debate about the double-standards surrounding male and female access to pornography (which culminates in the scene of a topless woman protesting the confinement of a woman in solitary confinement for possessing a photograph of a naked man); and a bizarre dream sequence in which the warden warns women that sexual injustice placed them behind bars.

33. Terry Curtis Fox, "Fully Female: Stephanie Rothman," *Film Comment* 12 (November–December 1976), pp. 46–50.

NOTES TO CHAPTER 6

1. Barbara Lawton, "Lupe—No Change!", *Photoplay*, December 1930, pp. 74ff.

260 I Notes to Chapter 6

2. Katherine Albert, "The Hot Baby of Hollywood, Otherwise Lupe Velez," *New Movie*, undated clipping (probably circa 1932), Lupe Velez file, Herbert Blum Collection, Wisconsin Center for Film and Theatre Research.

3. Ruth Biery, "The Love Life Story of Lupe Velez," unidentified clipping (probably circa 1930), Lupe Velez file, Herbert Blum Collection, Wisconsin Center for Film and Theatre Research.

4. Budd Schulberg, *Moving Pictures: Memoirs of a Hollywood Prince* (New York: Stein and Day, 1981), p. 339.

5. "Flirting with Dynamite," *New Movie*, June 1933, Lupe Velez File, Herbert Blum Collection, Wisconsin Center for Film and Theatre Research.

6. Biery, "The Love Life Story of Lupe Velez."

7. Ibid.

8. Kenneth Anger, *Hollywood Babylon* (New York: Dell, 1975), p. 332.

9. Ibid., p. 329.

10. Edward G. Robinson, as quoted in Floyd Conner, *Lupe Velez and Her Lovers* (New York: Barricade, 1993), p. 60.

11. Conner, *Lupe Velez and Her Lovers*, p. 50.

12. "She is gradually transforming herself into the sort of person her press agents paint her. This is never a happy metamorphosis, in as much as it is rarely achieved without overacting. She speaks of herself as Lupe, flashes her eyes extravagantly, avoids the conventional in speech and posture, and registers gaiety untrammeled at any cost." Malcolm H. Dettinger, "Just a Little Madcap," undated fan magazine clipping (circa 1929), Herbert Blum Collection, Wisconsin Center for Film and Theatre Research.

13. For feminist work on Madonna, see Cathy Schwichtenberg, ed., *The Madonna Connection: Representational Politics, Subcultural Identities, and Cultural Theory* (Boulder, CO: Westview, 1993); for feminist work on Annie Sprinkle, see Chris Straayer, "The Seduction of Boundaries: Feminist Fluidity in Annie Sprinkle's Art/Education/Sex," in Pamela Church Gibson, ed., *More Dirty Looks: Gender, Pornography, and Power* (London: British Film Institute, 2004), pp. 224–36; and Linda Williams, "A Provoking Agent: The Pornography and Performance Art of Annie Sprinkle," in Pamela Church Gibson and Roma Gibson, eds., *Dirty Looks: Women, Pornography, Power* (London: British Film Institute, 1993), pp. 176–92.

14. Kathleen Rowe, *The Unruly Woman: Gender and the Genres of Laughter* (Austin: University of Texas Press, 1995); Mary Russo, *The Female Grotesque: Risk, Excess and Modernity* (New York: Routledge, 1994).

15. Natalie Zemon Davis, *Society and Culture in Early Modern France* (Stanford: Stanford University Press, 1975), pp. 124–25.

16. "Misbehaving Ladies," unidentified fan magazine clipping (circa 1929–30), Lupe Velez file, Herbert Blum Collection, Wisconsin Center for Film and Theatre Research.

17. Anger, *Hollywood Babylon*, p. 328.

18. Biery, "The Love Life Story of Lupe Velez."

19. For more on Winnie Lightner and Charlotte Greenwood, see Henry Jenkins, *What Made Pistachio Nuts? Early Sound Comedy and the Vaudeville Aesthetic* (New York: Columbia University Press, 1992), pp. 245–76. This essay on Lupe Velez was originally intended to be a third case study in this chapter, but its creation has been delayed by almost a decade.

20. On Mae West, see Ramona Curry, *Too Much of a Good Thing: Mae West as Cultural Icon* (Minneapolis: University of Minnesota Press, 1996); Pamela Robertson, *Guilty Pleasures: Feminist Camp from Mae West to Madonna* (Durham, NC: Duke University Press, 1996).

21. Rowe, *The Unruly Woman*, p. 5.

22. Pamela Robertson Wojcik, "Mae West's Maids: Race, 'Authenticity,' and the Discourse of Camp," in Henry Jenkins, Tara McPherson, and Jane Shattuc, eds., *Hop on Pop: The Politics and Pleasure of Popular Culture* (Durham, NC: Duke University Press, 2003), pp. 287–99.

23. Michael Rogin, *Blackface, White Noise: Jewish Immigrants in the Hollywood Melting Pot* (Berkeley: University of California Press, 1996).

24. "Flirting with Dynamite," *New Movie*, June 1933, Lupe Velez file, Herbert Blum Collection, Wisconsin Center for Film and Theatre Research.

25. Richard Dyer, *White* (London: Routledge, 1997), p. 19.

26. "Misbehaving Ladies," unidentified fan magazine clipping (circa 1929–30), Lupe Velez file, Herbert Blum Collection, Wisconsin Center for Film and Theatre Research.

27. Roland Barthes, *Mythologies* (New York: Hill and Wang, 1983), pp. 56–57.

28. Robert K. Gluckson, "Sex Comics in the 1930s–1950s: A Genre History" (Master's thesis, University of Washington, 1992).

29. R. C. Harvey, "Getting Our Pornography Fixed," in R. C. Harvey, ed., *The Tijuana Bibles: America's Forgotten Comic Strips*, 2 vols. (Seattle: Eros Comics, 1996), vol. 1, p. 5.

30. "Hot Panties," in Harvey, ed., *The Tijuana Bibles*, vol. 1, pp. 39–43.

31. "Bigger Yet" in Harvey, ed., *The Tijuana Bibles*, vol. 2, pp. 62–66.

32. Peter Stallybrass and Allon White, *The Politics and Poetics of Transgression* (Ithaca, NY: Cornell University Press, 1986).

33. Mikhail Bakhtin, *Rabelais and His World* (Bloomington: Indiana University Press, 1984), p. 29.

34. Hardon Ever, "Nuts to Will Hays!," in Harvey, ed., *The Tijuana Bibles*, vol. 2, pp. 52–56.

35. "Eroll Sinn Shoots an Arrow" in Harvey, ed., *The Tijuana Bibles*, vol. 1, pp.104–8.

36. Russo, *The Female Grotesque*, p. 33.

37. Garson Kanin, *Hollywood: Stars and Starlets, Tycoons and Flesh-Ped-dlers, Moviemakers and Moneymakers, Frauds and Geniuses, Hopefuls and Has-Beens, Great Lovers and Sex Symbols* (New York: Bantam, 1974), pp. 390–411. Kanin's story probably provided the basis for the prostitute who looks like Veronica Lake, played by Kim Basinger, in *LA Confidential*.

38. Russo, *The Female Grotesque*, pp. 17–51.

39. "Mexicana," *Vanity Fair*, June 1932, p. 22, Lupe Velez file, Herbert Blum Collection, Wisconsin Center for Film and Theatre Research.

40. Ruth Biery, "The Best Showman in Town," *Photoplay*, November 1931, Lupe Velez file, Herbert Blum Collection, Wisconsin Center for Film and Theatre Research.

41. Conner, *Lupe Velez and Her Lovers*, p. 120.

42. Ibid., p. 5.

43. Biery, "The Best Showman in Town."

44. Unidentified clipping (circa 1936), Lupe Velez file, Herbert Blum Collection, Wisconsin Center for Film and Theatre Research.

45. Unidentified clipping, *Screen Guide*, date unknown, Lupe Velez file, Herbert Blum Collection, Wisconsin Center for Film and Theatre Research.

46. Unidentified clipping (circa 1936), Lupe Velez file, Herbert Blum Collection, Wisconsin Center for Film and Theatre Research.

47. Unidentified clipping, date unknown, Lupe Velez file, Herbert Blum Collection, Wisconsin Center for Film and Theatre Research.

48. "Flirting with Dynamite," *New Movie*, June 1932, Lupe Velez file, Herbert Blum Collection, Wisconsin Center for Film and Theatre Research.

49. All of the above gossip comes from Conner, *Lupe Velez and Her Lovers*.

50. Carlos Monsiváis, *Mexican Postcards*, trans. John Kraniauskas (London: Verso, 1997), p. 71.

51. Barthes, *Mythologies*, pp. 56–57.

52. Dyer, *White*, pp. 89–90.

53. Ibid., p. 29.

54. Monsiváis, *Mexican Postcards*, p. 75. Of course, this process worked in reverse as well, with the Polish-born Lydia Roberti cast as a Mexican woman in *Kid from Spain*. Here, an accent, more than skin color or facial features, cast Roberti as "non-white" and thus capable of passing for Mexican.

55. Duncan Underhill, "A Dash of Red Pepper," *Screen Life*, undated clipping (circa 1930), Lupe Velez file, Herbert Blum Collection, Wisconsin Center for Film and Theatre Research.

56. "Mexican Fire," undated clipping, Lupe Velez file, Herbert Blum Collection, Wisconsin Center for Film and Theatre Research.

57. Undated and unidentified clipping, Lupe Velez file, Herbert Blum Collection, Wisconsin Center for Film and Theatre Research.

58. Unidentified clipping (circa 1930), Lupe Velez file, Herbert Blum Collection, Wisconsin Center for Film and Theatre Research.

59. Biery, "The Best Showman in Town."

60. Ibid. "Lupe is full of hell and fire and earth and storm and sea. She is breathless and exciting and young, as simple as a nursery rhyme, as vital as passion." Katherine Albert, "The Hot Baby of Hollywood, Otherwise Known as Lupe Velez," Lupe Velez file, Herbert Blum Collection, Wisconsin Center for Film and Theatre Research.

61. Conner, *Lupe Velez and Her Lovers*, p. 1.

62. Walt Morton, "Tracking the Sign of Tarzan: Trans-Media Representation of a Pop-Culture Icon," in Pat Kirkham and Janet Thumim, eds., *You Tarzan: Masculinity, Movies, and Men* (New York: St. Martin's Press, 1993), p. 116.

63. Conner, *Lupe Velez and Her Lovers*, p. 139.

64. Undated and unidentified clipping (circa 1930), Lupe Velez file, Herbert Blum Collection, Wisconsin Center for Film and Theatre Research.

65. Conner, *Lupe Velez and Her Lovers*, p. 137.

66. Eric L. Ergenbright, "Lupe Talks about Her Johnny," undated clipping, Lupe Velez file, Herbert Blum Collection, Wisconsin Center for Film and Theatre Research.

67. Undated and unidentified clipping (circa 1934), Lupe Velez file, Herbert Blum Collection, Wisconsin Center for Film and Theatre Research.

68. James Oles, *South of the Border: Mexico in the American Imagination, 1914–1947* (Washington, DC: Smithsonian Institution Press, 1993), p. 49.

69. Conner, *Lupe Velez and Her Lovers*, pp. 1–3. Katherine Albert, "The Hot Baby of Hollywood, Otherwise Lupe Velez," undated clipping, Lupe Velez file, Herbert Blum Collection, Wisconsin Center for Film and Theatre Research, claims that Lupe's father was shot through the heart during the Mexican Revolution. The revolution appears as a reference point in several of the other fan magazine profiles.

70. Monsiváis, *Mexican Postcards*, p. 73.

71. Jean Franco, *Plotting Women: Gender and Representation in Mexico* (New York: Columbia University Press, 1989), p. xviii.

72. Dyer, *White*, p. 122.

73. Ana M. Lopez, "Are All Latins from Manhattan? Hollywood, Ethnography, and Cultural Colonialism," in Lester D. Friedman, ed., *Unspeakable Images: Ethnicity and the American Cinema* (Urbana: University of Illinois Press, 1991), p. 414. See also Shari Roberts, "'The Lady in the Tutti-Frutti Hat': Carmen Miranda, a Spectacle of Ethnicity," *Cinema Journal*, Spring 1993, pp. 3–19, who writes: "Latina actresses in Hollywood films generally fit neatly within one of two stereotypes of the foreign Other: the exotic sex object (such as Dolores Del Rio, the "female Valentino") or the ignorant comic actress (such

as Lupe Velez, the "Mexican Spitfire"). Miranda is unique in that she initially straddled both categories: she was perceived by contemporary audiences as simultaneously sexy and comic, a vamp and a joke" (p. 11). In fact, Roberts is mistaken—or at least reductive—about Velez's image, which, as we have seen, certainly was understood as "simultaneously sexy and comic, a vamp and a joke." There are significant differences in the ways Del Rio and Velez are sexy, having to do with the distinction between glamour and grotesque conceptions of feminine sexuality explored above, and they are both unique from Carmen Miranda. What this suggests is the need for a more complex vocabulary for speaking about the relations between comedy and sexuality.

74. John Kasson, *Rudeness and Civility: Manners in Nineteenth-Century Urban America* (New York: Hill and Wang, 1990), pp. 114–15.

75. Ibid., p. 165.

76. Schulberg, *Moving Pictures*, p. 338.

77. Ibid., p. 286. Schulberg's use of Velez to display his own sensitivity in response to violence has parallels in the ways that white writers used black conduct to describe the sexual excesses stirred up by jazz, while defining their own interests in the music in different terms. See Nicholas M. Evans, "Racial Cross-Dressing in the Jazz Age: Cultural Therapy and Its Discontents in Cabaret Nightlife," in Henry Jenkins, Tara McPherson, and Jane Shattuc, eds., *Hop on Pop: The Politics and Pleasures of Popular Culture* (Durham, NC: Duke University Press, 2002), pp. 388–414.

78. Biery, "The Love Life Story of Lupe Velez."

79. Gloria Anzaldua, "How to Tame a Wild Tongue," *Borderlands/La Frontera: The New Mestiza* (San Francisco: Aunt Lute Books, 1987), pp. 75–86.

80. Schulberg, *Moving Pictures*, p. 338.

81. This and subsequent quotes in this section are all taken from Anger, *Hollywood Babylon*, pp. 336–42.

NOTES TO PART III INTRODUCTION

1. For a fuller discussion of these issues, see Henry Jenkins, "Introduction: Childhood Innocence and Other Modern Myths," in Henry Jenkins, ed., *The Children's Culture Reader* (New York: New York University Press, 1998), pp. 1–38.

2. James R. Kincaid, "Producing Erotic Children," in Jenkins, ed., *The Children's Culture Reader*, pp. 241–53; Jacqueline S. Rose, *The Case of Peter Pan: Or the Impossibility of Children's Fiction* (London: Macmillan, 1984).

3. Justine Cassell and Henry Jenkins, eds., *From Barbie to Mortal Kombat: Gender and Computer Games* (Cambridge: MIT Press, 2000); Henry Jenkins, "From Barbie to Mortal Kombat: Further Reflections," in Anna Everett and

John T. Caldwell, eds., *New Media: Theories and Practices of Digitextuality*, AFI Readers (New York: Routledge, 2003), pp. 243–54.

NOTES TO CHAPTER 7

Acknowledgments: I am indebted to John Fiske, David Bordwell, Richard Lachman, Murray Smith, and Kristine Karnick for their helpful suggestion in preparing this manuscript for publication. I am especially grateful to the active inspiration and support of Cynthia Benson Jenkins and Henry Jenkins IV, without whom this project would not have been possible.

1. Roald Dahl, *Charlie and the Chocolate Factory* (New York: Alfred A. Knopf), pp. 145–46; cited hereafter by page number in the text.

2. Robert Hodge and David Tripp, *Children and Television: A Semiotic Approach* (Cambridge: Polity Press, 1986), pp. 2–3.

3. See Clifford Geertz, *The Interpretation of Cultures* (New York: Basic Books, 1973).

4. For examples of how adults might confront a similar problem—that of recounting their experience of a text—see David Bleich, "Gender Interests in Reading and Language," in Elizabeth A. Flynn and Patrocinio P. Schweickart, eds., *Gender and Reading: Essays on Readers, Texts and Contexts* (Baltimore: Johns Hopkins University Press, 1986), pp. 234–66. Although more research is needed here, my own experience with Henry's viewing of a variety of different types of texts suggests that the more fragmented structure of *Pee-Wee's Playhouse* is not a major determinant of this sensation-centered reading strategy. Even programs with more linear constructions, such as *Masters of the Universe*, are often read atomistically with little or no interest in the larger narrative context within which a particularly compelling scene might be embedded.

5. While the parents were informed that the party constituted a type of scholarly research and completed open-ended survey forms about their children and their viewing habits, they were asked to treat the gathering as any other that their son or daughter might attend. As far as the children were concerned, it was simply another opportunity to share a good time with some friends. My son, Henry, was active at all stages of the planning process, selecting which children to invite, designing and making the invitations, determining the menu, and deciding what program episodes we would show. Such a child-centered research design helped to eliminate, though not entirely, the youngster's tendencies to conform to the expectations of authorities, tendencies that unmistakably color more traditional approaches to children and the media.

6. See Patricia Palmer, *The Lively Audience: A Study of Children around the TV Set* (Sidney: Allen and Unwin, 1986).

7. David Bordwell, *Narration in the Fiction Film* (Madison: University of Wisconsin Press, 1986), p. 31.

8. Bruno Bettelheim, "The Importance of Play," *Atlantic* (March 1987): 35–46.

9. L. S. Vygotsky, "Play and Its Role in the Mental Development of the Child," in J. S. Bruner, A. Jolly, and K. Sylva, eds., *Play: Its Role in Development and Evolution* (New York: Penguin, 1976), pp. 537–54.

10. T. Gertler, "The Pee-Wee Perplex," *Rolling Stone*, February 12, 1987, pp. 37–41.

11. Ibid., p. 38.

12. Alison James, "Confections, Concoctions and Conceptions," in Henry Jenkins, ed., *The Children's Culture Reader* (New York: New York University Press, 1998), pp.394–405; cited hereafter by page number in the text.

13. Note how Bill's "knock-knock" joke follows adult rules only long enough to sucker his playmates into participation and then gleefully abandons them for a punch line that seems totally beside the point. His reference to *Silverhawks* here reflects Bill's general strategy throughout the party to deflect attention away from *Pee-Wee's Playhouse*, a show he was forbidden to watch by his father, onto the more comfortable terrain of his own favorite television program, and suggests rather vividly the degree to which the ability to make in-references to popular programs may be a real source of social power within kindergarten society.

14. Martha Wolfenstein, *Children's Humor: A Psychological Analysis* (Bloomington: Indiana University Press, 1954).

15. Ibid.; Erik H. Erikson, *Childhood and Society* (New York: W. W. Norton, 1950).

16. Henry Jenkins, "Star Trek Rerun, Reread, Rewritten: Fan Writing as Textual Poaching," *Critical Studies in Mass Communication* 5, no. 2 (1988): 85–107.

17. Hodge and Tripp, *Children and Television*, p. 85.

NOTES TO CHAPTER 8

1. Keith Feinstein and Steven Kent, "Towards a Definition of Videogames" (1997), http://www.videotopia.com/errata1.htm.

2. A. Booth and D. Johnson, "The Effect of Crowding on Child Health and Development," *American Behavioral Scientist* 18 (1975): 736–49; J. F. van Staden, "Urban Early Adolescents, Crowding and the Neighbourhood Experience: A Preliminary Investigation," *Journal of Environmental Psychology* 4 (1984): 97–118.

3. J. L. Kinchloe, "Home Alone and 'Bad to the Bone': The Advent of a Postmodern Childhood," in. S. R. Steinberg and J. L. Kinchloe, eds., *Kinder-Culture: The Corporate Construction of Childhood* (New York: Westview, 1997), pp. 31–52.

4. Elliott West, "Children on the Plains Frontier," in Elliott West and Paula Petrik, eds., *Small Worlds: Children and Adolescents in America, 1850–1950* (Lawrence: University Press of Kansas, 1992), pp. 26–41.

5. Dominick Cavallo, *Muscles and Morals: Organized Playgrounds and Urban Reform, 1880–1920* (Philadelphia: University of Pennsylvania Press, 1981).

6. Roger Hart, *Children's Experience of Place* (New York: John Wiley and Sons, 1979).

7. Ibid., pp. 9–14.

8. Robin C. Moore, *Childhood's Domain: Play and Place in Child Development* (London: Croom Helm, 1986); Willem Van Vliet, "Exploring the Fourth Environment: An Examination of the Home Range of City and Suburban Teenagers," *Environment and Behavior* 15 (1983), pp. 567–88.

9. M. H. Matthews, *Making Sense of Place: Children's Understanding of Large-Scale Environments* (Hertfordshire: Barnes and Noble, 1992).

10. Frederick Donaldson, "The Child in the City" (1970), cited in Matthews Making Sense of Place, p. 000.

11. Moore, *Childhood's Domain*, p. 72.

12. Hart, *Children's Experience of Place*, p. 65.

13. John Newson and Elizabeth Newson, *Seven Years Old in the Home Environment* (London: Allen and Unwin, 1976).

14. H. L. Rheingold and K. V. Cook, "The Content of Boys' and Girls' Rooms as an Index of Parents' Behavior," *Child Development* 46 (1975): 459–63.

15. Matthews, *Making Sense of Place*, pp. 163–74.

16. Miriam Formanek-Brunnel, "The Politics of Dollhood in Nineteenth-Century America," in Henry Jenkins, ed., *The Children's Culture Reader* (New York: New York University Press, 1998), pp. 363–81.

17. E. Anthony Rotundo, *American Manhood: Transformations in Masculinity from the Revolution to the Modern Era* (New York: Basic Books, 1994), pp. 31–55.

18. Ibid., p. 37.

19. Moore, *Childhood's Domain*, p. 000.

20. Rotundo, *American Manhood*, p. 45.

21. M. Kinder, "Contextualizing Video Game Violence: From 'Teenage Mutant Ninja Turtles 1' to 'Mortal Kombat 2,'" in Patricia M. Greenfield and Rodney R. Cocking, eds., *Interacting with Video*, Advances in Applied Developmental Psychology 11 (Norwood: Ablex, 1996), pp. 25–38.

22. Rotundo, *American Manhood*, p. 55.

23. Justine Cassell, "Storytelling as a Nexus of Change in the Relationship between Gender and Technology: A Feminist Approach," in Justine Cassell and Henry Jenkins, eds., *From Barbie to Mortal Kombat: Gender and Computer Games* (Cambridge, MA: MIT Press, 1998), pp. 298–327.

24. Justine Cassell and Henry Jenkins, "Chess for Girls? Feminism and Computer Games," in Cassell and Jenkins, eds, *From Barbie to Mortal Kombat*, pp. 2–45.

25. Elizabeth Segel, "'As the Twig Is Bent . . . ': Gender and Childhood Reading," in Flynn and Schweickart, eds., *Gender and Reading*, p. 171.

26. Ibid.

27. Walter Farley, *The Black Stallion* (New York: Random House, 1941), p. 27.

28. Frances Hodgson Burnett, *The Secret Garden* (New York: Harper Collins, 1911), p. 71; cited hereafter by page number in the text.

29. Segel, "As the Twig Is Bent," pp. 171–72.

30. Ibid., p. 173.

31. Norman N. Holland and Leona F. Sherman, "Gothic Possibilities," in Flynn and Schweickart, eds., *Gender and Reading*.

32. Ibid., p. 220.

33. Louise Fitzhugh, *Harriet the Spy* (New York: Harper and Row, 1964), pp. 3–5; cited hereafter by page number in the text.

34. T. Friedman, "Making Sense of Software: Computer Games and Interactive Textuality," in Steve Jones, ed., *Cybersociety: Computer-Mediated Communication and Community* (Thousand Oaks, CA.: Sage Publications, 1995).

35. Theresa Duncan, quoted in "Interviews with Theresa Duncan and Monica Gesue (Chop Suey)," in Cassell and Jenkins, eds., *From Barbie to Mortal Kombat*, pp. 172–91.

36. Ibid.

37. Segel, "As the Twig Is Bent," p. 171–72

38. Jenkins and Cassell, "Chess for Girls?"

39. Barrie Thorne, *Gender Play: Girls and Boys in School* (New Brunswick: Rutgers University Press), 64–65.

NOTES TO CHAPTER 9

1. Kathleen Kete, *The Beast in the Boudoir: Petkeeping in Nineteenth-Century Paris* (Berkeley: University of California Press, 1994).

2. On James Bond as a popular hero, see Tony Bennett and Janet Woollacott, *Bond and Beyond: The Political Career of a Popular Hero* (New York: Methuen, 1987). On Batman, see Roberta E. Pearson and William Uricchio,

eds., *The Many Lives of Batman: Critical Approaches to a Superhero and His Media* (New York: Routledge, Chapman and Hall, 1991).

3. Most of these images can be found in *Lassie Coloring Book* (Racine, WI.: Whitman, 1962).

4. Jacqueline Rose reminds us that fantasies of a transparent relationship between language and the world, and of a simple moral legibility, are at the heart of contemporary conceptions of children's fiction. Jacqueline Rose, *The Case of Peter Pan: Or the Impossibility of Children's Fiction* (London: Macmillan, 1984).

5. James R. Kincaid, *Child Loving: The Erotic Child and Victorian Culture* (New York: Routledge, 1992), p. 79.

6. Eric Knight, *Lassie Come-Home* (New York: Dell, 1940), i; cited hereafter by page number in the text.

7. Kete, *Beast in the Boudoir*, esp. pp. 39–55.

8. Harriet Ritvo argues that this shift reflected growing middle-class fantasies of upward mobility and class assimilation, as the lower orders mimicked the practices of those better off. Harriet Ritvo, *The Animal Estate: The English and Other Creatures in the Victorian Age* (Cambridge, MA: Harvard University Press, 1987), pp. 93–104.

9. Knight's writings helped to popularize the collie as the ideal pet for U.S. children. In 1944 there were fewer than 3,000 collies in the United States. Following the popularity of the book and the six MGM films that it spawned, sales skyrocketed, resulting in 18,400 registrations of purebred collies by 1949. See Susan M. Brown, "Forward: A Charismatic Collie and Her Fifty-Year Influence," in Susan M. Brown, ed., *Lassie: A Collie and Her Influence* (St. Louis: Dog Museum, 1993), p. 4.

10. Ritvo, *Animal Estate*, p. 89.

11. For an example of such a reading, see Emily D. Berkley, "Lassie and American Culture," in Brown, ed., *Lassie: A Collie and Her Influence*, pp. 6–17.

12. Background information on Eric Knight in this essay comes from Elizabeth Wasserman, "Eric Knight and *Lassie Come Home*," in Brown, ed., *Lassie: A Collie and Her Influence*, pp. 18–23.

13. Eric Knight, quoted in ibid., p. 22.

14. Ibid., p. 20.

15. Viviana A. Zelizer, *Pricing the Priceless Child: The Changing Social Value of Children* (New York: Basic Books, 1985).

16. Mary Lynn Stevens Heininger, "Children, Childhood, and Change in America, 1820–1920," in Mary Lynn Stevens Heininger et al., eds., *A Century of Childhood, 1820–1920* (Rochester, NY: Margaret Woodbury Strong Museum, 1984), p. 31.

17. See Harriet Ritvo, "Barring the Cross: Miscegenation and Purity in Eighteenth- and Nineteenth-Century Britain," in Diana Fuss, ed., *Human, All Too Human* (New York: Routledge, 1996), pp. 37–58.

18. For the most part, as Harriet Ritvo notes, those distinctions between breeds were emptied of meaningful content (having everything to do with the sentimental value and physical beauty of dogs, and nothing to do with their functionality or adaptability). Ritvo, *Animal Estate*, pp. 104–15.

19. Kete, *Beast in the Boudoir*, p. 94.

20. Ace Collins, *Lassie: A Dog's Life* (New York: Cader, 1993), p. 94.

21. The ideological motivations behind this prolonged transition are clearer when we recognize that the roles of the Martins, Timmy's adoptive parents, were recast, without acknowledgment or explanation, at the end of the first season of the Timmy years, since the producers were unhappy with the chemistry between Cloris Leachman and Jon Shepodd. Timmy's relationship with his parents was a minor footnote in the series; the focus was on the boy and his dog.

22. Richard Dyer, "Entertainment and Utopia," in Bill Nichols, ed., *Movies and Methods*, vol. 2 (Berkeley: University of California Press, 1985); and Fredric Jameson, "Reification and Utopia in Mass Culture," *Social Text* (Winter 1979): 130–48.

23. Sally Allen McNall, "American Children's Literature, 1880–Present," in Joseph M. Hawes and N. Ray Hiner, eds., *American Childhood: A Research Guide and Historical Handbook* (Westport, CT: Greenwood, 1985), p. 388.

24. Ibid., 393.

25. Berkley, "Lassie and American Culture," p. 8.

26. A similar fate befell the protagonists of *National Velvet*, which was adapted for television at about the same time.

27. Collins, *A Dog's Life*, 79.

28. Nina C. Leibman, *The Living-Room Lectures: The Fifties' Family in Film and Television* (Austin: University of Texas Press, 1995), p. 25.

29. Ace Collins notes that this time slot was initially seen as undesirable for family programming: "Viewership was low at this time and the demographic mix was bad. Many people were eating, throughout the Bible Belt people were in church, and television usually remained off until 8:00 p.m." (Collins, *A Dog's Life*, p. 83).

30. Cyclops, quoted in David Zinman, *Saturday Afternoon at the Bijou* (New York: Castle Books, 1973), p. 473. Zinman offers a detailed discussion of the production of the films, as well as the casting and training of the collies that played Lassie over the years.

31. Elizabeth Segal, "'As the Twig is Bent . . . ': Gender and Childhood Reading," in Elizabeth A. Flynn and Patrocinio P. Schweickart, eds., *Gender and Reading: Essays on Readers, Texts, and Contexts* (Baltimore: Johns Hopkins University Press, 1986), p. 171.

32. As Elizabeth Segal notes, American educational policy had typically favored the teaching of books predominantly aimed at boys, since girls would often read and enjoy boys' books, while boys consistently rejected girl-centered stories.

33. Jack London, *The Call of the Wild* (New York: Puffin, 1903), p. 120.

34. For a discussion of the sentimental tradition, see Jane Tompkins, "Sentimental Power: *Uncle Tom's Cabin* and the Politics of Literary History," in Robyn R. Warhol and Diane Price Herndl, eds., *Feminisms: An Anthology of Literary Theory and Criticism* (New Brunswick, NJ: Rutgers University Press, 1991), pp. 20–39.

35. Roger Hart, *Children's Experience of Place* (New York: John Wiley and Sons, 1979). See also Bernard Mergen, *Play and Playthings: A Reference Guide* (Westport, CT: Greenwood, 1982).

36. See Gayle Kaye, "Lassie Collectibles," in Brown, ed., *Lassie: A Collie and Her Influence*, pp. 24–31.

37. For a fuller discussion of this tradition and its influence on 1950s television, see Henry Jenkins, "Dennis the Menace: The All American Handful," in Lynn Spigel and Michael Curtin, eds., *The Revolution Wasn't Televised: Sixties Television and Social Conflict* (New York: Routledge, 1997), pp. 119–38.

38. Newton Minow, "Is TV Cheating Our Children," *Parents*, February 1962, pp. 52–54, 116. For a fuller discussion of the ways reformers constructed their cultural canons, see Lynn Spigel and Henry Jenkins, "Same Bat Channel, Different Bat Times: Mass Culture and Popular Memory," in Pearson and Uricchio, eds., *The Many Lives of the Batman*, pp. 117–48.

39. Nancy Larrick, *A Parent's Guide to Children's Reading for Parents and Teachers of Boys and Girls under Thirteen* (New York: Pocket Books, 1958). Sponsored by the National Book Committee, this guide is surprisingly sympathetic to television.

40. "The Mini-Wasteland," *Newsweek*, January 23, 1967, pp. 92–94.

41. "The Most Objectionable," *Newsweek*, July 30, 1956, p. 78.

42. Anna W. M. Wolf, "TV, Movies, Comics: Boon or Bane to Children?" *Parents*, April 1961, pp. 46–48.

43. Frank Orme, "TV for Children: What's Good? What's Bad?" *Parents*, February 1962, pp. 54ff.

44. "Time Out for Television," *PTA*, November 1967, p. 20.

45. Rudolf Dreikurs, *Children: The Challenge* (New York: Hawthorn, 1964), p. 153.

46. For more information on the Capra unit's influence on postwar children's culture, see Henry Jenkins, "'No Matter How Small': The Democratic Imagination of Dr. Seuss," in Henry Jenkins, Tara McPherson, and Jane Shattuc, eds., *Hop on Pop: The Pleasures and Politics of Popular Culture* (Durham, NC: Duke University Press, 2003), pp. 187–208.

47. Susan Stewart, *On Longing* (Durham, NC: Duke University Press, 1993), 23.

48. Marjorie Garber, "Heavy Petting," in Fuss, ed., *Human, All Too Human*, pp. 11–36.

49. Dylan Loeb McLain, "Dogs and Cats with Chips on Their Shoulders," *New York Times*, January 22, 1996, p. D5.

50. Ibid.

Index

About the Author

The founder and director of MIT's Comparative Media Studies Program, Henry Jenkins is the author or editor of more than ten books on various aspects of media and popular culture, including *Textual Poachers: Television Fans and Participatory Culture*; *From Barbie to Mortal Kombat: Gender and Computer Games*; *Hop on Pop: The Politics and Pleasures of Popular Culture*; and, for NYU Press, *Convergence Culture: Where Old and New Media Intersect* and *Fans, Bloggers, and Gamers: Exploring Participatory Culture*. His career so far has included testifying before the U.S. Senate Commerce Committee hearing into Marketing Violence for Youth following the Columbine shootings; promoting media literacy education before the Federal Communications Commission; speaking to the Governor's Board of the World Economic Forum about intellectual property and grassroots creativity; heading the Education Arcade, which promotes the educational uses of computer and video games; writing monthly columns for *Technology Review* and *Computer Games* magazine; and consulting with leading media companies about consumer relations.